QUICK FOOD

QUICK FOOD

Gourmet Food in Just 30 Minutes

Jenny Fanshaw, Annette Forrest

Reader's Digest

THE READER'S DIGEST ASSOCIATION, INC.

Pleasantville, New York / Montreal / Sydney / Singapore

A READER'S DIGEST BOOK

This edition published by
The Reader's Digest Association, Inc.,
by arrangement with McRae Books Srl

Quick Food was created and produced by
McRae Books Srl
Via del Salviatino, 1-50016 Fiesole
(Florence), Italy
Info@mccraebooks.com

FOR MCRAE BOOKS
Project Director: Anne McRae
Art Director: Marco Nardi
Photography: Brent Parker Jones
Photographic Art Direction: Neil Hargreaves
Texts: Jenny Fanshaw, Annette Forrest
Food Styling: Lee Blaycock, Neil Hargreaves
Layouts: Aurora Granata
Prepress: Filippo Delle Monache,
Davide Gasparri

FOR READER'S DIGEST
U.S. Project Editor: Andrea Chesman
Canadian Project Editor: Pamela Chichinskas
Australian Project Editor: Annette Carter
Copy Editor: Emily Bigelow
Senior Art Director: George McKeon
Executive Editor, Trade Publishing:
Dolores York
Associate Publisher, Trade Publishing:
Rosanne McManus
President and Publisher, Trade Publishing:
Harold Clarke

LIBRARY OF CONGRESS CATALOGING-IN-PUBLICATION DATA

Fanshaw, Jenny.
   Quick food : gourmet recipes in just 30 minutes
/ Jenny Fanshaw, Annette Forrest.
      p.   cm.
   Includes index.
   ISBN 978-0-7621-0981-4
   1. Quick and easy cookery. I. Forrest, Annette.
II. Title.
TX833.5.F334 2009
641.5'55--dc22

                                      2008040855

We are committed to both the quality of our
products and the service we provide to our
customers. We value your comments, so please
feel free to contact us.

The Reader's Digest Association, Inc.
Adult Trade Publishing
Reader's Digest Road
Pleasantville, NY 10570-7000

NOTE TO OUR READERS
Eating eggs or egg whites that are not completely
cooked poses the possibility of salmonella food
poisoning. The risk is greater for pregnant women,
the elderly, the very young, and persons with
impaired immune systems. If you are concerned
about salmonella, you can use reconstituted
powdered egg whites or pasteurized eggs.

For more Reader's Digest products and
information, visit our website:
   www.rd.com (in the United States)
   www.readersdigest.ca (in Canada)
   www.readersdigest.com.au (in Australia)
   www.readersdigest.com.nz (in New Zealand)

Printed in China

1 3 5 7 9 10 8 6 4 2

The level of difficulty for each recipe is given on a scale
from 1 (easy) to 3 (complicated).

CONTENTS

INTRODUCTION

This book is dedicated to busy people who enjoy simple, stylish food that can be prepared with a minimum of fuss and in less time than it takes to get takeouts. From comfort food like Spicy potato wedges and Meatballs with tomato salsa, to gourmet offerings such as Cherry tomato clafoutis and Chocolate fudge and amaretti sundaes, we have selected more than 300 dishes from a mixture of homestyle cooking and popular world cuisines such as Italian, Mexican, and Chinese. We have streamlined their preparation and cooking times so that they can all be prepared in 30 minutes or less, from start to finish.

The recipes have been organized into 11 chapters, from Snacks and Starters to Desserts. We have tried to choose dishes that are complete in themselves and hearty enough to be served on their own. Many of the salads and soups include serving suggestions for different types of bread or croutons so that you can whip up a healthy and satisfying light meal in less than half an hour. But you can also combine the recipes to prepare a more substantial family meal of two or three courses, all in less than an hour.

We believe that the key to preparing tasty food quickly, without sacrificing either flavor or nutritional value, lies in the use of fresh, high-quality ingredients. Quick food needn't be based on canned or pre-packaged foodstuffs—a handful of garden-

garden-fresh vegetables seared in a wok with vegetable oil and a spice or two, then sprinkled with fresh herbs and served over rice or noodles makes a delectable and healthy meal. We have included several Asian favorites of this type, most of which you will find in the Noodles chapter. Also included are several Italian dishes that can be prepared easily and quickly. Classics like risotto and gnocchi are among the many recipes featured in the Pasta chapter.

Fish and seafood are high in protein and other nutritional values and are quick to cook. Try our Tuna Steaks with Oranges and Capers (see page 380) or Pan-fried Salmon with Grapes and Zucchini (see page 392), or any of the other 24 recipes in the Seafood chapter. You will find more ideas for protein-packed meals in the chapters on Poultry, Meat, and Eggs and Cheese. To finish, we have included more than 25 recipes for desserts, from puddings and soufflés to grilled fruit and quick-fix Tiramisù.

To help you plan your meals, each recipe includes preparation and cooking times. We have also graded the recipes from 1 to 3 for difficulty (1=easy to 3=complicated), with almost all falling into the first category.

Within you will find a full range of dazzling ideas for every occasion, from impressive meals when you are entertaining, to simpler dishes you can fix for friends and family on busy weeknights or lazy weekends.

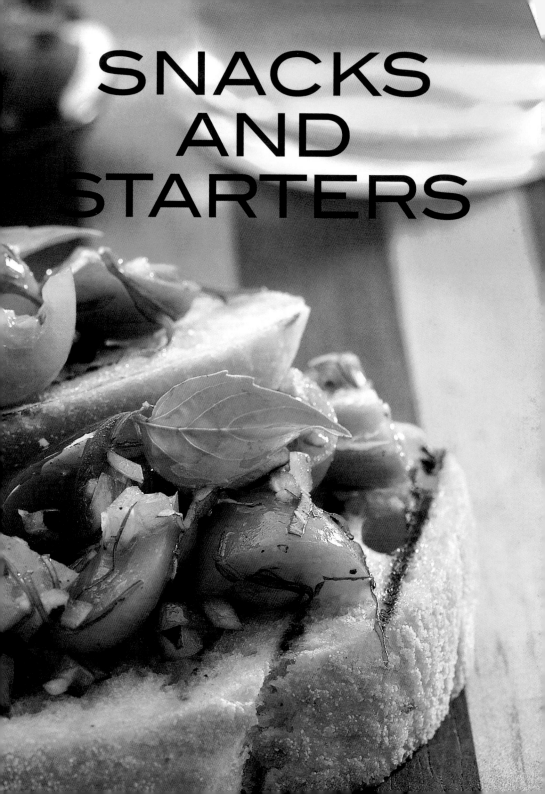

SNACKS AND STARTERS

SMOKED SALMON DIP

Process the smoked salmon, cream cheese, lemon juice, capers, and dill in a food processor until smooth. Season with salt and pepper. • Spoon the dip into a serving bowl, garnish with the dill, and serve with crackers.

5 ounces (150 g) smoked salmon (or smoked trout)

1 cup (250 g) light cream cheese, at room temperature

2 tablespoons freshly squeezed lemon juice

1$^1/_2$ tablespoons salt-cured capers, rinsed

2 tablespoons finely chopped fresh dill + a sprig to garnish

Salt and freshly ground black pepper

Crackers, to serve

Preparation: 10 minutes

Serves: 4
Level: 1

■■■ *Serve this dip with predinner drinks. It is great with thin, crisp crackers but can also be served with potato chips (crisps), corn chips, or thin slices of toasted bread.*

BACON AND MUSHROOM PIZZA

Preheat the oven to 450°F (230°C/ gas 8). • Sauté the bacon and mushrooms in the oil in a large frying pan over medium heat until the mushrooms are softened, about 5 minutes. • Remove from the heat and set aside. • Spread the pizza crust with the tomato paste. • Top with the mushrooms, bacon, shallots, and mozzarella. • Bake for 12–15 minutes, until golden brown and crisp. • Top with the arugula and season with salt and pepper. • Serve hot.

3   slices bacon, coarsely chopped

8   ounces (250 g) mushrooms, thinly sliced

1   tablespoon extra-virgin olive oil

1   12-inch (30-cm) store-bought pizza crust

1/4   cup (60 g) tomato paste

2   shallots, thinly sliced

1/2   cup (125 g) freshly grated mozzarella cheese

1   cup (30 g) arugula (rocket)

    Salt and freshly ground black pepper

Preparation: 10 minutes
Cooking: 17–20 minutes

Serves: 1–2
Level: 1

SALAMI, OLIVE, AND ANCHOVY PIZZA

Preheat the oven to 450°F (230°C/ gas 8). • Spread the pizza crust evenly with the tomato puree. Top with the tomatoes, salami, olives, anchovies, oregano, and mozzarella. • Bake for 12–15 minutes, until golden brown and crisp. • Cut the pizza into 6 or 8 slices. Serve hot with the arugula on the side.

1	10-inch (25-cm) store-bought pizza crust
1/3	cup (90 ml) tomato puree (passata)
4	ounces (125 g) cherry tomatoes, halved
6	slices hard salami, coarsely chopped
2	tablespoons pitted (stoned) kalamata olives, halved
6	salt-cured anchovies, rinsed and coarsely chopped
1	tablespoon finely chopped fresh oregano
6	slices mozzarella cheese
	Arugula (rocket), to serve

■■■ *Anchovies have a strong, salty flavor and not everyone likes them. If preferred, replace the anchovies in this recipe with a thinly sliced clove of garlic, or simply leave them out. You may also like to drizzle the freshly baked pizza with 1–2 tablespoons of top-quality extra-virgin olive oil.*

Preparation: 5 minutes

Cooking: 12–15 minutes

Serves: 1–2
Level: 1

HAM, CHEESE, AND AVOCADO QUESADILLAS

24

Lay out the tortillas on a clean work surface. • Place a slice of ham on each tortilla and spread with the mayonnaise. • Arrange the avocado, cheese, and arugula evenly over one half of the tortilla. • Season with salt and pepper. • Fold the tortillas in half. • Heat a large frying pan over medium heat. • Spray the tortillas with the oil. • Cook on each side until golden and crisp, for 2–3 minutes. • Serve warm.

4   **large flour tortillas or Mexican wraps**

4   **large slices ham**

2   **tablespoons mayonnaise**

1   **avocado, pitted (stoned) and thinly sliced**

8   **slices Swiss cheese**

2   **cups (60 g) arugula (rocket)**

     Salt and freshly ground black pepper

     Olive oil spray

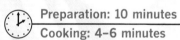

Preparation: 10 minutes
Cooking: 4–6 minutes

Serves: 4
Level: 1

SALAMI, ARTICHOKE, AND CHEESE FOCACCIA

Preheat a sandwich press. • Cut the focaccia in half. • Top the bottom slices with the salami, artichokes, provolone, and arugula. • Season with salt and pepper. • Replace the top halves of the bread to make sandwiches. Spray with the olive oil. • Place the focaccia in the sandwich press. • Cook for 3–4 minutes, until warmed through. • Serve warm.

4   focaccia rolls or
    1 large piece of
    focaccia, cut into 4
8   slices salami
4   artichoke hearts,
    thinly sliced
1   cup (125 g) freshly
    grated provolone
    cheese
1   bunch arugula
    (rocket)
    Salt and freshly
    ground black pepper
    Olive oil spray

Preparation: 10 minutes
Cooking: 4 minutes

Serves: 4
Level: 1

■■■ *If you don't have a sandwich press, flatten the focaccia and cook in a frying pan, pressing down with a spatula until golden and warmed through.*

SAUSAGE AND TABBOULEH WRAPS

Put the bulgur in a bowl and cover with cold water. Let stand for 25 minutes. • Sauté the sausages in 1 tablespoon of oil in a large frying pan over medium heat until cooked, about 10 minutes. • Remove from the heat and set aside. • Squeeze the excess moisture out of the bulgur and put into a bowl. • Stir in the parsley, mint, tomato, onion, remaining oil, and lemon juice. Season with salt and pepper. • Cut the sausages into long, thick slices. • Lay out the flat breads on a clean surface. • Spread evenly with the hummus and top with the tabbouleh and sausage. • Roll up carefully. Cut each wrap in half and serve.

1/4 cup (60 g) fine- or medium-grain bulgur

6 spicy sausages, such as pepperoni

2 tablespoons extra-virgin olive oil

1 cup (30 g) finely chopped fresh parsley

2 tablespoons finely chopped fresh mint

1 large tomato, finely chopped

1/2 small red onion, finely chopped

1/4 cup (60 ml) freshly squeezed lemon juice

Salt and freshly ground black pepper

4 Lebanese flat breads, pita breads, or flour wraps

2/3 cup (150 g) hummus

Preparation: 25 minutes
Cooking: 12 minutes

Serves: 4
Level: 1

BACON, LETTUCE, AND TOMATO SANDWICH

Sauté the bacon in the oil in a large frying pan over medium heat for 3 minutes. • Remove from the heat and drain on paper towels. • Lightly toast the bread on both sides, about 2 minutes. • Spread the toast with mayonnaise. • Top four slices of toast with bacon and top with the tomato and lettuce. • Top with the remaining slices of toast. Cut in half and serve warm.

8 slices rindless bacon

1 tablespoon extra-virgin olive oil

8 slices thickly sliced bread

2 tablespoons mayonnaise

2 tomatoes, thinly sliced

1 cup (30 g) finely shredded lettuce

Preparation: 10 minutes

Cooking: 5 minutes

Serves: 4
Level: 1

■■■ *This toasted sandwich is known as a BLT in many parts of the world.*

TURKEY, CAMEMBERT, AND CRANBERRY BAGELS

Place the bagel halves on a clean surface. • Spread each half with the cream cheese. Top evenly with the turkey, Camembert, cranberry sauce, and pea shoots. • Season with salt and pepper and serve.

4   bagels, cut in half

1/3   cup (90 ml) cream cheese

8   slices roasted or seasoned cooked turkey breast

8   thin slices Camembert cheese

1/3   cup (90 ml) cranberry sauce

1   cup (60 g) pea shoots or snow pea sprouts

Salt and freshly ground black pepper

 Preparation: 10 minutes

Serves: 4

Level: 1

■■■ *If preferred, toast the bagels lightly before assembling the sandwiches. Serve while still warm from toasting.*

SWEET AND SPICY CHICKEN WRAPS

Mix the chicken, mayonnaise, and sweet chili sauce in a bowl. • Lay the flat breads out on a clean surface. • Divide the chicken mixture, cucumber, tomatoes carrot, and lettuce evenly among the flat breads. Season with salt and pepper. • Roll up the bread and cut in half. Serve.

4	cups (400 g) shredded cooked chicken
1/3	cup (90 ml) mayonnaise
2	tablespoons Thai sweet chili sauce
4	Lebanese flat breads, pita breads, or flour wraps
1	cucumber, thinly sliced
2	tomatoes, finely chopped
1	large carrot, finely grated
2	cups (100 g) finely shredded lettuce
	Salt and freshly ground black pepper

 Preparation: 5 minutes

Serves: 4
Level: 1

TUNA PASTRY PIES

Preheat the oven to 375°F (190°C/gas 5).
• Lightly spray six muffin cups with olive
oil. • Place the phyllo pastry on a clean
work surface. • Lightly spray one sheet
with olive oil, fold in half lengthwise, and
spray again. • Fold again to form a
square. Repeat with the remaining phyllo
and olive oil. • Place the pastry squares
in the prepared muffin pans. • Mix the
tuna, arugula, scallions, eggs, and cream
in a large bowl. Season with salt and
pepper. • Spoon the mixture evenly into
the phyllo cases. • Bake for about
20 minutes, until golden brown
and crisp. • Serve hot.

Olive oil spray

6   sheets frozen phyllo
    (filo) pastry, thawed

2   cups (400 g)
    canned tuna,
    drained and flaked

1/2 cup (15 g) finely
    chopped arugula
    (rocket)

4   scallions (green
    onions), thinly sliced

5   large eggs,
    lightly beaten

1/3 cup (90 ml) light
    (single) cream

    Salt and freshly
    ground black pepper

Preparation: 10 minutes
Cooking: 20 minutes

Serves: 4–6
Level: 1

SAUSAGE ROLLS

Preheat the oven to 425°F (220°C/ gas 7). • Line a large baking sheet with parchment paper. • Mix the sausage, tomato paste, herbs, and bread crumbs until well blended. • Moisten your hands and shape the mixture into four long logs about 1 inch (2.5 cm) in diameter. • Cut each piece of pastry in half lengthwise to form two large rectangles. Place the sausage logs on one side of each piece of pastry. Brush the other edge of each piece of pastry with a little of the egg. Fold the pastry over the sausage, pressing down gently on the egg-brushed edges to seal. • Cut each pastry log into pieces about 3 inches (7.5 cm) long. • Arrange the sausage rolls on the prepared baking sheet. Brush with the remaining egg and sprinkle with sesame seeds. • Bake for 15–20 minutes, until golden brown and crisp. • Serve hot with tomato or barbecue sauce on the side.

1	pound (500 g) ground (minced) sausage
2	tablespoons tomato paste
2	teaspoons mixed dried herbs
2	cups (120 g) fresh bread crumbs
2	sheets frozen puff pastry, thawed and halved
1	large egg, lightly beaten
1	tablespoon sesame seeds
	Tomato or barbecue sauce, to serve

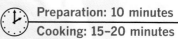

Preparation: 10 minutes
Cooking: 15–20 minutes

Serves: 6–8
Level: 1

■■■ Sausage rolls are a classic snack food the world over. They are easy to make and can be prepared in advance of a party, buffet, or other special occasion, and frozen uncooked. On the day they are to be served, they can be defrosted and baked just in time to serve while still warm. Tasty sausage rolls can be made by using highly-flavored fresh Italian sausages; just remove the casings and mix the sausage meat with the other ingredients.

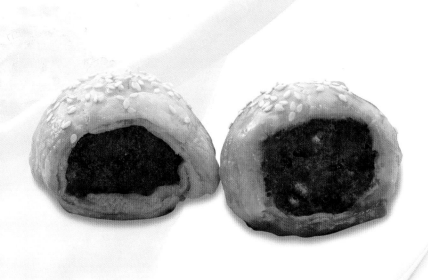

ASIAN CHICKEN ROLLS

Put the noodles in a medium bowl and let stand in boiling water for 5 minutes. • Drain and set aside. • Coarsely chop the noodles. • Mix the noodles, chicken, carrot, bean sprouts, pea shoots, cilantro, and mint in a large bowl. Mix the sweet chili sauce and lemon juice in a small bowl. • Pour over the chicken mixture and toss well. • Dip each rice paper sheet in hot water until just softened. • Place on a clean work surface and top with a little of the chicken mixture. • Roll up the rice paper sheets, tucking in the sides as you go. • Serve with the sweet chili sauce on the side.

■■■ *Rice paper sheets are made from rice flour, salt, and water. They are used to wrap spring rolls before frying but can also be used to wrap fillings without being cooked. They are widely available in Asian food stores and supermarkets.*

2 ounces (60 g) dried vermicelli rice noodles

2 cups (200 g) shredded barbecued or roast chicken breasts

1 carrot, coarsely grated

1 cup (50 g) fresh bean sprouts

1 cup (50 g) pea shoots or snow pea sprouts, trimmed

2 tablespoons cilantro (coriander) leaves

2 tablespoons mint leaves

2 tablespoons Thai sweet chili sauce + extra, to serve

2 tablespoons freshly squeezed lemon juice

12 rice paper sheets

Preparation: 15 minutes

Serves: 6–8
Level: 1

CORN AND RED BELL PEPPER CAKES

44

Mix the creamed corn, corn kernels, milk, eggs, bell pepper, scallions, parsley, and butter in a bowl. Add the flour and stir until smooth. Season with salt and pepper. • Heat the oil to very hot in a large, deep frying pan. • Drop tablespoons of the mixture into the oil. Fry in batches until golden brown all over and puffed, 3–4 minutes. • Drain well on paper towels. • Serve hot with the sour cream.

1¹/4 cups (300 g) canned creamed corn (sweet corn)

¹/2 cup (50 g) corn (sweet corn) kernels, drained

¹/3 cup (90 ml) milk

2 large eggs, lightly beaten

¹/2 cup (50 g) finely diced red bell pepper (capsicum)

2 scallions (spring onions), finely chopped

2 tablespoons finely chopped fresh parsley

1¹/2 tablespoons butter, melted

³/4 cup (125 g) self-rising flour

Salt and freshly ground black pepper

1 cup (250 ml) olive oil, for frying

¹/3 cup (90 ml) sour cream, to serve

Preparation: 5 minutes

Cooking: 10–15 minutes

Serves: 4–6
Level: 1

TUNA VOL-AU-VENTS

Preheat the oven to 350°F (180°C/gas 4).
• Bake the vol-au-vent cases on a baking sheet for 8–10 minutes until crisp.
• Remove from the oven and set aside.
• Sauté the scallions in the butter in a small saucepan over medium-low heat until softened, 2–3 minutes. • Add the flour and cook for 1 minute. • Gradually pour in the milk, stirring slowly until the mixture thickens and becomes smooth.
• Add the cheese, lemon zest and juice, and tuna. Stir until heated through. Season with salt and pepper. • Add a little more milk if mixture is too thick.
• Spoon the tuna mixture evenly into the vol-au-vents cases and sprinkle with the chives. Serve warm.

4 medium vol-au-vent pastry cases

2 scallions (spring onions), finely chopped

2 tablespoons butter

2 tablespoons all-purpose (plain) flour

1 cup (250 ml) milk + extra, if needed

1/3 cup (50 g) freshly grated mild cheese

Finely grated zest of 1 lemon

1/4 cup (60 ml) freshly squeezed lemon juice

1 cup (200 g) canned tuna, drained and flaked

Salt and freshly ground black pepper

1 tablespoon finely chopped chives

Preparation: 10 minutes

Cooking: 11–13 minutes

■■■ *Vol-au-vent is a French term that translates literally as "flying in the wind." The name refers to the fact that the puff pastry shells should be light enough to blow away in the wind.*

Serves: 2–4

Level: 1

MARJORAM BLINIS
WITH PROSCIUTTO

Beat the flour, baking powder, sugar, salt, egg yolks, butter, marjoram, and milk in a large bowl until smooth. • Beat the egg whites in a large bowl with a mixer at high speed until stiff peaks form. • In a separate bowl, beat the cream with a mixer at high speed until stiff. • Use a large rubber spatula to fold the beaten whites and cream into the batter. • Heat a large frying pan over medium heat. Brush the pan with a little butter. • Drop tablespoons of the batter into the frying pan. Cook in batches until golden brown on both sides. • Transfer the cooked blinis to a serving dish. • Top each blini with slices of melon and prosciutto. • Serve warm.

1¹/₂ cups (225 g) all-purpose (plain) flour

2 teaspoons baking powder

1 teaspoon sugar

¹/₂ teaspoon salt

2 large eggs, separated

3 tablespoons butter, melted

1 tablespoon finely chopped fresh marjoram

1 cup (250 ml) milk, hot

¹/₄ cup (60 ml) heavy (double) cream

1 small ripe cantaloupe (rock) melon, peeled, seeded, and cut into thin wedges

4 ounces (125 g) prosciutto (Parma ham)

Preparation: 10 minutes
Cooking: 5 minutes

Serves: 4–6
Level: 1

CROSTONI WITH PROSCIUTTO, PEACH, AND PECORINO

Spread each slice of toast lightly with butter. • Place a slice of prosciutto on top. Cover with the peach slices and arugula. Sprinkle with the chives and top with the pecorino. • Season generously with pepper, if preferred, and serve.

4 **large slices firm-textured bread, toasted**

2 **tablespoons butter**

4 **large thin slices prosciutto (Parma ham)**

1 **large ripe peach, peeled, pitted, and thinly sliced**

1 **cup (30 g) arugula (rocket)**

1 **tablespoon finely chopped fresh chives**

2 **ounces (60 g) pecorino cheese, thinly sliced**

Freshly ground black pepper (optional)

 Preparation: 5 minutes

Serves: 4
Level: 1

■■■ *You may already know that a crostino (plural "crostini") is a classic Italian appetizer made from day-old bread, usually toasted, and then spread with various toppings, such as sliced tomatoes, Parmesan, olive or chicken liver pâté, among others. A crostoni is just a larger version of the same thing.*

CHEESE CROSTONI WITH PEARS AND HAZELNUTS

Preheat the broiler (grill). • Sauté the scallion in the butter in a frying pan over medium heat until softened, 2–3 minutes. • Remove from the pan and set aside. • Add the pear to the pan and sauté for 2 minutes. • Add the wine and let it evaporate over high heat for 1 minute. • Remove from the heat and drain the pear on paper towels. Sprinkle with the cinnamon and let cool slightly. • Toast the bread under the broiler until brown. • Lay the brie on the toasted bread. Add a layer of scallions and a layer of the pear. • Broil until the cheese has melted, 2–3 minutes. Season with salt and pepper. • Transfer to a serving dish. Sprinkle with the parsley and hazelnuts. • Serve hot.

1	scallion (spring onion), finely chopped
3	tablespoons butter
1	large pear, peeled, cored, and thinly sliced
1/4	cup (60 ml) sweet white wine
1/4	teaspoon ground cinnamon
6	large slices whole-wheat (wholemeal) bread
8	ounces (250 g) brie cheese, thinly sliced
	Salt and freshly ground black pepper
1	tablespoon flat-leaf parsley leaves
2/3	cup (75 g) coarsely chopped hazelnuts

Preparation: 10 minutes

Cooking: 8 minutes

Serves: 4–6
Level: 1

■■■ *Pears originated in the Caucasus region a very long time ago. They spread around the world and there are now more than 1,000 varieties. Pears go well with many foods and are especially good with cheese. In this recipe the sweet flesh of the pears melds beautifully into the full, ripe flavor of the brie.*

TOMATO AND OLIVE BRUSCHETTA

Preheat the broiler (grill). • To prepare the tomato topping, sauté the tomatoes in the oil in a large frying pan over high heat for 5 minutes. • Transfer the tomatoes to a bowl. Mix in the onion, basil, and sugar. • To prepare the olive topping, place the black and green olives, oregano, and oil in a food processor and process until coarsely chopped. • To prepare the bruschette: Toast the bread until golden brown. Rub each piece of toast with garlic. • Arrange the toast on a serving dish and drizzle with the oil. • Spoon the tomato topping over the toast. Top with the olive topping. Season with salt and pepper and serve.

Preparation: 15 minutes
Cooking: 10 minutes

Serves: 6
Level: 1

Tomato Topping

2 large ripe tomatoes, finely chopped
1 tablespoon extra-virgin olive oil
1/4 onion, finely chopped
1 tablespoon torn basil
1/2 teaspoon sugar

Olive Topping

2/3 cup (60 g) black olives, pitted (stoned)
1/4 cup (30 g) green olives pitted (stoned)
1 tablespoon finely chopped fresh oregano
2 tablespoons extra-virgin olive oil

Bruschette

12 large slices firm-textured bread
3 cloves garlic, peeled
1/3 cup (90 ml) extra-virgin olive oil
Salt and freshly ground black pepper

YELLOW AND RED TOMATO BRUSCHETTA

Mix the tomatoes, onion, basil, garlic, olive oil, and balsamic vinegar in a medium bowl. Season with salt and pepper. • Cover with plastic wrap (cling film) and let stand for 20 minutes to let the flavor develop. • Cut the bread into ³/₄-inch (2-cm) slices. • Char-grill for 1–2 minutes on each side until toasted. • Spoon the tomato mixture over the bread and serve.

8	ounces (250 g) red tomatoes, coarsely chopped
8	ounces (250 g) yellow tomatoes, coarsely chopped
1	small red onion, finely chopped
2	tablespoons torn basil
1	clove garlic, finely chopped
2	tablespoons extra-virgin olive oil
1	tablespoon balsamic vinegar
	Salt and freshly ground black pepper
1	small loaf ciabatta bread or 1 crusty baguette (French loaf)

Preparation: 5 minutes
Cooking: 2–4 minutes

Serves: 4
Level: 1

■■■ *Bruschetta is a well-known Italian appetizer. In its simplest form, bruschetta consists of day-old bread, toasted, rubbed with garlic, and drizzled with extra-virgin olive oil. It can also be topped with tomatoes, cannellini beans, or spinach, among other things. Always remember to say the name correctly— it's pronounced "brusketta" (not brushetta)!*

SUN-DRIED TOMATO PESTO TOASTS

Preheat the oven to 350°F (180°C/gas 4).
• Arrange the bread on baking sheets
and drizzle with 1 tablespoon of olive oil.
• Bake for 5 minutes on each side, until
golden and crisp. • Arrange the toasts on
a large serving platter. • Process the sun-
dried tomatoes, remaining olive oil,
capers, garlic, lemon zest, lemon juice,
and thyme in a food processor until well
blended. • Arrange the arugula leaves
and sun-dried tomato pesto on top of the
toasts. Top with the sliced mozzarella
and serve.

1 **crusty baguette (French loaf), thickly sliced**

¹/₄ **cup (60 ml) extra-virgin olive oil**

³/₄ **cup (75 g) sun-dried tomatoes**

2 **tablespoons salt-cured capers, rinsed**

2 **cloves garlic, peeled**

Finely grated zest and juice of ¹/₂ lemon

1 **tablespoon thyme leaves**

1 **cup (30 g) arugula (rocket) leaves**

6 **ounces (180 g) small fresh mozzarella balls (bocconcini), drained and thinly sliced**

Preparation: 15 minutes
Cooking: 10 minutes

Serves: 4
Level: 1

CHERRY TOMATO AND MOZZARELLA SKEWERS

Thread half a cherry tomato onto a wooden skewer. Follow with a leaf of basil and a mozzarella ball. Repeat until all the mozzarella, tomatoes, and basil have been used. • Place the skewers on a serving plate. • Sprinkle with the chives. Season with salt and pepper and drizzle with the oil.

12 cherry tomatoes, halved

24 leaves fresh basil

24 small fresh mozzarella balls (bocconcini)

1 tablespoon finely chopped fresh chives

Salt and freshly ground black pepper

1/4 cup (60 ml) extra-virgin olive oil

 Preparation: 15 minutes

Serves: 4
Level: 1

■■■ *This is a healthy snack that also can be served as a starter or light lunch. Its flavor depends on top-quality ingredients, so use the freshest mozzarella cheese and tomatoes and a good quality extra-virgin olive oil to drizzle.*

STUFFED POTATOES

Pierce the potatoes four times with a skewer. • Arrange them around the outside of a microwave turntable.
• Microwave on high power for 4 minutes. Turn the potatoes over and microwave for 4 more minutes. • Remove the potatoes from the microwave and wrap in aluminum foil. • Let stand for 5 minutes. • Mix the sour cream, smoked salmon, and chives in a small bowl.
• Discard the foil. Cut two slits crosswise in the top of each potato and gently squeeze them open. Top with the smoked salmon mixture. Season with salt and pepper. Serve hot with the salad greens on the side.

4 medium potatoes, scrubbed

1/3 cup (90 ml) sour cream

4 ounces (125 g) smoked salmon, coarsely chopped

1 tablespoon finely chopped fresh chives

Salt and freshly ground black pepper

Salad greens, to serve

Preparation: 15 minutes
Cooking: 8 minutes

Serves: 4
Level: 1

CHINESE CHICKEN SALAD IN LETTUCE CUPS

66

Sauté the chicken, garlic, ginger, chiles, and shallots in the oil in a wok or large frying pan over medium-high heat until the chicken is cooked, about 5 minutes. • Stir in the water chestnuts, soy sauce, and sweet chili sauce. • Sauté for about 3 minutes, or until the liquid has been absorbed. • Remove from the heat. Stir in the mint and cilantro. • Spoon the mixture evenly into the lettuce leaves and serve hot.

1¼ pounds (650 g) ground (minced) chicken

2 cloves garlic, finely chopped

2 teaspoons freshly grated ginger

1–2 small red chiles, seeded and finely chopped

3 shallots, thinly sliced

1 tablespoon peanut oil

½ cup (50 g) water chestnuts, drained and thinly sliced

2 tablespoons soy sauce

2 tablespoons Thai sweet chili sauce

2 tablespoons finely chopped fresh mint

2 tablespoons finely chopped cilantro (coriander)

8 lettuce leaves, to serve

Preparation: 15 minutes
Cooking: 8 minutes

Serves: 4
Level: 1

MEATBALLS WITH TOMATO SALSA

68

Mix the beef, scallions, parsley, tomato paste, bread crumbs, and egg in a large bowl until well blended. Season with salt and pepper. • Form the mixture into balls the size of walnuts. • Heat the oil until very hot in a large, deep frying pan. • Fry the meatballs in batches for 5–7 minutes, until golden brown all over. • Drain well on paper towels. Serve hot with the tomato salsa on the side.

1   **pound (500 g) ground (minced) beef**

3   **scallions (spring onions), finely chopped**

2   **tablespoons finely chopped fresh parsley**

2   **tablespoons tomato paste**

3/4 **cup (45 g) fresh bread crumbs**

1   **large egg, lightly beaten**

    Salt and freshly ground black pepper

1   **cup (250 ml) olive oil, for frying**

1   **cup (250 ml) tomato salsa**

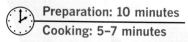

Preparation: 10 minutes

Cooking: 5–7 minutes

Serves: 8–10
Level: 1

SALMON FISH CAKES

Mix the salmon, mashed potatoes, scallions, dill, and egg in a large bowl. Season with salt and pepper. • Shape the mixture into eight fish cakes. Lightly dust with the flour. • Fry the fish cakes in the oil in a large frying pan over medium heat until golden brown, 3–4 minutes on each side. • Drain on paper towels. Garnish with the lemon wedges and dill and serve hot.

2 cups (400 g) canned pink salmon, drained and flaked

1¹/2 cups (350 g) leftover mashed potatoes

2 scallions (spring onions), thinly sliced

2 tablespoons finely chopped dill + extra, to garnish

1 large egg, lightly beaten

Salt and freshly ground black pepper

2 tablespoons all-purpose (plain) flour

1/4 cup (60 ml) extra-virgin olive oil

Lemon wedges, to serve

Preparation: 10 minutes
Cooking: 6–8 minutes

Serves: 4–6
Level: 1

SPICY POTATO WEDGES

Preheat the oven to 450°F (230°C/ gas 8). • Place the potato wedges in a microwave dish with the water. • Cover with plastic wrap (cling film) and microwave on high power for 5 minutes. • Drain the potatoes. • Place flour and Cajun seasoning in a plastic bag. • Add the potato wedges and toss well. • Place the wedges on a nonstick baking tray. Drizzle with the olive oil. • Bake for 15–20 minutes, until golden and crisp. • Serve hot with the sour cream and sweet chili sauce on the side.

4 large potatoes, scrubbed and cut into wedges

1 tablespoon water

2 tablespoons extra-virgin olive oil

1 tablespoon all-purpose (plain) flour

1 tablespoon Cajun seasoning

1/4 cup (60 ml) sour cream

1/4 cup (60 ml) Thai sweet chili sauce

Preparation: 5 minutes
Cooking: 25–30 minutes

Serves: 4
Level: 1

CHERRY TOMATO CLAFOUTIS

Preheat the oven to 400°F (200°C/ gas 6). • Grease four 1-cup (250-ml) ramekins or ovenproof dishes with oil. • Divide the tomatoes among the prepared ramekins and season with salt. • Beat the flour, eggs, milk, crème fraîche, and half the Parmesan in a large bowl until smooth. • Stir in the arugula. • Pour the mixture over the tomatoes. • Bake for 15 minutes, until set and golden brown on top. • Sprinkle with the remaining Parmesan. • Serve hot, with arugula on the side.

1	pound (500 g) cherry tomatoes, halved
	Salt
2	tablespoons all-purpose (plain) flour
4	large eggs
	Generous $1/3$ cup (100 ml) milk
	Generous $3/4$ cup (200 g) crème fraîche or half-and-half
	Generous $1/2$ cup (70 g) freshly grated Parmesan cheese
2	cups (60 g) arugula (rocket) leaves, torn + extra to serve

Preparation: 10 minutes
Cooking: 15 minutes

Serves: 4
Level: 1

HUMMUS WITH TOMATOES AND OLIVES

Combine the garbanzo beans, tahini, garlic, vinegar, and ¹/₄ cup (60 ml) of lemon juice in a food processor. Season with salt and pepper. • Process until smooth. If the mixture is too thick, add a little more lemon juice. • Mix the tomatoes, cucumber, olives, parsley, 1 tablespoon of oil, and 2 tablespoons of lemon juice in a large bowl. Season with salt and pepper. Toss well. • Spoon the hummus onto a serving plate and sprinkle with cayenne pepper. • Drizzle with a little oil. • Arrange the tomato salad in the center of the houmous and serve with the pita bread.

1   (14-ounce/400-g) can garbanzo beans (chick-peas), drained and rinsed

¹/₃ cup (90 ml) tahini

1   clove garlic, finely chopped

2   teaspoons white wine vinegar

¹/₃ cup (90 ml) freshly squeezed lemon juice

Salt and freshly ground black pepper

2   tomatoes, diced

1   cucumber, diced

¹/₃ cup (30 g) pitted kalamata olives

1   tablespoon finely chopped fresh parsley

2   tablespoons extra-virgin olive oil

¹/₈ teaspoon cayenne pepper

Pita or Lebanese flat breads, to serve

Preparation: 15 minutes

Serves: 4
Level: 1

NACHOS

Preheat the oven to 350°F (180°C/gas 4).
• Place the corn chips in a large baking
dish. • Arrange the kidney beans, chile
peppers, tomatoes, and cheese on top of
the corn chips. • Bake for about 10
minutes, until the cheese has melted.
• Serve warm with the avocado and
sour cream.

8 ounces (250 g) corn chips

1 (14-ounce/400-g) can red kidney beans, drained

2 jalapeño chiles, finely chopped

2 tomatoes, diced

1¹/₂ cups (185 g) freshly grated cheddar cheese

1 avocado, peeled and mashed

1 cup (250 ml) sour cream

Preparation: 10 minutes

Cooking: 10 minutes

Serves: 4
Level: 1

MEXICAN BEAN ENCHILADAS

Preheat the oven to 400°F (200°C/ gas 6). • Sauté the onion and bell pepper in the oil in a large frying pan over medium heat until softened, about 3 minutes. • Spread each tortilla evenly with the refried beans. • Arrange the onion, bell pepper, chile beans, tomatoes, and half the cheese evenly on the tortillas. Roll up tightly. • Arrange the enchiladas in a baking dish. • Sprinkle with the remaining cheese. • Bake for about 10 minutes, until the cheese has melted. • Serve hot.

1 onion, thinly sliced

1 green bell pepper (capsicum) seeded and thinly sliced

2 tablespoons vegetable oil

8 large flour tortillas

1 cup (250 g) refried beans

1 (14-ounce/400-g) can Mexican chile beans or pinto beans, drained and rinsed

2 tomatoes, diced

2 cups (250 g) freshly grated Monterey Jack or cheddar cheese

Preparation: 10 minutes
Cooking: 13 minutes

Serves: 4
Level: 1

GARBANZO BEAN PATTIES

Combine the garbanzo beans, garlic, cumin, scallions, and sour cream in a food processor. • Process until smooth. • Transfer to a large bowl and season with salt and pepper. • Shape the mixture into eight patties. • Dust lightly with flour. • Fry the patties in batches in the oil in a large frying pan until golden, about 3 minutes on each side. • Serve the patties with the tzatziki, salad, and lemon wedges.

1 (14-ounce/400-g) can garbanzo beans (chick-peas), drained and rinsed

1 clove garlic, finely chopped

1 teaspoon ground cumin

4 scallions (spring onions), thinly sliced

3 tablespoons sour cream

Salt and freshly ground black pepper

2 tablespoons all-purpose (plain) flour

1/4 cup (60 ml) extra-virgin olive oil

Tzatziki, to serve (see page 434)

Mixed salad greens, to serve

Lemon wedges, to serve

 Preparation: 10 minutes

Cooking: 12 minutes

Serves: 4

Level: 1

BAKED MUSHROOMS WITH FETA AND HERBS

Preheat the oven to 400°F (200°C/ gas 6). • Drizzle the tops of the mushrooms with half the oil. • Place the mushrooms cap-side down in a large baking dish. • Fill with the feta, parsley, and oregano. • Drizzle with the remaining oil and lemon juice. Season with salt and pepper. • Bake for about 15 minutes, until softened. • Arrange the ciabatta on serving plates. Top with the mushrooms and garnish with the arugula.
• Serve hot.

8	large portobello, field, or flat mushrooms
1/4	cup (60 ml) extra-virgin olive oil
4	ounces (125 g) feta cheese, crumbled
2	tablespoons finely chopped fresh parsley
2	tablespoons finely chopped fresh oregano
2	tablespoons freshly squeezed lemon juice
	Salt and freshly ground black pepper
	Toasted ciabatta bread, to serve
1	bunch arugula (rocket), trimmed

 Preparation: 10 minutes
Cooking: 15 minutes

Serves: 4
Level: 1

SALADS

SMOKED CHICKEN AND AVOCADO SALAD

For the salad: Toast the almonds in a large frying pan over medium heat for 3 minutes. • Remove from the heat and set aside. • Mix the chicken, avocado, cucumber, and lettuce in a large bowl. • For the dressing: Mix the lemon juice, olive oil, Dijon mustard, and sugar in a small bowl. Season with salt and pepper. • Drizzle over the salad and toss well.
• Serve with freshly baked, crusty bread.

Salad

- ¹/₄ cup (40 g) slivered almonds
- 1 pound (500 g) smoked chicken breasts, thinly sliced
- 2 small avocados, cut in half, pitted, and thinly sliced
- 1 cucumber, thinly sliced
- 1 head romaine lettuce, torn

Dressing

- ¹/₄ cup (60 ml) freshly squeezed lemon juice
- 2 tablespoons extra-virgin olive oil
- 1 tablespoon Dijon mustard
- 1 teaspoon superfine (caster) sugar

  Salt and freshly ground black pepper

Preparation: 5 minutes
Cooking: 3 minutes

Serves: 4
Level: 1

ARUGULA, PANCETTA, AND TOMATO SALAD

Preheat the oven to 400°F (200°C/ gas 6). • Arrange the tomatoes on a baking sheet cut side up. Drizzle with 1 tablespoon of oil and sprinkle with the sugar. Season with salt and pepper.
• Bake for about 10 minutes, until just softened. • Sauté the pine nuts in 1 tablespoon of oil in a small frying pan over medium heat until lightly browned, about 3 minutes. Remove from the heat and set aside. • Add the pancetta to the pan and sauté until crisp, about 3 minutes. Set aside. • Carefully toss the arugula, baked tomatoes, pine nuts, and pancetta in a large salad bowl.
• Season with salt and pepper. Drizzle with the remaining oil and balsamic vinegar. • Sprinkle with the Parmesan shavings and serve.

8 ounces (250 g) cherry tomatoes, halved

1/4 cup (60 ml) extra-virgin olive oil

1 teaspoon superfine (caster) sugar

Salt and freshly ground black pepper

1/4 cup (45 g) pine nuts

1 1/4 cups (150 g) coarsely chopped pancetta

5 ounces (150 g) arugula (rocket)

2 tablespoons balsamic vinegar

2 tablespoons Parmesan shavings

Preparation: 10 minutes
Cooking: 16 minutes

Serves: 4
Level: 1

ITALIAN SAUSAGE, ARTICHOKE, AND ASPARAGUS SALAD

Fry the sausages in a large nonstick frying pan over medium-high heat, turning occasionally, until cooked through, about 10 minutes. • Let cool slightly. • Cook the asparagus in a pan of salted boiling water until just tender, 3–5 minutes. The cooking time will depend on how thick the asparagus is. • Drain well and let cool. • Arrange the asparagus, lettuce, tomatoes, and artichokes in a large salad bowl. • Thickly slice the sausages and add to the salad. • Drizzle with the oil and balsamic vinegar. Season with salt and pepper. • Toss well and serve.

1¹/₂ pounds (750 g) Italian sausages

8 ounces (250 g) asparagus spears, trimmed

1 cup baby lettuce leaves

3 tomatoes, cut into quarters

6 artichoke hearts marinated in oil, drained and thinly sliced

2 tablespoons extra-virgin olive oil

1 tablespoon balsamic vinegar

Salt and freshly ground black pepper

 Preparation: 10 minutes
Cooking: 15 minutes

Serves: 4–6
Level: 1

POTATO, PROSCIUTTO, AND EGG SALAD

For the salad: Boil the potatoes in a large pot of salted water until just tender, 10–15 minutes. • Drain and rinse under cold water to stop the cooking process. • Cook the eggs in a medium saucepan of barely simmering water for 10 minutes. Drain well and cover with cold water. • Shell the eggs and chop coarsely. • Sauté the prosciutto in 1 tablespoon of the oil in a large frying pan over medium heat until crisp, 5 minutes. • Remove from the heat and set aside. Break each slice into 2–3 pieces. • Toss the potatoes, eggs, prosciutto, scallions, and parsley carefully in a large salad bowl. • For the dressing: Mix the mayonnaise, lemon juice, and Dijon mustard in a small bowl. Season with salt and pepper. • Drizzle over the salad and toss well.

Salad

1¹/2 pounds (750 g) new potatoes, sliced

3 large eggs

8 slices prosciutto (Parma ham)

2 tablespoons extra-virgin olive oil

3 scallions (spring onions), very thinly sliced

2 tablespoons finely chopped fresh parsley

Dressing

¹/2 cup (125 g) mayonnaise

2 tablespoons freshly squeezed lemon juice

2 teaspoons Dijon mustard

Salt and freshly ground black pepper

 Preparation: 5 minutes
Cooking: 20 minutes

Serves: 4
Level: 1

■■■ Prosciutto is an Italian deli meat made by air-curing the hindquarters of large pigs. The meat is a bright, rosy color, lightly veined with fat. The hams are treated with salt and then left to dry for about 12 months in well ventilated storerooms. Good prosciutto is worth its weight in gold so always buy the best available; the ham is so tasty that even small quantities will add heaps of flavor to any dish.

ROAST BEEF, ARUGULA, AND RED ONION SALAD

Place a grill pan over medium-high heat.
• Brush the onions with 1 tablespoon of oil and season with salt and pepper.
• Grill the onions until just tender, about 2 minutes on each side. • Mix the remaining oil, mustard, and white wine vinegar in a small bowl. Season with salt and pepper. • Arrange the arugula on individual serving plates. Top with the roast beef and onions. • Drizzle with the mustard dressing and serve with sourdough bread.

2   red onions, thickly sliced

1/3   cup (90 ml) extra-virgin olive oil

Salt and freshly ground black pepper

1   tablespoon whole-grain mustard

1   tablespoon white wine vinegar

1   bunch arugula (rocket)

12   thin slices rare roast beef

Sourdough bread, to serve

Preparation: 5 minutes

Cooking: 4 minutes

Serves: 4
Level: 1

ROAST PUMPKIN, SPINACH, AND GOAT CHEESE SALAD

Preheat the oven to 450°F (230°C/ gas 8). • Line a large roasting pan with parchment paper. • Cut the pumpkin into ¼-inch (5-mm) thick wedges. • Mix the olive oil, balsamic vinegar, and brown sugar in a large bowl. Season with salt and pepper. • Add the pumpkin and toss well. • Arrange the pumpkin in the prepared pan. • Roast for about 15 minutes, until tender and browned. • Let cool for 5 minutes. • Arrange the spinach and pumpkin on individual serving plates. • Sprinkle with the goat cheese. Drizzle with the pan juices and serve.

1½ pounds (750 g) pumpkin or winter squash, peeled and seeded

2 tablespoons extra-virgin olive oil

2 tablespoons balsamic vinegar

1 tablespoon light brown sugar

Salt and freshly ground black pepper

4 ounces (125 g) baby spinach leaves

5 ounces (150 g) goat cheese, crumbled

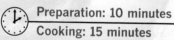 Preparation: 10 minutes
Cooking: 15 minutes

Serves: 4
Level: 1

CHICKEN AND PISTACHIO SALAD

Cook the snow peas in a small saucepan of boiling water for 1 minute. • Drain and rinse under cold water to stop the cooking process. Drain and pat dry with paper towels. • Shred the cooked chicken flesh, discarding the fat and bones. • Mix the chicken, snow peas, scallions, celery, pistachios, and lettuce in a large bowl. • Drizzle with the oil and lemon juice. Season with salt and pepper. • Toss gently and serve.

5 ounces (150 g) snow peas (mangetout), sliced lengthwise

1 roasted chicken, store-bought or homemade

3 scallions (spring onions), trimmed and thinly sliced on the diagonal

3 stalks celery, thinly sliced on the diagonal

1/2 cup (50 g) coarsely chopped pistachios

8 ounces (250 g) romaine lettuce leaves

1 tablespoon extra-virgin olive oil

2 tablespoons freshly squeezed lemon juice

Salt and freshly ground black pepper

Preparation: 10 minutes
Cooking: 1 minutes

Serves: 4
Level: 1

PEAR AND BLUE CHEESE SALAD

Sauté the walnuts in 1 tablespoon of oil in a small frying pan over medium heat for 1 minute. • Add the honey and cook over low heat for 2 minutes. • Transfer to a small bowl. • Add the remaining olive oil and lemon juice. Let cool. • Mix the baby spinach, pears, and blue cheese in a large bowl. • Add the honeyed walnuts. Toss well and serve.

$1/3$ cup (50 g) walnuts

$1/4$ cup (60 ml) extra-virgin olive oil

1 tablespoon honey

2 tablespoons freshly squeezed lemon juice

5 ounces (150 g) baby spinach leaves

3 pears, halved, cored, and thinly sliced

8 ounces (250 g) blue cheese, such as Gorgonzola or Stilton, crumbled

Preparation: 15 minutes

Cooking: 3 minutes

Serves: 4
Level: 1

SPINACH AND FETA SALAD WITH CROUTONS

Sauté the bread cubes in 1 tablespoon of oil in a large frying pan over medium heat until crisp and golden, 5–7 minutes. • Drain well on paper towels. • Toss the sun-dried tomatoes, spinach, and feta in a large salad bowl. Drizzle with the remaining oil and white wine vinegar. Season with salt and pepper. • Add the croutons. Toss well and serve.

1/2 small baguette (French loaf), cut into small cubes

3 tablespoons extra-virgin olive oil

5 ounces (150 g) sun-dried tomatoes in oil, drained

5 ounces (150 g) baby spinach leaves

5 ounces (150 g) feta cheese, thinly sliced

1 tablespoon white wine vinegar

Salt and freshly ground black pepper

Preparation: 5 minutes
Cooking: 5–7 minutes

Serves: 4
Level: 1

TUNA AND ROASTED VEGETABLE SALAD

Preheat the oven to 450°F (230°C/ gas 8). • Place the onions, bell peppers, and tomatoes in a large roasting pan. Drizzle with 1 tablespoon of oil and the balsamic vinegar. Season with salt and pepper. • Roast for about 20 minutes, until tender. • Arrange the vegetables and olives on a serving plate. Top with the tuna and drizzle with the remaining oil. • Serve warm with the bread.

2	red onions, cut into thick wedges
1	yellow bell pepper (capsicum), halved, seeded, and cut into strips
1	red bell pepper (capsicum), halved, seeded, and cut into strips
1	pound (500 g) cherry tomatoes
2	tablespoons extra-virgin olive oil
1	tablespoon balsamic vinegar
	Salt and freshly ground black pepper
1¼ cups (125 g)	black olives
1	(14-ounce/400-g) can tuna in oil, drained
	Ciabatta or other freshly baked bread, to serve

Preparation: 10 minutes
Cooking: 20 minutes

Serves: 4
Level: 1

FIG, PROSCIUTTO, AND MOZZARELLA SALAD

Arrange the arugula and figs on serving plates. • Top with the prosciutto and mozzarella. • Drizzle with the oil and balsamic vinegar. Season with salt and pepper. • Serve.

3   ounces (90 g) arugula (rocket) leaves

8   firm-ripe figs, cut into quarters

12 thin slices prosciutto (Parma ham)

8   small fresh mozzarella balls (bocconcini), drained and thinly sliced

1/4 cup (60 ml) extra-virgin olive oil

1 1/2 tablespoons balsamic vinegar

Salt and freshly ground black pepper

 Preparation: 5 minutes

Serves: 4
Level: 1

WARM LAMB, TOMATO, AND PARSLEY SALAD

Heat a nonstick frying pan over medium-high heat. • Rub the lamb with 1 tablespoon of oil and season with salt and pepper. • Cook the lamb for 8–10 minutes, turning occasionally, until cooked to your liking. • Transfer to a plate, cover with aluminum foil, and let rest. • Mix the scallions, parsley, tomatoes, and cucumber in a large salad bowl. • Mix the remaining oil, mustard, and honey in a small bowl. Season with salt and pepper. • Thinly slice the lamb and add to the salad. • Pour the dressing over the salad and toss gently. • Serve with the hummus on the side.

1 pound (500 g) boneless lamb steaks or lamb tenderloin

1/3 cup (90 ml) extra-virgin olive oil

Salt and freshly ground black pepper

4 scallions (spring onions), thinly sliced on the diagonal

2 cups (100 g) coarsely chopped flat-leaf parsley

8 ounces (250 g) yellow tomatoes, halved

1 cucumber, diced

2 teaspoons whole-grain mustard

1 tablespoon honey

Hummus, to serve

Preparation: 10 minutes
Cooking: 8–10 minutes

Serves: 4
Level: 1

CRISP BACON, ASPARAGUS, AND EGG SALAD

Cook the eggs in a medium saucepan of barely simmering water for 10 minutes. Drain and refill the saucepan with cold water. Let cool for 5 minutes. • Shell the eggs and cut each one in half. • Sauté the bacon in 1 tablespoon of oil in a large frying pan over medium heat until crisp, about 5 minutes. • Remove from the heat and set aside. • Sauté the garlic and bread crumbs in the same pan until golden, about 4 minutes. • Remove from the heat and set aside. • Cook the asparagus and wax beans in a pan of salted boiling water until tender, about 2 minutes. • Drain and transfer to a large salad bowl. • Add the bacon and bread crumb mixture. Toss gently. • Arrange the salad on serving plates and top with the eggs. • Season with salt and pepper and serve.

4 large eggs

2 cups (240 g) coarsely chopped bacon

2 tablespoons extra-virgin olive oil

1 clove garlic, finely chopped

1½ cups (90 g) fresh bread crumbs

12 ounces (350 g) asparagus, trimmed

8 ounces (250 g) wax (butter) beans

Salt and freshly ground black pepper

 Preparation: 10 minutes
Cooking: 20 minutes

Serves: 4
Level: 1

MUSHROOM, PINE NUT, AND PARMESAN SALAD

Dry-fry the pine nuts in a small frying pan over medium heat until golden, about 3 minutes. • Remove from the heat and set aside. • Add the oil, balsamic vinegar, and mustard to the pan. • Cook over low heat, stirring constantly, until it starts to boil, about 1 minute. • Add the mushrooms and toss until well coated. • Add the pine nuts and chives. Season with salt and pepper. • Arrange the salad greens in a large serving bowl. • Top with the mushrooms and Parmesan and serve.

- ¹/₃ cup (60 g) pine nuts
- ¹/₄ cup (60 ml) extra-virgin olive oil
- 2 tablespoons balsamic vinegar
- 1 tablespoon whole-grain mustard
- 1 pound (500 g) button mushrooms, thinly sliced
- 2 tablespoons finely chopped chives
- Salt and freshly ground black pepper
- 5 ounces (150 g) baby Asian salad greens
- 3 ounces (90 g) Parmesan cheese, in shavings

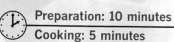

Preparation: 10 minutes
Cooking: 5 minutes

Serves: 4
Level: 1

CHILE PORK
AND SNOW PEA SALAD

Place a grill pan over medium-high heat. • Season the pork with salt and pepper. • Grill the pork until cooked through, about 10–15 minutes. • Transfer to a plate and cover with aluminum foil. • Mix the chiles, lime juice, peanut oil, sugar, fish sauce, and sesame oil in a small bowl. • Set aside. • Cook the snow peas in salted boiling water for 1 minute. Drain well. • Mix the snow peas, scallions, and chile dressing in a large bowl. • Thinly slice the pork and add to the salad. • Add the cilantro and peanuts. Toss gently and serve.

1	pound (500 g) pork fillets
	Salt and freshly ground black pepper
2	red Thai (bird's eye) chiles, seeded and finely chopped
1/4	cup (60 ml) freshly squeezed lime juice
1/4	cup (60 ml) peanut oil
2	tablespoons super-fine (caster) sugar
1	tablespoon Asian fish sauce
1	teaspoon Asian sesame oil
4	oz (125 g) snow peas (mangetout), thinly sliced lengthwise
4	scallions (spring onions), trimmed and thinly sliced
1	cup (30 g) fresh cilantro (coriander) leaves
1	cup (40 g) roasted peanuts, chopped

Preparation: 10 minutes
Cooking: 11–16 minutes

Serves: 4
Level: 1

CHICKEN CAESAR SALAD

To prepare the salad, preheat the broiler (grill). • Place the bread on a baking sheet and drizzle with 1 tablespoon of oil. • Toast about 2 minutes each side, until golden and crisp. • Cook the eggs in a medium saucepan of barely simmering water for 10 minutes. Drain well. Fill the saucepan with cold water and leave the eggs in it for 5 minutes. • Shell the eggs and chop coarsely. • Sauté the bacon in the remaining oil in a large frying pan over medium heat until crisp, about 5 minutes. Set aside to cool a little and until ready to assemble the salad. • Sprinkle the chicken with the seasoning. • Sauté the chicken in the same pan used to cook the bacon until cooked through, about 4 minutes each side. Let cool a little. • Mix the lettuce, cucumber, scallions, bacon, chicken, baguette, and egg in a large salad bowl. Season with salt and pepper.

Salad

1 baguette (French loaf), thinly sliced
2 tablespoons extra-virgin olive oil
2 large eggs
4 slices bacon, coarsely chopped
2 boneless, skinless chicken breasts, thinly sliced
2 teaspoons Cajun seasoning
1 romaine lettuce, torn
1 cucumber, sliced
3 scallions (spring onions), thinly sliced
Salt and freshly ground black pepper

Preparation: 10 minutes
Cooking: 20 minutes

Serves: 4
Level: 1

Dressing

¼ cup (60 ml) mayonnaise

2 tablespoons freshly squeezed lemon juice

1 teaspoon Djion mustard

1 tablespoon water

2 salt-cured anchovy fillets, finely chopped

4 tablespoons freshly grated Parmesan

For the dressing: Mix the mayonnaise, lemon juice, mustard, water, and anchovies in a small bowl. • Drizzle over the salad and toss well. Sprinkle with the Parmesan and serve.

■■■ *Caesar salad is a favorite the world over. It is said to have been invented by Rosa Cardini, the daughter of an Italian immigrant named Cesare Cardini. The Cardinis lived in San Diego, but, during Prohibition, they ran a restaurant just over the border in Tijuana, Mexico. One hot July 4th in 1924, the restaurant was crowded with customers and ingredients were running short. Rosa just used what she had on hand and concocted a salad directly at customers' tables. The salad, which became known as Caesar Salad, became popular, especially with movie stars of the time who were always looking for ways to maintain a trim waistline.*

SMOKED SALMON AND AVOCADO SALAD

Dry-fry the sesame seeds in a small frying pan over medium heat until browned, about 4 minutes. • Remove from the heat and set aside. • Mix the mirin, soy sauce, oil, and sugar in a small saucepan. • Bring to a boil over medium-high heat, stirring until the sugar has dissolved. • Boil for 1 minute. • Let cool slightly. • Peel and pit (stone) the avocados. Cut into thin slices. • Arrange the spinach and avocado on individual serving plates. • Top with the smoked salmon. • Drizzle with the warm soy dressing. Sprinkle with the sesame seeds and serve.

2	tablespoons sesame seeds
1/4	cup (60 ml) mirin
1/4	cup (60 ml) soy sauce
2	tablespoons vegetable oil
1	tablespoon superfine (caster) sugar
2	medium ripe avocados
8	ounces (250 g) baby spinach leaves
10	ounces (300 g) smoked salmon, thinly sliced

Preparation: 10 minutes
Cooking: 5 minutes

Serves: 4
Level: 1

■■■ *Mirin is a sweet Japanese rice wine similar to sake, but with less alcohol. It has quite a strong flavor and is generally used with fish dishes.*

GARBANZO BEAN AND FETA COUSCOUS SALAD

Put the couscous in a large bowl.
• Pour the boiling water over the couscous. • Cover the bowl with plastic wrap (cling film) and let stand for 10 minutes, until the couscous has completely absorbed the liquid. • Stir in the oil, lemon juice, and zest with a fork. • Add the scallions, bell pepper, garbanzo beans, feta, olives, parsley, and mint. Season with salt and pepper. • Serve.

1¹/2 cups (300 g) instant couscous

1¹/2 cups (375 ml) boiling water

2 tablespoons extra-virgin olive oil

2 tablespoons freshly squeezed lemon juice

1 teaspoon finely grated lemon zest

2 scallions (spring onions), thinly sliced

1 small yellow bell pepper (capsicum), seeded, and finely chopped

1 (14-ounce/400-g) can garbanzo beans (chick-peas), drained and rinsed

3 ounces (90 g) feta cheese, crumbled

1 cup (100 g) black olives

¹/2 cup (25 g) finely chopped flat-leaf parsley

1 sprig fresh mint leaves, finely chopped

Salt and freshly ground black pepper

Preparation: 20 minutes

Serves: 4
Level: 1

EGGPLANT AND BUFFALO MOZZARELLA SALAD

Preheat the oven to 450°F (230°C/ gas 8). • Mix the oil and garlic in a small bowl. • Arrange the eggplant slices on a baking sheet. Brush with the oil mixture and season with salt and pepper. • Bake for about 20 minutes, until softened.
• Arrange layers of eggplant, mozzarella, arugula, and tomatoes on individual serving plates. Top with the pesto.
• Serve with crusty bread.

¹/₄ cup (60 ml) extra-virgin olive oil

2 cloves garlic, finely chopped

Salt and freshly ground black pepper

1 medium eggplant (aubergine), trimmed and cut into ¹/₂-inch (1-cm) thick slices

4 balls fresh buffalo-milk mozzarella cheese, thinly sliced

1 small bunch arugula (rocket)

2 tomatoes, thinly sliced

¹/₄ cup (60 ml) basil or arugula (rocket) pesto

Crusty bread, to serve

Preparation: 10 minutes

Cooking: 20 minutes

Serves: 4

Level: 1

■■■ *The most highly prized mozzarella cheese in Italy is made using buffalo milk. Some cheesemakers in other countries also make buffalo-milk mozzarella. if you can't find it, replace with the same quantity of top quality fresh cows' milk mozzarella.*

SHRIMP AND AVOCADO SALAD

To prepare the dill dressing, beat the egg yolk and Dijon mustard in a double boiler over barely simmering water with an electric mixer at high speed until pale. • Gradually beat in the oil in a thin steady trickle until thick. • Add the lemon juice and dill. • Stir in the sour cream and season with salt and pepper. • To prepare the salad, arrange the lettuce, shrimp, and avocado on individual serving plates. • Drizzle with the dill dressing and serve.

Dill Dressing

1   large egg yolk

1   teaspoon Dijon mustard

1/2 cup (125 ml) extra-virgin olive oil

2   teaspoons freshly squeezed lemon juice

2   tablespoons finely chopped fresh dill

1/4 cup (60 ml) sour cream

Salt and freshly ground black pepper

Salad

1   head baby romaine lettuce

24 cooked large shrimp (prawns), peeled and deveined

2   medium ripe avocados, peeled and sliced lengthwise

 Preparation: 25 minutes

Serves: 4
Level: 1

FENNEL, GREEN BEAN, AND RICOTTA SALAD

Mix the fennel, lemon juice, and ¼ cup (60 ml) of oil in a large bowl. • Cover with plastic wrap (cling film) and let marinate for 10 minutes. • Sauté the pine nuts in the remaining oil in a small frying pan over medium heat until golden, about 3 minutes. • Remove from the heat and set aside. • Cook the green beans in salted boiling water for 2 minutes. • Drain and rinse under cold water. Dry with a clean kitchen towel. • Add the pine nuts, green beans, and ricotta to the fennel mixture. Season with salt and pepper. • Toss gently and serve.

2 **bulbs baby fennel, trimmed and very thinly sliced**

2 **tablespoons freshly squeezed lemon juice**

⅓ **cup (90 ml) extra-virgin olive oil**

¼ **cup (45 g) pine nuts**

12 **ounces (350 g) green beans**

1 **cup (250 g) ricotta salata cheese**

Salt and freshly ground black pepper

 Preparation: 15 minutes
Cooking: 5 minutes

Serves: 4
Level: 1

INDIAN RICE SALAD

Cook the rice with the turmeric, cardamom pods, and cinnamon stick in a large pan of salted boiling water until tender, 10–15 minutes. • Drain well and transfer to a large bowl. • Dry-fry the mustard seeds in a small frying pan over low heat until aromatic. • Transfer to a small bowl and mix in the oil, white wine vinegar, and sugar. • Add the almonds, golden raisins, garbanzo beans, and cilantro to the rice. • Drizzle with the dressing. • Toss well and serve.

- 1$\frac{1}{2}$ cups (300 g) basmati rice
- $\frac{1}{2}$ teaspoon ground turmeric
- 2 pods cardamom, lightly crushed
- 1 stick cinnamon
- 2 tablespoons mustard seeds
- $\frac{1}{4}$ cup (60 ml) grape seed oil
- 2 tablespoons white wine vinegar
- 1 tablespoon superfine (caster) sugar
- $\frac{1}{3}$ cup (50 g) slivered almonds, roasted
- $\frac{1}{3}$ cup (60 g) golden raisins (sultanas)
- 1 (14-ounce/400-g) can garbanzo beans (chick-peas), drained and rinsed
- $\frac{1}{2}$ cup (15 g) coarsely chopped fresh cilantro (coriander)

Preparation: 10 minutes

Cooking: 10–15 minutes

Serves: 4

Level: 1

PASTA SALAD WITH TOMATOES, BASIL, AND PARMESAN

Cook the penne in a large pot of salted boiling water until al dente. • Mix the tomatoes, garlic, basil, and oil in a large bowl. Season with salt and pepper. • Preheat the oven to 425°F (220°C/gas 7). • Line a baking sheet with parchment paper. • Sprinkle the cheese onto the sheet. • Bake for 5 minutes until melted and lightly browned. • Remove from the oven and let cool slightly. • Drain the pasta and rinse under cold water to stop the cooking process. Dry well on a clean kitchen towel. • Add the pasta to the bowl with the tomatoes. Mix well and transfer to a serving dish. • Break up the cheese and sprinkle it over the pasta. Garnish with the basil and pine nuts.

1	pound (500 g) penne pasta
8	ounces (250 g) cherry tomatoes, cut into quarters
4	cloves garlic, finely chopped
1	ounce (30 g) basil leaves, torn
1/4	cup (60 ml) extra-virgin olive oil
	Salt and freshly ground black pepper
1	cup (125 g) freshly grated Parmesan cheese
	Sprigs of basil, to garnish
2	tablespoons pine nuts, toasted

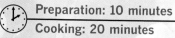

Preparation: 10 minutes
Cooking: 20 minutes

Serves: 4–6
Level: 1

TUNA, ARTICHOKE AND WATERCRESS PASTA SALAD

Cook the farfalle in a large pot of salted boiling water until al dente. • Drain the pasta and rinse under cold water to stop the cooking process. Dry well on a clean kitchen towel. Place in a large pasta bowl. • Add the tuna, artichokes, onion, olives, tomatoes, and watercress.
• Drizzle with the oil and lemon juice. Season with salt and pepper. • Gently toss to combine.

1	pound (500 g) farfalle pasta
1	(14-oz/400-g) can tuna in oil, drained and flaked
6	marinated artichoke hearts, drained and thickly sliced
1/2	small red onion, thinly sliced
1/2	cup (50 g) kalamata olives
8	ounces (250 g) cherry tomatoes, halved
2	cups (60 g) watercress sprigs
1/4	cup (60 ml) extra-virgin olive oil
2	tablespoons freshly squeezed lemon juice
	Salt and freshly ground black pepper

Preparation: 15 minutes
Cooking: 12 minutes

Serves: 4
Level: 1

■■■ *Farfalle pasta is also known as bow-tie pasta. You can also make this pasta salad with penne or another short pasta shape.*

GARBANZO BEAN AND SALMON SALAD

Mix the salmon, garbanzo beans, cucumbers, red onion, and spinach in a large bowl. • Toss well. • Season with salt and pepper. • Mix the yogurt, lemon juice, tahini, and chives in a small bowl. • Spoon the salad onto serving plates and drizzle with the dressing.

1   (8-ounce/250-g) can pink salmon, drained and flaked

1   (14-ounce/400-g) can garbanzo beans (chick-peas), drained and rinsed

2   cucumbers, halved and sliced

1   red onion, thinly sliced

3   cups (100 g) baby spinach leaves

    Salt and freshly ground black pepper

1/2 cup (125 ml) plain yogurt

2   tablespoons freshly squeezed lemon juice

1   tablespoon tahini

1   tablespoon finely chopped fresh chives

 Preparation: 15 minutes

Serves: 4
Level: 1

BUTTER BEANS WITH ARTICHOKES AND TOMATOES

Sauté the garlic in the oil in a large frying pan over medium-low heat until softened, about 2 minutes. • Stir in the cayenne pepper. • Remove from the heat and add the white wine vinegar and sugar. • Combine the butter beans, artichokes, tomatoes, scallions, parsley, and watercress in a large bowl. • Pour the dressing over the top and toss well. • Season with salt and pepper and serve.

2 cloves garlic, finely chopped

1/4 cup (60 ml) extra-virgin olive oil

1/4 teaspoon cayenne pepper

1 tablespoon white wine vinegar

1/8 teaspoon sugar

1 (14-ounce/400-g) can butter beans or lima beans, drained and rinsed

4 marinated artichokes, drained and quartered

8 ounces (250 g) cherry tomatoes, halved

3 scallions (spring onions), thinly sliced

3 tablespoons finely chopped fresh parsley

8 ounces (250 g) watercress

Salt and freshly ground black pepper

Preparation: 10 minutes

Cooking: 1 minute

Serves: 4

Level: 1

SOYBEAN AND VEGETABLE SALAD

Blanch the snow peas in a large saucepan of salted water for 1 minute. • Use a slotted spoon to remove the snow peas and rinse them under ice-cold water to stop the cooking process. • Add the broccoli and carrot. • Cook until just tender, 2–3 minutes. • Drain and rinse under cold water. • Mix the snow peas, broccoli, carrot, soybeans, olive oil, lemon juice, and parsley in a large bowl. • Season with salt and pepper. • Spoon into bowls and serve.

4 ounces (125 g) snow peas, trimmed and cut in half

8 ounces (250 g) broccoli, cut into florets

1 large carrot, peeled, halved lengthwise, and thinly sliced

2 (14-ounce/400-g) cans soybeans, drained

2 tablespoons extra-virgin olive oil

2 tablespoons freshly squeezed lemon juice

2 tablespoons finely chopped fresh parsley

Salt and freshly ground black pepper

Preparation: 10 minutes
Cooking: 4 minutes

Serves: 4–6
Level: 1

BEAN AND SPINACH SALAD

Mix the cannellini beans, onion, bell pepper, tomatoes, and spinach in a large bowl. • Mix the oil, lemon juice, and sugar in a small bowl. • Drizzle the dressing over the salad and toss well. • Season with salt and pepper. • Spoon into bowls and serve.

1   (14-ounce/400-g) can cannellini beans, drained and rinsed

1   small red onion, thinly sliced

1   red bell pepper (capsicum), seeded and diced

4   tomatoes, cut into wedges

4   ounces (125 g) baby spinach leaves, shredded

2   tablespoons extra-virgin olive oil

2   tablespoons freshly squeezed lemon juice

1/8 teaspoon sugar

Salt and freshly ground black pepper

 Preparation: 10 minutes

Serves: 4
Level: 1

SOUPS

THAI TOFU AND MUSHROOM SOUP

Sauté the mushrooms in the oil in a large saucepan over medium heat until softened, about 3 minutes. • Add the curry paste and cook for 1 minute while stirring until aromatic. • Stir in the vegetable stock, coconut milk, fish sauce, lime juice, tofu, and scallions. Bring to a boil. • Cover and simmer over medium-low heat for 5 minutes. • Ladle the soup into bowls. Garnish with the cilantro and serve hot.

8   ounces (250 g) button mushrooms, thinly sliced

¹/₄ cup (60 ml) peanut oil

¹/₃ cup (90 ml) Thai red curry paste

4   cups (1 liter) vegetable stock

2   cups (500 ml) coconut milk

1   tablespoon Asian fish sauce

1   tablespoon freshly squeezed lime juice

8   ounces (250 g) firm tofu, cut into small cubes

3   scallions (spring onions), thinly sliced

1   bunch fresh cilantro (coriander) leaves

 Preparation: 10 minutes
Cooking: 10 minutes

Serves: 4
Level: 1

■■■ *Red curry paste is a Thai condiment used to flavor soups, curries, and stir-fries. You can buy it at Asian food stores or online.*

CREAMY MUSHROOM SOUP WITH THYME

Sauté the onion, garlic, and mushrooms in the oil in a large saucepan over medium heat until softened, about 3 minutes. • Pour in the stock and cream. Bring to a boil. • Cover and simmer over low heat for 5 minutes. • Pour the mixture into a food processor and process until smooth. • Stir in the thyme and season with salt and pepper. • Ladle the soup into bowls. • Garnish with the thyme leaves and serve hot.

1 onion, finely chopped

2 cloves garlic, finely chopped

1 pound (500 g) white mushrooms, coarsely chopped

2 tablespoons extra-virgin olive oil

4 cups (1 liter) vegetable stock

1 cup (250 ml) light (single) cream

2 tablespoons fresh thyme leaves, + extra leaves to garnish

Salt and freshly ground black pepper

Preparation: 10 minutes
Cooking: 10 minutes

Serves: 4
Level: 1

■ ■ ■ *The fresh thyme sets off the flavors of the mushrooms beautifully in this creamy soup. For the best flavor, use homemade vegetable stock. Although making stock takes time, remember that it can be made ahead of time and frozen for future use.*

CHICKEN AND CORN SOUP

Sauté the garlic and ginger in the oil in a large saucepan over medium-low heat until aromatic, about 1 minute. • Pour in the chicken stock and creamed corn. Add the chicken and soy sauce. Bring to a boil. • Simmer over medium heat for 5 minutes. • Mix the cornstarch and cold water in a small bowl until smooth. • Add the cornstarch mixture to the soup and stir until it starts to thicken, about 30 seconds. • Gradually pour in the egg, stirring constantly. Cook for about 1 minute, until the egg is cooked. • Ladle the soup into bowls. • Garnish with the scallions and serve hot.

2   cloves garlic, finely chopped

2   teaspoons finely grated ginger

2   teaspoons peanut oil

$2^{1}/_{2}$ cups (625 ml) chicken stock

$2^{1}/_{2}$ cups (625 ml) canned creamed corn (sweet corn)

2   cups (200 g) shredded cooked chicken

1   tablespoon light soy sauce

2   teaspoons cornstarch (cornflour)

2   tablespoons cold water

1   large egg, lightly beaten

2   scallions (spring onions), thinly sliced

Preparation: 10 minutes

Cooking: 8 minutes

Serves: 4

Level: 1

THAI SWEET POTATO SOUP

Sauté the onion and garlic in the oil in a large saucepan over medium-low heat until softened, about 3 minutes. • Add the curry paste and cook, stirring, for 1 minute until aromatic. • Add the sweet potatoes, stirring well to coat them with the curry paste. • Pour in the stock and coconut milk. Bring to a boil. • Cover and simmer over medium-low heat until the sweet potatoes are tender, about 20 minutes. • Pour the mixture into a food processor and process until smooth. • Ladle the soup into bowls. Garnish with the cilantro and serve hot.

1   onion, finely chopped

2   cloves garlic, finely chopped

1   tablespoon extra-virgin olive oil

1/4 cup (60 ml) Thai red curry paste

2   pounds (1 kg) sweet potatoes, peeled and cut into small cubes

5   cups (1.25 liters) chicken stock

1   cup (250 ml) coconut milk

Fresh cilantro (coriander) leaves, to garnish

 Preparation: 5 minutes
Cooking: 25 minutes

Serves: 4
Level: 1

TOMATO, VEGETABLE, AND BEAN SOUP

Sauté the onion and garlic in the oil in a large saucepan over medium-low heat until softened, about 3 minutes. • Add the vegetable stock, tomatoes, tomato paste, zucchini, carrot, and celery. Bring to a boil. • Cover and simmer over medium-low heat until the zucchini are tender, about 15 minutes. • Add the borlotti beans and basil. Season with salt and pepper. • Simmer for 2 minutes. • Ladle the soup into bowls and serve hot.

1	onion, finely chopped
2	cloves garlic, finely chopped
1	tablespoon extra-virgin olive oil
4	cups (1 liter) vegetable stock
2	pounds (1 kg) tomatoes, chopped
2	tablespoons tomato paste
2	zucchini (courgettes), halved lengthwise and thinly sliced
1	large carrot, finely chopped
2	stalks celery, thinly sliced
1	(14-ounce/400-g) can borlotti or red kidney beans, drained and rinsed
1	small sprig basil leaves
	Salt and freshly ground black pepper

Preparation: 10 minutes
Cooking: 20 minutes

Serves: 4
Level: 1

SPICY PUMPKIN SOUP

Sauté the onion and garlic in the oil in a large saucepan over medium-low heat until softened, about 3 minutes. • Add the Cajun spices and cook, stirring, for 1 minute. • Add the pumpkin, stirring well to coat it with the Cajun spices.
• Pour in the vegetable stock and bring to a boil. • Cover and simmer over low heat until the pumpkin is tender, 15–20 minutes. • Pour the mixture into a food processor and process until smooth.
• Season with salt and pepper. • Ladle the soup into bowls. Garnish with the chives and serve hot.

1   onion, finely chopped

2   cloves garlic, finely chopped

1   tablespoon extra-virgin olive oil

2   teaspoons Cajun spices

2   pounds (1 kg) pumpkin or winter squash, cut into small cubes

5   cups (1.25 liters) vegetable stock

    Salt and freshly ground black pepper

1   tablespoon finely chopped fresh chives

 Preparation: 10 minutes
Cooking: 20 minutes

Serves: 4
Level: 1

LEEK AND POTATO SOUP

Sauté the leeks and garlic in the oil in a large saucepan over medium-low heat until softened, about 3 minutes. • Pour in the chicken stock. Add the potatoes and rosemary. Bring to a boil. • Cover and simmer over low heat until the potatoes are tender, about 15 minutes. • Stir in the lemon juice and season with salt and pepper. • Ladle the soup into bowls and serve hot.

2   leeks, thinly sliced

2   cloves garlic, finely chopped

1   tablespoon extra-virgin olive oil

5   cups (1.25 liters) chicken stock

2   pounds (1 kg) potatoes, peeled and cut into small cubes

1   tablespoon finely chopped fresh rosemary

2   tablespoons freshly squeezed lemon juice

Salt and freshly ground black pepper

 Preparation: 10 minutes
Cooking: 20 minutes

Serves: 4
Level: 1

TOMATO AND LENTIL SOUP

Sauté the onion and garlic in the oil in a large saucepan over medium-low heat until softened, about 3 minutes. • Add the curry paste and cook, stirring, for 1 minute. • Pour in the vegetable stock, tomatoes, and lentils. Bring to a boil. • Cover and simmer over low heat, stirring from time to time, until the lentils are tender, about 20 minutes. • Season with salt and pepper. • Ladle the soup into bowls and serve hot.

1   onion, finely chopped

2   cloves garlic, finely chopped

2   tablespoons extra-virgin olive oil

2   tablespoons mild curry paste

4   cups (1 liter) vegetable stock

2   (14-ounce/400-g) can tomatoes, with juice

1   cup (100 g) red lentils

    Salt and freshly ground black pepper

Preparation: 5 minutes
Cooking: 25 minutes

Serves: 4
Level: 1

VEGETABLE, LENTIL, AND PESTO SOUP

Sauté the onion and garlic in the oil in a large saucepan over medium-low heat until softened, about 3 minutes. • Add the carrot, celery, potatoes, sweet potatoes, lentils, and vegetable stock. Bring to a boil. • Cover and simmer over low heat until the vegetables are tender, about 15 minutes. • Stir in the pesto and lentils. • Cook until the lentils are heated through, about 2 minutes. • Season with salt and pepper. • Ladle the soup into bowls and serve hot.

1   onion, finely chopped

2   cloves garlic, finely chopped

1   tablespoon extra-virgin olive oil

1   carrot, peeled and cut into cubes

2   stalks celery, thinly sliced

2   potatoes, peeled and cut into cubes

10 ounces (300 g) sweet potatoes, peeled and cut into cubes

14 ounces (400 g) frozen brown lentils

4   cups (1 liter) vegetable stock

2   tablespoons basil pesto

    Salt and freshly ground black pepper

 Preparation: 10 minutes
Cooking: 20 minutes

Serves: 4
Level: 1

CURRIED SPINACH SOUP

Sauté the onion and garlic in the oil in a large saucepan over medium-low heat until softened, about 3 minutes. • Add the curry paste and cook for 1 minute while stirring. • Add the stock and spinach. Bring to a boil. • Stir in the coconut milk. Cover and simmer over low heat for 5 minutes, stirring from time to time. • Pour the mixture into a food processor and process until smooth. • Season with salt and pepper. • Ladle the soup into bowls. • Serve hot with the pappadams on the side.

1	onion, finely chopped
2	cloves garlic, finely chopped
1	tablespoon extra-virgin olive oil
2	tablespoons Thai green curry or mild curry paste
2	cups (500 ml) chicken or vegetable stock
8	ounces (250 g) frozen spinach, thawed
2	cups (500 ml) coconut milk
	Salt and freshly ground black pepper
	Pappadams, to serve

Preparation: 10 minutes
Cooking: 10 minutes

Serves: 4
Level: 1

■■■ *Pappadams are a crisp, wafer-thin Indian bread made from lentil flour. They are available in Indian food markets. If preferred, substitute with crusty, freshly baked bread.*

MINTED PEA SOUP

Sauté the onion and garlic in the oil in a large saucepan over medium-low heat until softened, about 3 minutes. • Pour in the stock. Bring to a boil. • Add the peas and mint, reserving a little for a garnish. • Cover and simmer over low heat for 5 minutes. • Pour the mixture into a food processor and process until smooth. • Return the soup to the saucepan. Stir in the sour cream. Season with salt and pepper. • Simmer over low heat for 5 minutes. • Ladle the soup into bowls, garnish with the reserved mint, and serve hot.

1   onion, finely chopped

2   cloves garlic, finely chopped

2   tablespoons extra-virgin olive oil

2¹/₂ cups (625 ml) chicken stock

2   pounds (1 kg) frozen peas, thawed

1   small bunch fresh mint, coarsely chopped

¹/₃ cup (90 ml) sour cream

   Salt and freshly ground black pepper

Preparation: 10 minutes
Cooking: 15 minutes

Serves: 4
Level: 1

JERUSALEM ARTICHOKE AND LEEK SOUP

Sauté the leeks and garlic in the oil in a large saucepan over medium-low heat until softened, about 3 minutes. • Add the Jerusalem artichokes and stock. Bring to a boil. • Cover and simmer over low heat until the artichokes are tender, 12–15 minutes. • Stir in the lemon juice and season with salt and pepper. • Pour the mixture into a food processor and process until smooth. • Ladle the soup into bowls. • Garnish with the parsley and serve hot with the bread.

2 leeks, cut in half lengthwise and thinly sliced

2 cloves garlic, finely chopped

2 tablespoons extra-virgin olive oil

1 pound (500 g) Jerusalem artichokes, peeled and cut into cubes

4 cups (1 liter) chicken or vegetable stock

2 tablespoons freshly squeezed lemon juice

Salt and freshly ground black pepper

Sprigs of parsley, to garnish

Whole-wheat (wholemeal) bread, to serve

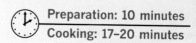

Preparation: 10 minutes
Cooking: 17–20 minutes

Serves: 4
Level: 1

HOT AND SOUR CHICKEN SOUP

Bring the chicken stock to a boil in a large saucepan over high heat. • Add the garlic, lemon grass, 1 chile pepper, and half the kaffir lime leaves. Bring to a boil. • Strain the stock into a large bowl. • Return the stock to the saucepan. • Cover and simmer over medium-low heat for 10 minutes. • Add the lime juice, fish sauce, jaggery, and remaining chile pepper to the soup. • Stir in half the cilantro. • Divide the shredded chicken among the serving bowls. • Ladle the soup over the chicken. • Garnish with the remaining kaffir lime leaves and cilantro and serve hot.

6	cups (1.5 liters) chicken stock
2	cloves garlic, finely chopped
2	stems lemon grass, coarsely chopped
2	small red Thai chiles, seeded and finely sliced
6	kaffir lime leaves, finely shredded
2	tablespoons freshly squeezed lime juice
2	tablespoons Asian fish sauce
2	teaspoons jaggery (palm sugar) or brown sugar
2	cups (200 g) shredded cooked chicken
1/2	cup (25 g) cilantro (coriander) leaves

Preparation: 10 minutes
Cooking: 15 minutes

Serves: 4–6
Level: 1

■■■ *Kaffir lime, also known as makrut lime, is a member of the citrus family. The fruit is knobbly and bitter-tasting, and it is the leaves that are most commonly used to flavor food. If you can't find the lime leaves for this dish, it is okay to leave them out.*

SPICED CAULIFLOWER SOUP

Sauté the onion and garlic in the oil in a large saucepan over medium-low heat until softened, about 3 minutes. • Stir in the turmeric, coriander, and cumin and cook for 1 minute. • Add the cauliflower and potato. Pour in the stock. Bring to a boil. • Cover and simmer over low heat until the cauliflower and potato are tender, 10–12 minutes. • Pour the mixture into a food processor and process until smooth. • Stir in the yogurt and season with salt and pepper. • Ladle the soup into bowls. • Garnish with the parsley and serve hot with the toast.

1   onion, finely chopped

2   cloves garlic, finely chopped

2   tablespoons vegetable oil

1   teaspoon ground turmeric

1   teaspoon ground coriander

1   teaspoon ground cumin

1¹/₂ pounds (750 g) cauliflower, cut into florets

1   potato, peeled and cut into cubes

4   cups (1 liter) chicken or vegetable stock

¹/₃ cup (90 ml) plain yogurt

    Salt and freshly ground black pepper

    Sprigs of parsley, to garnish

    Toast, to serve

Preparation: 10 minutes
Cooking: 15–17 minutes

Serves: 4
Level: 1

CREAMY TOMATO SOUP

Sauté the onion and garlic in the oil in a large saucepan over medium-low heat until softened, about 3 minutes. • Add the tomatoes, stock, bay leaves, and sugar. • Break the tomatoes up using a wooden spoon. • Bring to a boil. • Cover and simmer over low heat for 10 minutes. • Discard the bay leaves. • Pour the mixture into a food processor and process until smooth. • Return the soup to the saucepan. Stir in the cream. Season with salt and pepper. • Simmer over low heat for 5 minutes. • Ladle the soup into bowls. • Garnish with the basil and serve hot.

1 onion, finely chopped

3 cloves garlic, finely chopped

2 tablespoons extra-virgin olive oil

2 (14-ounce/400-g) cans tomatoes, with juice

1 1/2 cups (375 ml) vegetable or chicken stock

2 bay leaves

1 teaspoon sugar

1/2 cup (125 ml) light (single) cream

Salt and freshly ground black pepper

Sprigs of basil, to garnish

Preparation: 10 minutes
Cooking: 20 minutes

Serves: 4
Level: 1

MOROCCAN CARROT AND GARBANZO BEAN SOUP

Sauté the onion and garlic in the oil in a large saucepan over medium-low heat until softened, about 3 minutes. • Add the ras el hanout and cook for 1 minute while stirring. • Add the carrots and cook for 3 minutes, stirring from time to time. • Add the stock and garbanzo beans. Bring to a boil. • Cover and simmer over low heat until the carrots are tender, 10–12 minutes. • Pour the mixture into a food processor and process until smooth. • Stir in the parsley and season with salt and pepper. • Ladle the soup into bowls and serve hot with bread.

1 **onion, finely chopped**

2 **cloves garlic, finely chopped**

2 **tablespoons extra-virgin olive oil**

2 **teaspoons ras el hanout (mixed Moroccan spices)**

1 **pound (500 g) carrots, thinly sliced**

5 **cups (1.25 liters) chicken stock**

1 **(14-ounce/400-g) can garbanzo beans (chick-peas), drained and rinsed**

2 **tablespoons finely chopped fresh flat-leaf parsley**

Salt and freshly ground black pepper

Freshly baked bread, to serve

 Preparation: 10 minutes
Cooking: 18–20 minutes

Serves: 4
Level: 1

CREAMY TOMATO SOUP WITH SOUR CREAM

Sauté the onions and thyme in the oil in a large saucepan over medium-low heat until softened, about 3 minutes. • Stir in the tomatoes and season with salt and pepper. • Cook for 2 minutes. • Pour in the water and bring to a boil. • Simmer over medium heat for 10 minutes.
• Discard the thyme. • Pour the mixture into a food processor and process until smooth. • Return the soup to the saucepan. Stir in the cream. • Simmer over low heat for 5 minutes. • Ladle the soup into bowls. • Garnish with the sour cream and cilantro. Serve hot.

2	large onions, finely chopped
1	sprig thyme
1/4	cup (60 ml) extra-virgin olive oil
4	pounds (2 kg) ripe tomatoes, peeled and coarsely chopped
	Salt and freshly ground black pepper
	Generous 3/4 cup (200 ml) boiling water
3/4	cup (180 ml) heavy (double) cream
2/3	cup (150 g) sour cream
	Sprigs of cilantro (coriander), to garnish

Preparation: 10 minutes
Cooking: 20 minutes

Serves: 6–8
Level: 1

■■■ *Tomatoes are so widely used today in almost every cuisine that it is hard to believe that they were unknown outside of South and Central America until the 16th century. They did not become popular in European cooking until the 18th century. By the end of the 19th century, both Italians and Americans were growing tomatoes on a large scale. Tomato ketchup was invented in the United States in the 1830s and quickly spread around the globe. Tomatoes are a healthy food; they are an excellent source of vitamin C and a good source of vitamin A. They also contain a chemical called lycopene which many doctors believe can help to protect against cancer.*

BROCCOLI AND HAM SOUP

Sauté the scallions and garlic in the oil in a large saucepan over medium-low heat until softened, about 3 minutes. • Add the potatoes, broccoli, and chicken stock. Bring to a boil. • Cover and simmer over medium-low heat until the potatoes and broccoli are tender, about 10 minutes. • Pour the mixture into a food processor and process until smooth. • Return the soup to the saucepan. Stir in the sour cream and ham. Season with salt and pepper. • Simmer over low heat for 5 minutes. • Ladle the soup into bowls and serve hot.

- **3** scallions (spring onions), thinly sliced
- **2** cloves garlic, finely chopped
- **1** tablespoon extra-virgin olive oil
- **2** potatoes, peeled and cut into small cubes
- **12** ounces (350 g) broccoli, cut into florets
- **5** cups (1.25 liters) chicken stock
- **1/2** cup (125 ml) sour cream
- **1** cup (180 g) diced smoked ham

  Salt and freshly ground black pepper

Preparation: 10 minutes

Cooking: 20 minutes

Serves: 4

Level: 1

VIETNAMESE BEEF NOODLE SOUP

Cook the noodles according to the instructions on the package. • Drain and set aside. • Mix the beef stock, star anise, cinnamon stick, ginger, and brown sugar in a large saucepan. Bring to a boil over high heat, stirring until the sugar has dissolved. • Cover and simmer over medium-low heat for 5 minutes.
• Discard the cinnamon stick and star anise. • Stir in the fish sauce and rice vinegar. • Divide the noodles among serving bowls. Top with the sliced beef.
• Bring the stock mixture to a boil and ladle over the beef. • Garnish with the bean sprouts and cilantro. Serve hot with the lime wedges.

10 ounces (300 g) dried rice vermicelli noodles
6 cups (1.5 liters) beef stock
4 star anise
1 stick cinnamon
1¹/₂-inch (1.5-cm) piece fresh ginger, peeled and thinly sliced
2 teaspoons brown sugar
2 tablespoons Asian fish sauce
2 tablespoons rice vinegar
1 pound (500 g) beef fillet steak, very thinly sliced across the grain
3 ounces (90 g) fresh bean sprouts
¹/₂ cup (25 g) cilantro (coriander) leaves
1 lime, cut into wedges

Preparation: 10 minutes
Cooking: 10 minutes

Serves: 4
Level: 1

CHORIZO, BEAN, AND SPINACH SOUP

Sauté the chorizo and onion in the oil in a large saucepan over medium-high heat until the onion is softened, about 5 minutes. • Add the garlic and tomato paste. • Sauté for 1 minute. • Pour in the chicken stock, tomatoes, and beans. Bring to a boil. • Simmer over medium heat for 10 minutes. • Stir in the spinach and season with salt and pepper. • Cook until the spinach has wilted, about 3 minutes. • Ladle the soup into bowls and serve hot.

12	ounces (350 g) dried Spanish chorizo sausage, diced
1	onion, finely chopped
1	tablespoon extra-virgin olive oil
2	cloves garlic, finely chopped
2	tablespoons tomato paste
5	cups (1.25 liters) chicken stock
1	(14-ounce/400 g) can tomatoes, with juice
1	(14-ounce/400 g) can cannellini beans, drained and rinsed
4	ounces (125 g) baby spinach leaves
	Salt and freshly ground black pepper

Preparation: 5 minutes

Cooking: 20 minutes

Serves: 4

Level: 1

GAZPACHO

Combine the tomatoes, bell pepper, cucumber, scallion, bread crumbs, almonds, and garlic in a food processor and process until smooth. • Add the oil, vinegar, and water. Season with salt and pepper. • Process for a few seconds more until well mixed. • Ladle the soup into serving bowls. • Garnish with the remaining thinly sliced bell pepper and cilantro. • Serve at once.

192

■■■ *Make sure all the ingredients for this cool soup are well chilled in the refrigerator. Take them out just before you make the soup and keep it well chilled until you serve it.*

1	pound (500 g) firm-ripe tomatoes, peeled
1	red bell pepper (capsicum), seeded, cored, and coarsely chopped, + extra to garnish
1	cucumber, peeled and finely chopped
1	scallion (spring onion), finely chopped
4	cups (250 g) fresh bread crumbs
1/2	cup (75 g) almonds, toasted
1	clove garlic, peeled
1/4	cup (60 ml) extra-virgin olive oil
2	tablespoons white wine vinegar
4	cups (1 liter) ice-cold water
	Salt and freshly ground black pepper
	Fresh cilantro (coriander) leaves, to garnish

Preparation: 5 minutes

Serves: 4
Level: 1

PASTA

SPAGHETTI WITH MINT, GARLIC, AND OLIVES

Sauté the garlic in the oil in a large frying pan over medium heat until pale gold, 2–3 minutes. • Add the anchovies and sauté—crushing with the tines of a fork—until they have dissolved into the oil, about 5 minutes. • Remove from the heat and add the mint and parsley. • Meanwhile, cook the pasta in a large pot of salted boiling water until al dente, 10–12 minutes. • Drain and add to the sauce. • Sprinkle with the capers and olives, toss well, and serve hot.

2	cloves garlic, finely chopped
1/3	cup (90 ml) extra-virgin olive oil
6	anchovy fillets
2	tablespoons finely chopped fresh mint
4	tablespoons finely chopped fresh parsley
1	pound (500 g) spaghetti
2	tablespoons capers in brine, rinsed
12	black olives, pitted and coarsely chopped

 Preparation: 10 minutes
Cooking: 20 minutes

Serves: 4–6
Level: 1

SPAGHETTI WITH PEAS, CRISP BACON, AND PARMESAN

Cook the spaghetti in a large saucepan of salted boiling water, until al dente, about 10 minutes • Meanwhile, heat the oil in a large frying pan over medium-high heat. • Sauté the bacon and onion, until the bacon is crisp, about 5 minutes. Remove from the pan and keep warm. • Add the chicken stock to the pan and bring to a boil. • Add the peas and mint. Cover and simmer until the peas are tender, about 2 minutes. • Drain the pasta and return to the pan. • Add the pea mixture, bacon and onion mixture, and Parmesan.
• Season with salt and pepper. Toss over low heat until well combined.
Serve hot.

1   pound (500 g) spaghetti

1   tablespoon extra-virgin olive oil

6   ounces (180 g) bacon slices, coarsely chopped

1   onion, finely chopped

1/2 cup (125 ml) chicken stock

1   cup (150 g) frozen peas

2   tablespoons finely chopped fresh mint

5   ounces (150 g) Parmesan cheese, shaved

Salt and freshly ground black pepper

Preparation: 10 minutes
Cooking: 15 minutes

Serves: 4
Level: 1

SPAGHETTI WITH BUTTER AND SAGE BREAD CRUMBS

Cook the spaghetti in a large saucepan of salted boiling water until al dente, 10–12 minutes. • Meanwhile, heat the butter and oil in a medium frying pan over medium-high heat. • Sauté the garlic and sage until tender, about 1 minute. • Add the bread crumbs and cook, stirring from time to time, until crisp and golden, 3–5 minutes. • Drain the spaghetti and return to the pan.
• Add the bread crumb mixture.
• Season with salt and pepper.
• Toss until well combined. Serve hot with the grated Parmesan.

1 pound (500 g) spaghetti

1/4 cup (60 g) butter

1 tablespoon extra-virgin olive oil

3 cloves garlic, finely chopped

1/4 cup (10 g) fresh sage leaves

1 cup (60 g) fresh bread crumbs

Salt and freshly ground black pepper

Freshly grated Parmesan cheese, to serve

Preparation: 10 minutes
Cooking: 15 minutes

Serves: 4
Level: 1

SPAGHETTI WITH PANCETTA, TOMATOES, AND BASIL

Cook the spaghetti in a large saucepan of salted boiling water until al dente, about 10 minutes. Drain the spaghetti, reserving 1 cup (250 ml) of the cooking water.
• Meanwhile, heat the oil in a large frying pan over medium-high heat. • Sauté the pancetta until golden, about 2 minutes.
• Add the tomatoes and garlic. Cook, stirring occasionally, until the tomatoes are soft, about 5 minutes. • Add the drained spaghetti to the pan. • Add the basil and enough of the reserved cooking water to make a thick sauce. • Season with salt and pepper. • Toss over low heat until hot, 1–2 minutes. • Spoon into bowls and serve hot with the Parmesan cheese.

1 **pound (500 g) spaghetti**

1 **tablespoon extra-virgin olive oil**

5 **ounces (150 g) pancetta or bacon, coarsely chopped**

1 **pound (500 g) cherry tomatoes, halved**

3 **cloves garlic, crushed**

4 **tablespoons coarsely chopped fresh basil**

Salt and freshly ground black pepper

Freshly grated Parmesan cheese, to serve

 Preparation: 10 minutes
Cooking: 12 minutes

Serves: 4
Level: 1

LEMON, CHILE, AND BASIL ANGEL HAIR PASTA

204

Cook the angel hair pasta in a large saucepan of salted boiling water until al dente, 2–3 minutes. • Meanwhile, combine the lemon juice, oil, chiles, and Parmesan in a medium bowl. Whisk until well combined. • Drain the pasta and return to the pan. • Add the lemon mixture, basil, and lemon zest. • Season with salt and pepper. • Toss over low heat until well combined. Serve hot.

1 **pound (500 g) angel hair pasta**

1/2 **cup (125 ml) freshly squeezed lemon juice**

1/3 **cup (90 ml) extra-virgin olive oil**

2 **small fresh, red chiles, seeded and finely sliced**

3 **ounces (90 g) Parmesan cheese, freshly grated**

1 **cup (30 g) basil leaves**

2 **teaspoons finely grated lemon zest**

Salt and freshly ground black pepper

 Preparation: 10 minutes

Cooking: 2–3 minutes

Serves: 4
Level: 1

BUCATINI WITH GARLIC, TUNA, AND CHERRY TOMATOES

Cook the bucatini in a large saucepan of salted boiling water until al dente, 10–12 minutes. • Drain and keep warm. • Heat the oil in a saucepan over high heat. • Sauté the tomatoes, garlic, and sugar until the tomatoes are just soft, about 5 minutes. • Stir in oregano and season with salt and pepper. • Add the bucatini and tuna to the tomato mixture. • Toss over low heat until well combined. Serve hot.

1	pound (500 g) bucatini or spaghetti
3	tablespoons extra-virgin olive oil
1	pound (500 g) cherry tomatoes, halved
3	cloves garlic, finely chopped
1/2	teaspoon sugar
2	tablespoons fresh oregano leaves
	Salt and freshly ground black pepper
1	(14-ounce/400-g) can tuna in oil, drained and flaked

Preparation: 5 minutes
Cooking: 15 minutes

Serves: 4
Level: 1

SPAGHETTI WITH ZUCCHINI AND PINE NUTS

208

Cook the pasta in a large saucepan of salted boiling water until al dente, about 10 minutes. • Drain and set aside. • Heat 1 tablespoon of oil in a large saucepan over medium heat. • Sauté the pine nuts until golden, about 1 minute. Remove with a slotted spoon. • Heat the remaining oil and the butter in the same pan. Sauté the garlic and zucchini until soft, about 2 minutes. • Return the pasta and pine nuts to the pan. Add the basil and cream. • Season with salt and pepper. • Toss the pasta until heated through, about 3 minutes. • Serve hot with the Parmesan cheese.

1	pound (500 g) spaghetti
3	tablespoons extra-virgin olive oil
1/2	cup (90 g) pine nuts
3	tablespoons butter
3	cloves garlic, crushed
3	medium zucchini (courgettes), shredded or grated
4	tablespoons finely chopped basil
1/2	cup (125 ml) light (single) cream
1	cup (125 g) freshly grated Parmesan cheese

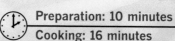

Preparation: 10 minutes
Cooking: 16 minutes

Serves: 4
Level: 1

SPAGHETTI WITH CHERRY TOMATOES

Cook the spaghetti in a large pot of salted, boiling water until al dente, 10–12 minutes. • Mix the oil, oregano, chile pepper, and garlic in a small bowl. • Heat a large frying pan over medium heat. Add the oil mixture and sauté until the garlic is pale gold, about 2 minutes. • Add the tomatoes and sauté for 3 minutes. • Drain the pasta and add to the tomatoes. Season with salt. Add the mozzarella and toss well. • Serve hot.

1	pound (500 g) spaghetti
1/3	cup (90 ml) extra-virgin olive oil
1	tablespoons finely chopped fresh oregano
1	dried red chile, finely chopped
2	cloves garlic, lightly crushed but left whole
2	pounds (1 kg) cherry tomatoes, halved
	Salt
8	ounces (250 g) small mozzarella balls (bocconcini), halved

Preparation: 10 minutes
Cooking: 10–15 minutes

Serves: 4–6
Level: 1

SPAGHETTI WITH SPICY TUNA AND THYME

Toss the tuna in the flour, shaking to remove the excess. • Heat the oil in a large frying pan over medium heat. Add the garlic, olives, chiles, and 1 tablespoon of thyme. Sauté for 2 minutes. • Season with salt and pepper. Add the tuna and zucchini. Cook over medium heat until the fish is cooked through, 5–6 minutes. • Drizzle with the wine and let it evaporate for 2 minutes. • Meanwhile, cook the pasta in a large pot of salted, boiling water until al dente, 10–12 minutes. • Drain and add to the tuna. Toss well. Sprinkle with the extra thyme. • Serve hot.

1	pound (500 g) tuna steak, cut into small pieces
2	tablespoons all-purpose (plain) flour
1/4	cup (60 ml) extra-virgin olive oil
1	clove garlic, finely chopped
20	black olives, pitted and finely chopped
2	fresh red or green chiles, seeded and finely chopped
1	tablespoon finely chopped fresh thyme or parsley + extra, to garnish
	Salt and freshly ground black pepper
4	medium zucchini (courgettes), diced
1/2	cup (125 ml) dry white wine
1	pound (500 g) spaghetti

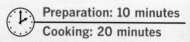

Preparation: 10 minutes
Cooking: 20 minutes

Serves: 4
Level: 1

SPICY SPAGHETTI WITH GARLIC, PINE NUTS, AND RAISINS

Cook the pasta in a large pot of salted, boiling water until al dente, 10–12 minutes. • Sauté the garlic and chile in the oil in a large frying pan over medium heat until the garlic turns pale gold. • Add the pine nuts and golden raisins. Season with salt and pepper. Sauté for 1 minute more. • Drain the pasta well and add to the pan with the sauce. Add the parsley and toss over high heat for 1 minute. • Serve hot.

2 cloves garlic, finely chopped

1 fresh red chile, seeded and finely chopped

1/3 cup (90 ml) extra-virgin olive oil

1/2 cup (90 g) pine nuts

1/2 cup (90 g) golden raisins (sultanas)

Salt and freshly ground black pepper

1 pound (500 g) spaghetti

4 tablespoons finely chopped fresh parsley

Preparation: 10 minutes
Cooking: 15 minutes

Serves: 4
Level: 1

SPAGHETTI WITH CLAMS

Place 1 clove of garlic and half the parsley in 2 tablespoons of oil in a large saucepan. Add the clams and cook over high heat until open, 5–10 minutes. Discard any clams that do not open.
• Cook the remaining garlic, chile pepper, and chopped tomatoes in a large saucepan over medium heat for 10 minutes. • Season with salt and pepper. Add the clams and their cooking liquid.
• Meanwhile, cook the pasta in a large pot of salted, boiling water until al dente, 10–12 minutes. • Drain and add to the clam sauce. Season generously with pepper. Toss well. • Serve hot.

3 cloves garlic, finely chopped

2 tablespoons finely chopped fresh parsley

1/3 cup (90 ml) extra-virgin olive oil

2 pounds (1 kg) clams, in shell

1 pound (500 g) ripe tomatoes, peeled and chopped

1 fresh red chile, seeded and finely chopped

Salt and freshly ground black pepper

1 pound (500 g) spaghetti

Preparation: 15 minutes
Cooking: 15 minutes

Serves: 4–6
Level: 2

PAPPARDELLE WITH SWEET POTATO, SAGE, AND PROSCIUTTO

Cook the pasta in a large saucepan of salted boiling water until al dente, about 5 minutes. • Drain and set aside. • Using a vegetable peeler, cut the sweet potato into thin strips. • Meanwhile, heat the oil in a large frying pan over high heat. • Cook the sweet potato in batches until crisp, 1–2 minutes for each batch. • Drain on paper towels. • Add the garlic, proscuitto, and sage leaves. • Cook until golden and crisp, about 2 minutes. • Stir in the wine and cook for 2 minutes. • Add the cream, Parmesan, and pasta. Season with salt and pepper. • Toss over low heat for 2 minutes. Serve hot.

14 ounces (400 g) pappardelle

1/2 cup (125 ml) extra-virgin olive oil

1 large sweet potato (kumara), peeled

10 thin slices prosciutto (Parma ham)

2 cloves garlic, crushed

1 small bunch fresh sage leaves

1/2 cup (125 ml) dry white wine

1 cup (250 ml) heavy (double) cream

Freshly grated Parmesan cheese, to serve

Salt and freshly ground black pepper

Preparation: 10 minutes
Cooking: 8–10 minutes

Serves: 4
Level: 1

PENNE WITH ASPARAGUS, MUSHROOMS, AND CHILE

Cook the pasta in a large saucepan of salted boiling water until al dente, about 10 minutes. • Drain and set aside. • Heat the oil in a large frying pan over medium heat. • Sauté the garlic, chiles, mushrooms, and asparagus until soft, about 3 minutes. • Return the pasta to the pan. • Stir in the stock, spinach, thyme, and mushroom mixture. Season with salt and pepper. • Stir until heated through, about 2 minutes. Serve hot.

1	pound (500 g) penne
3	tablespoons extra-virgin olive oil
2	cloves garlic, crushed
2	small fresh red chiles, seeds removed and finely chopped
8	ounces (250 g) button mushrooms, sliced
1	bunch asparagus, cut into short lengths
1	cup (250 ml) chicken stock
3	ounces (90 g) baby spinach leaves
2	tablespoons fresh thyme leaves
	Salt and freshly ground black pepper

 Preparation: 10 minutes

Cooking: 10 minutes

Serves: 4
Level: 1

FETTUCCINE WITH SALMON AND CAPERS

Cook the pasta in a large saucepan of salted boiling water until al dente, about 3–5 minutes. • Drain and place in a large heated bowl. • Meanwhile, heat the oil in a large saucepan over medium heat. • Sauté the salmon until nearly cooked, about 3 minutes each side. Stir in the lemon juice. • Transfer the salmon to a plate and flake. • Add the scallions, cream, capers, salmon, and parsley to the pasta in the bowl. • Season with salt and pepper. Toss thoroughly and serve hot.

222

1   pound (500 g) fettuccine

3   tablespoons extra-virgin olive oil

14 ounces (400 g) salmon fillet

$1/3$ cup (90 ml) freshly squeezed lemon juice

4   scallions (green onions), thinly sliced

$1^1/2$ cups (375 ml) light (single) cream

$1^1/2$ tablespoons capers

2   tablespoons finely chopped fresh flat-leaf parsley

Salt and freshly ground black pepper

 Preparation: 10 minutes
Cooking: 3–5 minutes

Serves: 4
Level: 1

GRILLED ASPARAGUS, SPINACH, AND RICOTTA SALATA PASTA

Cook the fusilli in a large saucepan of boiling salted water until al dente, 10–12 minutes. • While the pasta is cooking, preheat a grill on high heat. • Brush the asparagus with 1 tablespoon of oil. • Grill the asparagus, turning from time to time, until just tender, about 3 minutes. • Remove and cut the asparagus into 2-inch (5-cm) lengths. Set aside. • Drain the pasta, reserving 3 tablespoons of the cooking water. Return the pasta and reserved water to the pan. • Add the remaining oil, scallions, asparagus, spinach, and ricotta. • Season with salt and pepper. • Toss to combine over low heat until the spinach just wilts. Serve hot.

1	pound (500 g) fusilli
2	bunches asparagus, trimmed
1/4	cup (60 ml) extra-virgin olive oil
4	scallions (green onions), thinly sliced diagonally
4	ounces (125 g) baby spinach leaves
8	ounces (250 g) ricotta salata cheese, crumbled
	Salt and freshly ground black pepper

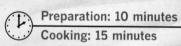

Preparation: 10 minutes
Cooking: 15 minutes

Serves: 4
Level: 1

FETTUCCINE WITH CHICKEN, CREAM, AND CHIVES

Cook the fettuccine in a large saucepan of salted boiling water, until al dente, 3–5 minutes. • Meanwhile, heat the oil in a large frying pan over medium-high heat. • Sauté the garlic and leek until tender, about 5 minutes. • Add the wine and simmer for 1 minute. • Add the cream, chives, and chicken. • Season with salt and pepper. • Cover and simmer over medium heat until warmed through, 3–5 minutes. • Drain the fettuccine and return to pan. • Add the cream sauce. • Toss over low heat until well combined. Serve hot.

1   pound (500 g) fettuccine

3   tablespoons extra-virgin olive oil

2   cloves garlic, crushed

1   leek, trimmed, halved lengthwise, and thinly sliced

1/2   cup (125 ml) dry white wine

1 1/2   cups (375 ml) light (single) cream

2   tablespoons finely chopped fresh chives

2   cups (300 g) cooked shredded chicken

Salt and freshly ground black pepper

Preparation: 15 minutes
Cooking: 10 minutes

Serves: 4
Level: 1

EGGPLANT, MUSHROOM, AND ZUCCHINI PENNE

Cook the penne in a large saucepan of salted boiling water until al dente, 10–12 minutes. • Meanwhile, heat the oil in a large frying pan over medium-high heat. • Sauté the onion, garlic, and eggplant until tender, 3–5 minutes. • Add the mushrooms, zucchini, and tomato sauce. • Season with salt and pepper. • Cover and simmer, stirring occasionally, for 10 minutes or until the vegetables are tender. • Drain the penne and return to the pan. • Add the vegetable mixture. • Toss over low heat until well combined. Serve hot.

1 pound (500 g) penne

3 tablespoons extra-virgin olive oil

1 onion, finely chopped

3 cloves garlic, crushed

1 medium eggplant (aubergine), trimmed and cut into $1/2$-inch (1-cm) cubes

8 ounces (250 g) button mushrooms, thinly sliced

8 ounces (250 g) zucchini (courgettes), thinly sliced

2 cups (500 ml) tomato pasta sauce

Salt and freshly ground black pepper

Preparation: 10 minutes
Cooking: 20 minutes

Serves: 4
Level: 1

PEPPERED MUSHROOM MACARONI

Cook the macaroni in a large saucepan of salted boiling water until al dente, about 10 minutes. • Meanwhile, heat the butter and oil in a large frying pan over medium-high heat. • Sauté the mushrooms and scallions until tender, 4–5 minutes. • Season with salt and stir in the cracked pepper. • Stir in the cream and cook until heated through, about 3 minutes. • Drain the macaroni and return to the pan. • Add the mushroom mixture, parsley, and cheese. • Toss over low heat until the cheese melts. Serve hot.

1	pound (500 g) macaroni
2	tablespoons butter
3	tablespoons extra-virgin olive oil
10	ounces (300 g) button mushrooms, thinly sliced
4	scallions (green onions), thinly sliced
	Salt
1	teaspoon cracked black pepper
1	cup (250 ml) heavy (double) cream
2	tablespoons coarsely chopped fresh flat-leaf parsley
8	ounces (250 g) freshly grated mozzarella cheese

Preparation: 10 minutes
Cooking: 15 minutes

Serves: 4
Level: 1

RIGATONI WITH PANCETTA AND SPRING VEGETABLES

Cook the rigatoni in a large saucepan of salted boiling water until al dente, 10–12 minutes. • Meanwhile, heat the oil in a frying pan over high heat. • Sauté the pancetta until crisp, about 3 minutes. • Remove with a slotted spoon and set aside. • Add the garlic, asparagus, and squash to the pan and cook, stirring from time to time, for 2 minutes. • Stir in the peas and stock. Season with salt and pepper. • Cover and simmer until the vegetables are just tender, 4–5 minutes. • Drain the rigatoni and return to the pan. Stir in the vegetable mixture and pancetta. • Toss until well combined. Serve hot.

1	pound (500 g) rigatoni
2	tablespoons extra-virgin olive oil
5	ounces (150 g) pancetta, coarsely chopped
2	cloves garlic, crushed
1	bunch asparagus, trimmed and cut into 1-inch (2.5-cm) pieces
8	ounces (250 g) yellow squash, sliced
4	ounces (125 g) sugar snap peas, trimmed
1/3	cup (90 ml) chicken or vegetable stock
	Salt and freshly ground black pepper

Preparation: 15 minutes

Cooking: 15 minutes

Serves: 4
Level: 1

THREE-CHEESE PENNE

Cook the penne in a large saucepan of salted boiling water until al dente, 10–12 minutes. • Drain the penne and return to the pan. • Add the cheeses, cream, and chives. • Toss gently to combine. • Season with salt and pepper. • Spoon into four 2-cup (500-ml) greased shallow ovenproof dishes. • Preheat a broiler (grill) on high heat. • Place the dishes under the broiler and cook until hot and bubbling, 3–5 minutes. • Sprinkle with the basil leaves and serve hot.

1   **pound (500 g) penne**
5   **ounces (150 g) Gruyère cheese, freshly grated**
3   **ounces (90 g) cheddar cheese, freshly grated**
5   **ounces (150 g) goat cheese, crumbled**
1/2   **cup (125 ml) light (single) cream**
2   **tablespoons chopped chives**
    Salt and freshly ground black pepper
1/2   **cup basil leaves, to serve**

 Preparation: 10 minutes
Cooking: 20 minutes

Serves: 4
Level: 1

SPINACH ARRABBIATA PASTA

Cook the pasta in a large saucepan of salted boiling water until al dente, 10–12 minutes. • Meanwhile, heat the oil in a large frying pan over medium heat. • Sauté the onion, garlic, and chiles until tender, about 3 minutes. • Add the tomatoes. • Gently simmer, stirring from time to time, until thick, 5–8 minutes. • Stir in the balsamic vinegar. • Season with salt and pepper. • Drain the pasta and return to the pan. • Add the tomato sauce and spinach. • Toss over low heat until well combined. Serve hot.

1	pound (500 g) casarecce or rotini
2	tablespoons extra-virgin olive oil
1	onion, finely chopped
2	cloves garlic, finely chopped
3	small fresh red chiles, seeded and finely chopped
1	(14-ounce/400-g) can tomatoes, with juice
1	tablespoon balsamic vinegar
	Salt and freshly ground black pepper
4	ounces (125 g) baby spinach leaves

Preparation: 10 minutes
Cooking: 15 minutes

Serves: 4
Level: 1

PASTA ALLA PUTTANESCA

Cook the pasta in a large saucepan of salted boiling water until al dente, 10–12 minutes. • Heat the oil in a large frying pan over medium heat. Sauté the garlic, chile, and tomatoes until tender, about 5 minutes. • Stir in the olives, anchovies, and capers. • Simmer, stirring from time to time, until boiling, about 5 minutes. • Drain the pasta and return to the pan. • Add the tomato mixture and the basil. Season with salt and pepper. • Toss over low heat until well combined. Serve hot.

1 pound (500 g) tortiglioni or rigatoni

1/4 cup (60 ml) extra-virgin olive oil

2 cloves garlic, finely chopped

1 long red fresh chile, seeded and finely sliced

6 ripe tomatoes, seeded and coarsely chopped

1/2 cup (75 g) black olives

4 anchovy fillets, drained and coarsely chopped

2 tablespoons salt-cured capers, rinsed

1 cup (30 g) small basil leaves

Salt and freshly ground black pepper

Preparation: 15 minutes
Cooking: 12 minutes

Serves: 4
Level: 1

TOMATO, ARUGULA, AND BLACK OLIVE LINGUINE

Cook the linguine in a large saucepan of salted boiling water until al dente, 10–12 minutes. • Meanwhile, combine the tomato sauce, sugar, and bay leaves in a saucepan. • Cover and simmer over low heat, stirring from time to time, for 10 minutes. • Season with salt and pepper. • Remove the bay leaves. • Drain the linguine and return to the pan. • Add the tomato sauce, olives, and arugula. • Toss until well combined. Serve hot.

1	pound (500 g) linguine
2	cups (500 ml) tomato pasta sauce
1	teaspoon sugar
2	bay leaves
	Salt and freshly ground black pepper
1/2	cup (90 g) small black olives
3	ounces (90 g) baby arugula (rocket) leaves

 Preparation: 10 minutes
Cooking: 12 minutes

Serves: 4
Level: 1

PAPPARDELLE MARINARA

Cook the pappardelle in a large saucepan of salted boiling water until al dente, 3–5 minutes. • Meanwhile, heat the oil in a large frying pan over medium-high heat. • Sauté the onion and garlic until tender, about 3 minutes. • Add the wine and simmer for 1 minute. • Stir in the stock, tomato sauce, and tomato paste. • Bring to a boil, stirring from time to time. • Add the mixed seafood. • Cover and cook until the seafood is cooked through, 3–5 minutes. • Season with salt and pepper. • Drain the pappardelle and return to the pan. Add the marinara sauce and parsley. • Toss until well combined. Serve hot.

1	**pound (500 g) pappardelle**
1/3	**cup (90 ml) extra-virgin olive oil**
1	**onion, finely chopped**
2	**garlic cloves, finely chopped**
2/3	**cup (150 ml) dry white wine**
1/2	**cup (125 ml) fish stock or clam juice**
2	**cups (500 ml) tomato pasta sauce**
3	**tablespoons tomato paste**
2	**pounds (1 kg) mixed fresh seafood (shrimp, fish filets, shelled mussels)**
	Salt and freshly ground black pepper
1/3	**cup (10 g) coarsely chopped fresh flat-leaf parsley**

Preparation: 10 minutes
Cooking: 15 minutes

Serves: 4
Level: 1

FARFALLE WITH BEANS AND PESTO

To prepare the pasta: Bring a large pot of salted water to a boil. Add the green beans and return to a boil. • Add the pasta and cook for 5 minutes. • Add the peas and cook until the pasta is al dente. • To make the pesto: Chop the basil, pine nuts, garlic, oil, and salt in a food processor until smooth. Stir in the cheese. • Drain the pasta and vegetables and toss gently with the pesto. Stir in the kidney beans and walnuts. Drizzle with the oil and garnish with the basil leaves. • Serve hot.

Pasta

- 5 ounces (150 g) green beans, cut into short lengths
- 1 pound (500 g) farfalle
- 1 cup (150 g) fresh or frozen peas
- 1 cup (200 g) canned red kidney beans, drained and rinsed
- 1/2 cup (50 g) chopped walnuts
- 1/4 cup (60 ml) extra-virgin olive oil

  Basil leaves, to garnish

Preparation: 10 minutes

Cooking: 15 minutes

Serves: 4–6

Level: 1

Pesto

1   **large bunch fresh basil**

2   **tablespoons pine nuts**

2   **cloves garlic**

1/2   **cup (125 ml) extra-virgin olive oil**

     Salt

4   **tablespoons freshly grated Parmesan cheese**

■■■ *Pesto is made from basil, garlic, pine nuts, Parmesan, salt, and extra-virgin olive oil. It is quick and simple to prepare and delicious with pasta and fish. It comes from Liguria, the region in Italy that stretches along the northwestern coast to Provence, in France. The same sauce exists in Provence, where it is known as* pistou.

PENNE WITH PESTO

Cook the penne in a large saucepan of salted boiling water until al dente, 10–12 minutes. • Meanwhile, to make the pesto, combine the pine nuts, garlic, and salt in a food processor. • Process until finely chopped. • Add the basil and oil. Process until almost smooth. • Season with salt and pepper. • Stir in the Parmesan. • Drain the penne and return to the pan. • Add the pesto. • Toss over low heat until well combined. Serve hot garnished with basil.

1   **pound (500 g) penne**

1/3   **cup (60 g) pine nuts, toasted**

2   **cloves garlic, coarsely chopped**

1/2   **teaspoon sea salt**

2   **cups (60 g) basil leaves + extra, to garnish**

1/2   **cup (125 ml) extra-virgin olive oil**

1/2   **cup (60 g) freshly grated Parmesan cheese**

Preparation: 15 minutes

Cooking: 12 minutes

Serves: 4

Level: 1

FUSILLI WITH RICOTTA AND ORANGE

Beat the ricotta, orange zest and juice, and water in a small bowl. • Stir in the oil and season with salt and pepper. • Cook the pasta in a large pot of salted, boiling water for 5 minutes. • Add the zucchini and cook until the pasta is al dente and the zucchini are tender, 5–7 minutes. • Drain well and transfer to a large bowl. • Add the sauce and toss well. • Garnish with the slices of orange and serve hot.

2   cups (500 g) fresh ricotta cheese, drained

Finely grated zest and juice of 1 orange

1/3   cup (90 ml) hot water

1/4   cup (60 ml) extra-virgin olive oil

Salt and freshly ground white pepper

1   pound (500 g) fusilli

3   medium zucchini (courgettes), thinly sliced

1   orange, with skin, very thinly sliced, to garnish

 Preparation: 10 minutes
Cooking: 10 minutes

Serves: 4
Level: 1

TAGLIATELLE WITH WALNUT SAUCE

Blanch the walnuts in boiling water for 1 minute. Drain and transfer to a cloth. Roll the nuts firmly under your fingers to remove the skins. • Put the walnuts, garlic, and bread crumbs in the bowl of a food processor and process until finely chopped. • Add the cream, Parmesan, oil, and cinnamon and process until smooth. Season with salt and pepper. • Cook the pasta in a large pot of salted, boiling water until al dente, 3–5 minutes. • Drain and transfer to a large bowl. Add the walnut sauce and toss gently. Garnish with walnut halves and serve hot.

1	cup (125 g) walnuts + extra walnut halves, to garnish
1	clove garlic, peeled
1	cup (60 g) fresh bread crumbs
3/4	cup (180 ml) heavy (double) cream
1/2	cup (60 g) freshly grated Parmesan cheese
3	tablespoons extra-virgin olive oil
1/4	teaspoon ground cinnamon
	Salt and freshly ground black pepper
1	pound (500 g) fresh tagliatelle or fettuccine

Preparation: 20 minutes
Cooking: 4–6 minutes

Serves: 4
Level: 2

TAGLIATELLE WITH VEGETABLE SAUCE

Sauté the onion and garlic in half the oil in a large frying pan over medium heat until softened. • Add the zucchini, bell pepper, carrot, and basil. Sauté for 2–3 minutes. • Stir in the tomatoes. Cover and simmer for 10 minutes until all the vegetables are tender. • Discard the garlic. Season with salt and pepper. • Meanwhile, cook the pasta in a large pot of salted, boiling water until al dente, 3–5 minutes. • Drain and add to the sauce. Toss over medium heat for 1 minute. • Sprinkle with the parsley and drizzle with the remaining oil. Garnish with the extra basil and serve hot.

1 onion, finely chopped

2 cloves garlic, lightly crushed but left whole

1/3 cup (90 ml) extra-virgin olive oil

2 zucchini (courgettes), very thinly sliced

1 red bell pepper (capsicum), seeded and thinly sliced

1 large carrot, very thinly sliced

2 sprigs basil, torn + extra, to garnish

1 pound (500 g) tomatoes, peeled and chopped

Salt and freshly ground black pepper

1 pound (500 g) fresh tagliatelle or fettuccine

1 tablespoon finely chopped fresh parsley

Preparation: 15 minutes

Cooking: 15 minutes

Serves: 4
Level: 1

TAGLIATELLE WITH BLACK PEPPER AND CHEESE

Cook the pasta in a large pot of salted, boiling water until al dente, 2–3 minutes. • Drain, reserving 3 tablespoons of the cooking water. • Sauté the garlic in the oil in a large frying pan over low heat until pale gold. • Add the butter and let it melt. • Remove from the heat and add the parsley. • Add the pasta and reserved cooking water. Season with the pepper. • Sprinkle with the Parmesan and serve hot.

1   pound (500 g) fresh tagliatelle

1   clove garlic, finely chopped

2   tablespoons extra-virgin olive oil

1/4 cup (60 g) butter

2   tablespoons finely chopped fresh parsley

2   tablespoons crushed black peppercorns

3   ounces (90 g) Parmesan cheese, cut into flakes

 Preparation: 10 minutes

Cooking: 10 minutes

Serves: 4–6
Level: 1

TORTELLINI ALLA BOSCAIOLA

Cook the tortellini in a large saucepan of salted boiling water until al dente, 5–10 minutes. • Drain and set aside. • Meanwhile, heat the oil in a large frying pan over medium heat. • Sauté the mushrooms until soft, about 3 minutes. • Add the ham and cook for 2 minutes. • Add the tortellini to the pan with the mushrooms. Add the cream, lemon zest, and parsley. Season with salt and pepper. • Stir until heated through, about 2 minutes. • Spoon into bowls and serve hot.

14 ounces (400 g) tortellini

2 tablespoons extra-virgin olive oil

8 ounces (250 g) button mushrooms, sliced

8 ounces (250 g) ham, coarsely chopped

1¹/₄ cups (300 ml) light (single) cream

Finely grated zest of 1 lemon

2 tablespoons finely chopped flat-leaf parsley

Salt and freshly ground black pepper

Preparation: 10 minutes
Cooking: 5–10 minutes

Serves: 4
Level: 1

TORTELLINI WITH FAVA BEANS, FETA, AND ARUGULA

Cook the tortellini in a large saucepan of salted boiling water until al dente, 5–10 minutes. • Drain and return to the pan. • Meanwhile, cook the fava beans in a saucepan of boiling water until just tender, 3–5 minutes. • Drain and rinse in cold water. • Remove and discard the tough outer skins. Add the fava beans to the hot tortellini. • Season with salt and pepper. • Add the oil, arugula, and feta. • Toss over low heat until well combined. Serve hot.

$1^{1}/_{2}$ pounds (750 g) fresh cheese tortellini

$1^{1}/_{2}$ pounds (750 g) fresh fava (broad) beans, hulled

Salt and freshly ground black pepper

$^{1}/_{3}$ cup (90 ml) extra-virgin olive oil

2 ounces (60 g) wild arugula (rocket) leaves

5 ounces (150 g) feta cheese, crumbled

Preparation: 15 minutes
Cooking: 15 minutes

Serves: 4
Level: 1

GNOCCHI WITH CHORIZO AND TOMATOES

Cook the gnocchi in a large saucepan of salted boiling water until they bob up to the surface, 3–4 minutes. • Drain, reserving ¹/₂ cup (125 ml) of the cooking water. • Heat the oil in a large frying pan over medium heat. • Sauté the sausages until brown, about 3 minutes. • Add the sauce and gnocchi and stir until heated through. • Add a little of the reserved cooking water if the sauce is too thick. • Stir in the parsley and season with freshly ground black pepper. • Spoon into bowls and serve hot.

1¹/₂ **pounds (750 g) fresh or frozen potato gnocchi**

1 **tablespoon extra-virgin olive oil**

1 **pound (500 g) dried chorizo sausages, sliced**

1 **(26-ounce/750 g) jar napoletana pasta sauce**

2 **tablespoons finely chopped fresh flat-leaf parsley**

Freshly ground black pepper

Preparation: 8 minutes

Cooking: 5–7 minutes

Serves: 4
Level: 1

GNOCCHI WITH BLUE CHEESE, SPINACH, AND WALNUTS

Cook the gnocchi in large saucepan of salted boiling water until they bob up to the surface, 3–4 minutes. • Drain and set aside. • Heat the oil in a saucepan over high heat. • Sauté the walnuts until toasted, 2–3 minutes. • Add the gnocchi, spinach, and blue cheese to the pan. • Season with salt and pepper. • Toss over low heat until the cheese begins to melt. Serve hot.

1¹/2 pounds (750 g) fresh or frozen potato gnocchi

¹/4 cup (60 ml) extra-virgin olive oil

3 ounces (90 g) walnuts, coarsely chopped

2 ounces (60 g) baby spinach leaves

5 ounces (150 g) soft blue cheese, crumbled

Salt and freshly ground black pepper

 Preparation: 5 minutes

Cooking: 10 minutes

Serves: 4
Level: 1

NOODLES

SOY NOODLE TOFU SOUP

Bring the chicken stock to a boil in a large saucepan. • Stir in the soy sauce, mirin, oil, and brown sugar. • Add the noodles and choy sum stems. • Cook for 1 minute. • Add the choy sum leaves and tofu. Simmer for 2 minutes. • Ladle the soup into individual serving bowls. • Top with the scallions and serve hot.

2 **quarts (2 liters) chicken stock**

3 **tablespoons dark soy sauce**

2 **tablespoons mirin or sweet sherry**

1 **teaspoon Asian sesame oil**

2 **teaspoons brown sugar**

1 **pound (500 g) fresh thin Chinese egg noodles**

1 **bunch baby choy sum or bok choy, stems sliced and leaves coarsely chopped**

8 **ounces (250 g) firm tofu, diced**

3 **scallions (spring onions), finely shredded**

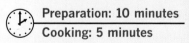

Preparation: 10 minutes

Cooking: 5 minutes

Serves: 4
Level: 1

CHICKEN UDON NOODLE SOUP

Bring the stock to a boil in a large saucepan. Add the chicken. • Decrease the heat to medium and simmer until cooked, 12–15 minutes. • Remove the chicken from the pan and shred it finely. • Bring the stock back to a boil over high heat. • Add the soy sauce and dashi granules. Cook, stirring until the granules have dissolved. • Add the noodles and broccoli. Cook until tender, about 4 minutes. • Add the chicken and bring to a boil. • Ladle the soup into individual serving bowls. • Add the eggs and scallions. Serve hot.

8	**cups (2 liters) chicken stock**
2	**boneless, skinless chicken breasts**
2	**tablespoons dark soy sauce**
1/2	**teaspoon dashi granules or miso paste**
8	**ounces (250 g) dried udon noodles**
1	**bunch kai-lan or Chinese broccoli, cut into short lengths**
3	**hard-boiled eggs, shelled and quartered lengthwise**
2	**scallions (spring onions), trimmed and thinly sliced**

Preparation: 10 minutes
Cooking: 20 minutes

Serves: 4
Level: 1

■■■ *Dashi is a basic stock used in Japanese cooking which is made from boiled seaweed and dried fish. Instant dashi granules are available at Asian food stores and online.*

CHICKEN LAKSA

To prepare the chicken laksa, heat a wok over high heat. • When it is very hot, add the oil. • Sauté the chicken for 5 minutes. • Add the laksa paste and cook until aromatic, about 30 seconds.
• Add the coconut milk, chicken stock, lime juice, fish sauce, and brown sugar. Bring to a boil. • Add the noodles and cook for 3 minutes. • Add the bean sprouts and scallions. • Ladle into individual serving bowls. Garnish with the cilantro and serve hot.

Chicken Laksa

1 **tablespoon peanut oil**

1 **pound (500 g) boneless, skinless chicken breasts, diced**

½ **cup (125 ml) laksa paste**

1½ **cups (375 ml) coconut milk**

4 **cups (1 liter) chicken stock, boiling**

2 **tablespoons freshly squeezed lime juice**

1 **tablespoon Asian fish sauce**

2 **teaspoons brown sugar**

8 **ounces (250 g) thin Chinese dried egg noodles**

■■■ *Laksa paste is available in many Asian supermarkets. However, if you can't find it you can make your own at home by following the recipe on the next page.*

 Preparation: 10 minutes
Cooking: 10 minutes

Serves: 4
Level: 1

8 ounces (250 g) fresh bean sprouts

4 scallions (spring onions), thinly sliced

Fresh cilantro (coriander) leaves, to serve

Laksa Paste

1 teaspoon finely chopped fresh ginger

3 cloves garlic

1 (1-inch/2.5-cm) piece lemon grass

1 tablespoon cilantro (coriander) leaves

2 small, fresh red chiles

1 teaspoon shrimp paste

1 teaspoon ground tumeric

3 tablespoons peanut oil

To prepare the laksa paste, place all the ingredients in a food processor and process until smooth.

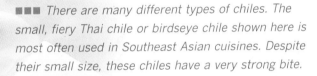

273

■■■ *There are many different types of chiles. The small, fiery Thai chile or birdseye chile shown here is most often used in Southeast Asian cuisines. Despite their small size, these chiles have a very strong bite.*

CHILE AND LIME SHRIMP NOODLE SALAD

Cook the noodles according to the instructions on the package. • Drain and rinse under cold running water. • Place the noodles in a large bowl. • Add the shrimp, cilantro, mint, chile, and scallions. • Mix the lime juice, sweet chili sauce, sugar, and oil in a small bowl. • Pour the dressing over the noodle salad. • Toss gently and serve.

8 ounces (250 g) dried rice noodles

2 pounds (1 kg) cooked shrimp (prawns), peeled and deveined

1 cup (60 g) fresh cilantro (coriander) leaves

1 cup (60 g) fresh mint leaves

1 fresh red chile, seeded and thinly sliced

3 scallions (spring onions), trimmed and thinly sliced

1/4 cup (60 ml) freshly squeezed lime juice

1/3 cup (90 ml) Thai sweet chili sauce

2 teaspoons superfine (caster) sugar

2 tablespoons peanut oil

 Preparation: 20 minutes

Serves: 4
Level: 1

SOBA NOODLE DUCK SALAD

Cook the noodles according to the instructions on the package. • Drain and rinse under cold running water. • Place the noodles in a large bowl. • Add the duck, scallions, cucumber, and mizuna. • Mix the rice vinegar, vegetable oil, soy sauce, ginger, sesame oil, sugar, and red pepper flakes in a small bowl. • Pour the dressing over the noodle salad. • Toss gently and serve.

8 ounces (250 g) dried soba noodles

2 cups (300 g) shredded Chinese barbecued duck

3 scallions (spring onions), trimmed and thinly sliced

1 cucumber, thinly sliced

2 ounces (60 g) mizuna

1/4 cup (60 ml) rice vinegar

2 tablespoons vegetable oil

1 tablespoon dark soy sauce

2 teaspoons finely grated ginger

1 teaspoon Asian sesame oil

2 teaspoons superfine (caster) sugar

1 teaspoon dried red pepper flakes

■■■ Soba noodles are Japanese noodles made from buckwheat flour. Mizuna is a leafy salad green grown in China and Japan. It has a sweet, slightly mustard-flavored tang. It can be found in Asian markets. If unavailable, replace with the same amount of arugula (rocket). Chinese barbecued duck can be found in Asian delicatessens.

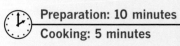

Preparation: 10 minutes
Cooking: 5 minutes

Serves: 4
Level: 1

WARM BLACK BEAN LAMB AND RICE NOODLE SALAD

Cook the noodles in plenty of boiling water. Refer to the package for the exact cooking time. • Drain and set aside. • Mix 2 tablespoons of peanut oil, the mirin, sesame oil, and brown sugar in a small bowl. • Pour the mixture over the noodles and toss well. • Mix the black bean sauce, the remaining peanut oil, and lamb in a medium bowl. • Place a grill pan over medium-high heat. • Grill the lamb on each side for 5 minutes. • Let rest for 5 minutes. Slice the lamb thinly. • Add the lamb and spinach to the noodles. • Toss well and serve warm.

8	ounces (250 g) dried rice stick noodles
1/4	cup (60 ml) peanut oil
2	tablespoons mirin or sweet sherry
1	teaspoon Asian sesame oil
2	teaspoons brown sugar
2	tablespoons Chinese black bean sauce
1	pound (500 g) boneless leg of lamb or lamb tenderloin
3	ounces (90 g) baby spinach leaves

Preparation: 20 minutes
Cooking: 10 minutes

Serves: 4
Level: 1

BLACK BEAN BEEF NOODLES

Cook the noodles according to the instructions on the package. Drain and set aside. • Place a wok over high heat. When it is very hot, add 2 tablespoons of oil. • Add the beef and stir-fry for 3 minutes. Remove from the pan and set aside. • Add the remaining oil and stir-fry the garlic and onion over medium heat until softened, about 3 minutes. • Pour in the black bean sauce, mirin, and green beans. • Stir-fry for 3 minutes. • Return the beef and noodles to the wok. Stir-fry for 1 minute. • Toss well and serve hot.

15 ounces (450 g) flat Thai fresh egg noodles or fresh tagliatelle

1/4 cup (60 ml) peanut oil

1 pound (500 g) fillet beef, cut into thin strips

2 cloves garlic, finely chopped

1 onion, thinly sliced

1/4 cup (60 ml) Chinese black bean sauce

1 tablespoon mirin or sweet sherry

5 ounces (150 g) green beans

Preparation: 10 minutes

Cooking: 13 minutes

Serves: 4

Level: 1

STIR-FRIED BEEF WITH ASPARAGUS AND BABY CORN

Cook the hokkien noodles in plenty of boiling water. Refer to the package for the exact cooking time. • Drain and set aside. • Place a wok over high heat. • When it is very hot, add 2 tablespoons of oil. • Add the beef and stir-fry for 3 minutes. • Remove from the pan and set aside. • Add the remaining oil and stir-fry the garlic over medium heat until pale gold, about 1 minute. • Add the asparagus and corn. Stir-fry for 3 minutes. • Return the beef to the wok. • Add the oyster sauce, Shaoxing wine, and water. • Stir-fry for 2 minutes. • Serve hot.

15	ounces (450 g) hokkien noodles
1/4	cup (60 ml) peanut oil
1	pound (500 g) fillet beef, cut into thin strips
2	cloves garlic, finely chopped
12	ounces (350 g) asparagus, trimmed and cut into short lengths
12	ounces (350 g) baby corn (sweetcorn), halved
3	tablespoons Chinese oyster sauce
1	tablespoon Shaoxing wine or sherry
1/4	cup (60 ml) water

 Preparation: 10 minutes
Cooking: 14 minutes

Serves: 4
Level: 1

■■■ Hokkien noodles are sold fresh, in refrigerated packages. If unavailable, substitute with 1 pound (500 g) of egg noodles and cook according to the package instructions.

MEE GORENG

Cook the hokkien noodles in plenty of boiling water. Refer to the package for the exact cooking time. • Place a wok over high heat. • When it is very hot, add 1 tablespoon of oil. • Pour in the eggs. • Slide a wooden spatula under the eggs to loosen them from the pan. Shake the pan with a rotating movement to spread. Cook until nicely browned on the underside. • Remove from the heat and cut into thin strips. • Add 1 tablespoon of oil to the wok. • Add the beef and stir-fry for 3 minutes. • Remove from the pan and set aside. • Add the remaining oil and stir-fry the garlic, scallions, shrimp paste, and sambal oelek for 1 minute. • Stir in the kecap manis, stock, noodles, and beef. • Stir-fry for 2 minutes. • Add the cilantro, strips of egg, and peanuts. • Serve hot.

$1^{1}/_{2}$ pounds (750 g) hokkien noodles

3 tablespoons peanut oil

3 large eggs, lightly beaten

1 pound (500 g) fillet beef, cut into thin strips

2 cloves garlic, finely chopped

4 scallions (spring onions), thinly sliced

2 tablespoons dried shrimp paste

2 teaspoons sambal oelek

$1/_4$ cup (60 ml) kecap manis

$1/_4$ cup (60 ml) beef stock

2 tablespoons coarsely chopped fresh cilantro (coriander)

$3/_4$ cup (80 g) coarsely chopped unsalted peanuts

Preparation: 10 minutes
Cooking: 15 minutes

Serves: 4–6
Level: 1

■■■ Mee goreng is the name for "fried noodles" in Indonesia and Malaysia, where it is a common dish. Many different types of noodles are prepared this way. Sambal oelek is a spicy chile paste used to flavor dishes in many parts of Asia. It is available in Asian food stores or online, as is the dried shrimp paste. Kecap manis is a thick, Indonesian sweet soy sauce. It is available in Asian supermarkets and food stores. Hokkien noodles can be substituted in this recipe with fresh Chinese egg noodles or fresh Italian-style tagliatelle or fettuccine.

287

SPICY STIR-FRIED BEEF

Cook the noodles according to the instructions on the package. Drain and set aside. • Place a wok over high heat. • When it is very hot, add the oil. • Add the beef and stir-fry for 3 minutes. • Add the garlic, ginger, scallions, and chiles. Stir-fry for 1 minute. • Stir in the oyster sauce, soy sauce, and noodles. • Stir-fry for 2 minutes. • Toss well and serve hot.

15 ounces (450 g) flat Thai fresh egg noodles or pappardalle

2 tablespoons peanut oil

1 pound (500 g) fillet beef, cut into thin strips

2 cloves garlic, finely chopped

2 teaspoons finely grated ginger

6 scallions (spring onions), cut into short lengths

2 fresh red chiles, seeded and thinly sliced

1/4 cup (60 ml) Chinese oyster sauce

2 tablespoons dark soy sauce

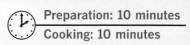

Preparation: 10 minutes

Cooking: 10 minutes

Serves: 4
Level: 1

FIVE SPICE PORK WITH HOKKIEN NOODLES

Cook the hokkien noodles in plenty of boiling water. Refer to the package for the exact cooking time. • Drain and set aside. • Place a wok over high heat. • When it is very hot, add 1 tablespoon of oil. • Add the five-spice powder, garlic, and ginger. Stir-fry for about 30 seconds. • Add the pork and stir-fry until cooked, about 5 minutes. • Remove from the pan and set aside. • Add the remaining oil to the wok. • Add the scallions and stir-fry for 2 minutes. • Add the noodles, pork, and hoisin and oyster sauces. • Stir-fry for 2 minutes. • Toss well and serve hot.

1 pound (500 g) hokkien noodles

2 tablespoons peanut oil

1 teaspoon Chinese five-spice powder

2 cloves garlic, finely chopped

1 tablespoon finely grated ginger

1 pound (500 g) pork fillet, cut into small pieces

4 scallions (spring onions), cut into 2-inch (5-cm) lengths

2 tablespoons hoisin sauce

2 tablespoons oyster sauce

Preparation: 10 minutes
Cooking: 15 minutes

Serves: 4
Level: 1

■■■ *Hokkien noodles are sold fresh in refrigerated packages. If unavailable, substitute with 1 pound (500 g) of Chinese egg noodles or tagliatelle and cook according to the package instructions.*

NOODLES WITH SPICY GROUND PORK

Cook the noodles in plenty of boiling water. Refer to the package for the exact cooking time. • Drain and set aside. • Place a wok over high heat. • When it is very hot, add the oil. • Stir-fry the pork for 4 minutes. • Add the garlic, ginger, and chiles. Stir-fry for 1 minute. • Add the laksa paste, fish sauce, brown sugar, and scallions. • Stir-fry for 2 minutes. • Add the noodles. Stir-fry for 2 minutes. • Toss well and serve hot.

1	pound (500 g) fresh rice noodles or tagliatelle
1	tablespoon peanut oil
1^{1}/2	pounds (750 g) ground (minced) pork
2	cloves garlic, finely chopped
2	teaspoons finely grated ginger
2	small fresh green chiles, seeded and finely chopped
3	tablespoons laksa paste
1	tablespoon Asian fish sauce
1	tablespoon brown sugar
4	scallions (spring onions), thinly sliced

■■■ *Laksa paste and chiles vary in heat. Adjust the amount according to your taste. Laksa paste is available in many Asian supermarkets. If you can't find it you can make your own at home by following the recipe on page 273.*

Preparation: 15 minutes
Cooking: 10 minutes

Serves: 4
Level: 1

HOKKIEN NOODLES WITH PORK AND SNOW PEAS

Cook the hokkien noodles in plenty of boiling water. Refer to the package for the exact cooking time. • Drain and set aside. • Place a wok over high heat. • When it is very hot, add the oil. • Stir-fry the pork for 4 minutes. • Add the curry paste and cook for 30 seconds. • Stir in the lime juice, fish sauce, brown sugar, kaffir lime leaves, snow peas, and chiles. • Stir-fry for 3 minutes. • Serve hot with the noodles.

1	pound (500 g) hokkien noodles
2	tablespoons peanut oil
1	pound (500 g) pork fillet, thinly sliced
2	tablespoons Thai red curry paste
2	tablespoons freshly squeezed lime juice
1	tablespoon Asian fish sauce
2	tablespoons brown sugar
4	kaffir lime leaves, thinly sliced
5	ounces (150 g) snow peas (mangetout), trimmed and halved
2	fresh red chiles, seeded and very thinly sliced

■■■ Hokkien noodles are sold fresh, in refrigerated packages. If unavailable, substitute with 1 pound (500 g) of Chinese egg noodles or tagliatelle and cook according to the package instructions. Kaffir lime, also known as makrut lime, is a member of the citrus family. The fruit is knobbly and bitter-tasting, and it is the leaves that are most commonly used to flavor food. If you can't find the lime leaves for this dish, it is okay to leave them out.

Preparation: 10 minutes
Cooking: 13 minutes

Serves: 4
Level: 1

SATAY LAMB AND NOODLE STIR-FRY

Place the noodles in a medium bowl and let stand in boiling water for 5 minutes. • Drain and set aside. • Place a wok over high heat. • When it is very hot, add 1 tablespoon of oil. • Add the lamb and stir-fry for 3 minutes. • Remove from the pan and set aside. • Add the remaining oil and stir-fry the garlic and onion over medium heat until softened, about 3 minutes. • Add the yard-long beans and stir-fry for 1 minute. • Stir in the coconut milk, satay sauce, and lamb. • Cook for 2 minutes. • Add the noodles and toss well. Serve hot.

1	pound (500 g) fresh thin rice noodles or tagliatelle
2	tablespoons peanut oil
1	pound (500 g) fillet lamb, cut into thin strips
2	cloves garlic, finely chopped
1	onion, cut into thin wedges
8	ounces (250 g) yard-long beans, cut into short lengths
1	cup (250 ml) coconut milk
1/2	cup (125 ml) satay sauce

Preparation: 15 minutes
Cooking: 10 minutes

Serves: 4
Level: 1

■■■ *Satay sauce is a sweet, spicy peanut sauce that is widely used in Indonesian, Malaysian, and Thai cuisines. It is available in Asian food markets and on line. Yard-long beans, also known as snake beans, asparagus beans, or China peas, are the fresh beans from which black-eyed peas are derived. If unavailable, replace with green beans.*

CHICKEN PAD THAI

Soak the noodles in a medium bowl of boiling water for 5–10 minutes. • Drain and set aside. • Place a wok over high heat. • When it is very hot, add 1 tablespoon of oil. • Beat the eggs lightly in a small bowl. Pour them into the wok. • Cook, stirring, until scrambled and cooked, about 2 minutes. • Remove from the pan and set aside. • Add the remaining oil to the wok and stir-fry the chicken for 3 minutes. • Add the garlic and scallions. Stir-fry for 1 minute. • Add the noodles, lime juice, fish sauce, brown sugar, soy sauce, and tofu. • Stir-fry for 3 minutes. • Add the bean sprouts and peanuts. • Garnish with the cilantro and lime wedges. Serve hot.

8	ounces (250 g) dried rice noodles
2	tablespoons peanut oil
2	large eggs
12	ounces (350 g) boneless, skinless chicken breasts, diced
2	cloves garlic, finely chopped
4	scallions (spring onions), thinly sliced
1/4	cup (60 ml) freshly squeezed lime juice
1/4	cup (60 ml) Asian fish sauce
1	tablespoon brown sugar
1	tablespoon light soy sauce
8	ounces (250 g) firm tofu, diced
8	ounces (250 g) fresh bean sprouts
1/3	cup (50 g) roasted peanuts, chopped
	Fresh cilantro (coriander) leaves, to garnish
	Lime wedges, to serve

■■■ *Pad Thai is a classic Thai street-food dish based on stir-fried noodles, eggs, and fish sauce and any combination of many other ingredients, such as chicken, tofu, and bean sprouts.*

Preparation: 20 minutes
Cooking: 10 minutes

Serves: 4
Level: 1

SWEET SPICY CHICKEN WITH BOK CHOY

Cook the hokkien noodles in plenty of boiling water. Refer to the package for the exact cooking time. • Drain and set aside. • Place a wok over high heat. • When it is very hot, add the oil. • Stir-fry the chicken until cooked, about 5 minutes. • Add the sweet chili sauce, soy sauce, bok choy, and noodles. • Cook for 2 minutes. • Serve hot.

15	ounces (450 g) hokkien noodles
2	tablespoons peanut oil
1	pound (500 g) boneless, skinless chicken breasts, thinly sliced
1/3	cup (90 ml) Thai sweet chili sauce
2	tablespoons dark soy sauce
1	bunch baby bok choy, leaves separated and stems coarsely chopped

Preparation: 10 minutes

Cooking: 7 minutes

Serves: 4
Level: 1

■■■ *Bok choy is a common Chinese leaf vegetable. It is widely available at Asian food markets. However, if you can't find it fresh, substitute with the same amount of fresh spinach or Swiss chard (silverbeet). Hokkien noodles are sold fresh, in refrigerated packages. If unavailable, substitute with 1 pound (500 g) of Chinese egg noodles or tagliatelle and cook according to the package instructions.*

NOODLES WITH CHICKEN AND VEGETABLES

Cook the noodles according ot the instructions on the package. • Drain and set aside. • Place a wok over high heat. • When it is very hot, add 2 tablespoons of oil. • Stir-fry the chicken until cooked, about 5 minutes. • Remove from the pan and set aside. • Add the remaining oil and stir-fry the garlic, carrot, and cabbage for 1 minute. • Add the kecap manis, noodles, and chicken. • Stir-fry for 2 minutes. • Garnish with the scallions and serve hot.

14 ounces (400 g) flat rice noodles or tagliatelle

3 tablespoons peanut oil

1 pound (500 g) boneless, skinless chicken breasts, thinly sliced

2 cloves garlic, finely chopped

1 carrot, shredded

8 ounces (250 g) Chinese cabbage (wombok), coarsely shredded

1/3 cup (90 ml) kecap manis

4 scallions (spring onions), thinly sliced

Preparation: 15 minutes
Cooking: 10 minutes

Serves: 4
Level: 1

■■■ *Kecap manis is a thick, Indonesian sweet soy sauce. It is available in Asian supermarkets and food stores.*

INSTANT NOODLE, CHICKEN, AND SUGAR SNAP STIR-FRY

Cook the noodles according to the instructions on the package. • Drain and set aside. • Heat a wok over high heat. • When it is very hot, add the oil. • Stir-fry the scallions and garlic for 1 minute. • Add the chicken, sugar snap peas, and oyster sauce. • Stir-fry for 3 minutes. • Add the noodles and cook for 2 minutes. • Toss well and serve hot.

14 ounces (400 g) instant noodles or 4 ramen noodle packages with flavor packet discarded

2 tablespoons peanut oil

4 scallions (spring onions), finely sliced

2 cloves garlic, finely chopped

2 cups (300 g) shredded cooked chicken

8 ounces (250 g) sugar snap peas, trimmed

1/3 cup (90 ml) Chinese oyster sauce

Preparation: 10 minutes
Cooking: 7 minutes

Serves: 4
Level: 1

SWEET SOY MUSHROOM AND CASHEW NOODLES

Cook the noodles according to the instructions on the package. • Drain and set aside. • Mix the mushrooms and 2 tablespoons of kecap manis in a bowl. Toss well. • Heat a wok over high heat. • When it is very hot, add the cashews. Toast for about 2 minutes until golden. Remove from the pan and set aside. • Add the oil to the pan. • Stir-fry the onion until softened, about 3 minutes. • Add the mushroom mixture and stir-fry until the mushrooms have just softened, about 3 minutes. • Add the noodles and the remaining kecap manis. • Stir-fry for 2 minutes. • Add the bean sprouts and toasted cashews. Toss well and serve hot.

8 ounces (250 g) dried rice noodles

1 pound (500 g) mixed mushrooms, thickly sliced

1/4 cup (60 ml) kecap manis

1/2 cup (80 g) cashews, coarsely chopped

2 tablespoons peanut oil

1 red onion, coarsely chopped

4 ounces (125 g) fresh bean sprouts

Preparation: 15 minutes
Cooking: 10 minutes

Serves: 4
Level: 1

■■■ Kecap manis is a thick, Indonesian sweet soy sauce. It is available in Asian supermarkets and food stores.

SHRIMP AND MUSHROOM NOODLES

Cook the noodles according to the instructions on the package. • Drain and set aside. • Mix the soy sauce, mirin, 1 tablespoon of oil, and sugar in a small bowl. • Add the shrimp. • Let marinate for 10 minutes. • Drain the shrimp, reserving the marinade. • Place a wok over high heat. • When it is very hot, add 1 tablespoon of oil. • Add the shrimp and stir-fry until they have turned pink, about 2 minutes. Remove from the pan and set aside. • Add the remaining oil to the pan. Stir-fry the shiitake mushrooms for 1 minute. • Add the reserved marinade, enoki mushrooms, scallions, and shrimp. • Stir-fry for 2 minutes. • Add the noodles. Stir-fry for 2 minutes. • Toss well and serve hot.

■■■ *Enoki mushrooms come from Japan.*
They have a delicate, fruity flavor. If you can't
find them, substitute with oyster mushrooms
or white mushrooms.

1 **pound (500 g) fresh rice noodles or tagliatelle**

1/4 **cup (60 ml) dark soy sauce**

2 **tablespoons mirin or sweet sherry**

3 **tablespoons peanut oil**

2 **tablespoons superfine (caster) sugar**

1 1/2 **pounds (750 g) large shrimps (prawns), peeled and deveined**

5 **ounces (150 g) fresh shiitake mushrooms, caps thinly sliced**

4 **ounces (125 g) enoki mushrooms**

4 **scallions (spring onions), trimmed and thinly sliced**

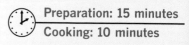

Preparation: 15 minutes
Cooking: 10 minutes

Serves: 4
Level: 1

SPICY SCALLOP AND SNOW PEA NOODLES

Cook the noodles according to the instructions on the package. • Drain and set aside. • Heat a wok over high heat. • When it is very hot, add the oil. • Add the chiles, garlic, lemon grass, scallions, snow peas, and asparagus. Stir-fry for 2 minutes. • Add the stock and scallops. • Cover and simmer until the scallops are cooked, about 2 minutes. • Add the noodles and basil. • Cook for 2 minutes and serve hot.

1	pound (500 g) fresh round egg noodles or fresh Chinese egg noodles
1	tablespoon peanut oil
2	small fresh red chiles, chopped
2	cloves garlic, finely chopped
1	stem lemon grass, trimmed, crushed, and thinly sliced
3	scallions (spring onions), thinly sliced
5	ounces (150 g) snow peas (mangetout)
1	bunch asparagus, cut into short lengths
1/3	cup (90 ml) fish stock or clam juice
20	large fresh scallops
1	cup (60 g) Thai basil or regular basil leaves

 Preparation: 15 minutes

Cooking: 10 minutes

Serves: 4
Level: 1

BEEF NOODLES

Cook the noodles according to the instructions on the package. • Drain and transfer to a large bowl. • Place a grill pan over medium-high heat. • Season the beef with salt and pepper. • Grill the beef until just pink in the center, about 5 minutes on each side. • Transfer to a plate, cover with aluminum foil, and let rest. • Mix the kecap manis, lime juice, sugar, and oil in a small bowl. • Pour the mixture over the noodles and toss well. • Slice the beef into 1/4-inch (5-mm) thick slices. • Add the beef, scallions, chiles, salad greens, and half the peanuts to the noodles and mix well. • Arrange the noodles in individual serving bowls. Sprinkle with the remaining peanuts and serve with the lime wedges.

12 ounces (350 g) fresh thick Chinese egg noodles

1 1/2 pounds (750 g) beef steak

Salt and freshly ground black pepper

2 tablespoons kecap manis

2 tablespoons freshly squeezed lime juice

2 tablespoons superfine (caster) sugar

1 tablespoon peanut oil

6 scallions (spring onions), trimmed and thinly shredded

2 fresh red Thai chiles, seeded and thinly sliced

2 ounces (60 g) baby Asian salad greens, thinly sliced

1/2 cup (70 g) unsalted roasted peanuts, coarsely chopped

Lime wedges, to serve

■■■ *Kecap manis is an Indonesian thick, sweet soy sauce. It is widely available in Asian supermarkets and food stores.*

Preparation: 10 minutes
Cooking: 13 minutes

Serves: 4
Level: 1

DUCK AND NOODLE RICE ROLLS

Cook the noodles according to the instructions on the package. • Drain and transfer to a large bowl. Chop the noodles coarsely. • Mix the noodles, duck, cucumber, cilantro, mint, sweet chili sauce, and lime juice in a large bowl. • Briefly dip a rice wrapper into a dish of hot water until it softens. • Place the wrapper on a clean work surface. Spoon the duck mixture onto the center and roll up tightly. • Repeat using remaining rolls and filling. • Serve with the sweet chili sauce for dipping.

- 2 ounces (60 g) dried rice vermicelli noodles
- 2 cups (300 g) shredded Chinese barbecued duck
- 1 cucumber, cut into thin lengths
- 3 tablespoons coarsely chopped fresh cilantro (coriander)
- 1 tablespoon coarsely chopped fesh mint
- 1/4 cup (60 ml) Thai sweet chili sauce
- 1 tablespoon freshly squeezed lime juice
- 8 large round rice paper wrappers

  Thai sweet chili sauce, to serve

Preparation: 20 minutes
Cooking: 5 minutes

Serves: 4–6
Level: 1

GRAINS

MUSHROOM AND ASPARAGUS RISOTTO

Sauté the onion and garlic in the oil in a large, deep frying pan over medium heat until softened, about 3 minutes. • Add the rice and mushrooms and cook for 2 minutes, stirring constantly. • Gradually add the stock, ½ cup (125 ml) at a time. Cook and stir until each addition has been absorbed. • Add the asparagus about 5 minutes before the rice is done. • Cook and stir until the rice and asparagus are tender. The whole process should take 15–18 minutes. • Stir in the feta and parsley. Season with pepper. • Serve hot.

1   onion, finely chopped

2   cloves garlic, finely chopped

¼   cup (60 ml) extra-virgin olive oil

2   cups (400 g) Italian risotto rice (Arborio, Carnaroli, or Vialone Nano)

4   cups (1 liter) chicken or vegetable stock, boiling

1   bunch asparagus, cut into short lengths

10 ounces (300 g) mushrooms, thinly sliced

4   ounces (100 g) feta cheese, crumbled

2   tablespoons finely chopped fresh parsley

Freshly ground black pepper

Preparation: 10 minutes

Cooking: 20 minutes

Serves: 4

Level: 1

ROAST PUMPKIN AND ARUGULA RISOTTO

Preheat the oven to 450°F (230°C/gas 8). • Place the pumpkin in a roasting pan. Drizzle with 1 tablespoon of oil. • Bake for 20 minutes, until tender. • Meanwhile, sauté the onion and garlic in the remaining oil in a large, deep frying pan over medium heat until softened, about 3 minutes. • Add the rice and cook for 2 minutes, stirring constantly. • Gradually add the stock, 1/2 cup (125 ml) at a time. Cook and stir until each addition has been absorbed. • Add the roasted pumpkin and arugula with the last 1/2 cup of stock. • Cook and stir until the rice is tender. The whole process should take 15–18 minutes. • Season with pepper. • Sprinkle with the Parmesan and serve hot.

1	pound (500 g) pumpkin or winter squash, peeled and cut into 1/2-inch (1-cm) cubes
2	tablespoons extra-virgin olive oil
1	onion, finely chopped
2	cloves garlic, finely chopped
2	cups (400 g) Italian risotto rice (Arborio, Carnaroli, or Vialone Nano)
4	cups (1 liter) vegetable stock, boiling
5	ounces (150 g) arugula (rocket), finely shredded
	Freshly ground black pepper
1/2	cup (60 g) freshly grated Parmesan cheese

Preparation: 10 minutes
Cooking: 20 minutes

Serves: 4
Level: 1

APPLE RISOTTO

Blanch the apples in boiling water for 1 minute. • Drain and drizzle with the lemon juice and wine. • Sauté the onion and garlic in the oil and butter in a large, deep, frying pan over medium heat until softened, about 3 minutes. • Add the rice and cook for 2 minutes, stirring constantly. • Stir in the apple mixture. • Gradually add the stock, $^{1}/_{2}$ cup (125 ml) at a time. Cook and stir until each addition has been absorbed and the rice is tender, 15–18 minutes. • Stir in the cream and Parmesan. • Let stand for 5 minutes. • Garnish with the apple slices and sprinkle with the paprika. • Serve hot.

2	tart apples, peeled, cored, and cut into small cubes
	Freshly squeezed juice of $^{1}/_{2}$ lemon
$^{1}/_{3}$	cup (90 ml) dry white wine
1	large onion, finely chopped
1	clove garlic, finely chopped
3	tablespoons extra-virgin olive oil
3	tablespoons butter
2	cups (400 g) Italian risotto rice (Arborio, Carnaroli, or Vialone Nano)
4	cups (1 liter) vegetable stock, boiling
2	tablespoons heavy (double) cream
$^{1}/_{2}$	cup (60 g) freshly grated Parmesan
	Slices of apple, to garnish
$^{1}/_{4}$	teaspoon paprika

Preparation: 10 minutes
Cooking: 20 minutes

Serves: 4
Level: 1

CHAMPAGNE AND CILANTRO RISOTTO

Sauté the onion in 2 tablespoons of butter in a large, deep frying pan over medium heat until softened, about 3 minutes. • Add the rice and cook for 2 minutes, stirring constantly. • Pour in the Champagne and cook over high heat for 3 minutes. • Gradually add the stock, 1/2 cup (125 ml) at a time. Cook and stir until each addition has been absorbed and the rice is tender, 15–18 minutes. • Season with salt and pepper. Stir in the remaining butter. • Sprinkle with the cilantro and Parmesan. • Serve hot.

1　large onion, finely chopped

1/4　cup (60 g) butter

2　cups (400 g) Italian risotto rice (Arborio, Carnaroli, or Vialone Nano)

3/4　cup (180 ml) Champagne or dry sparkling white wine

3　cups (750 ml) vegetable stock, boiling

　　Salt and freshly ground black pepper

2　tablespoons finely chopped fresh cilantro (coriander)

3　ounces (90 g) Parmesan cheese, cut into shavings

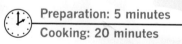

Preparation: 5 minutes

Cooking: 20 minutes

Serves: 4
Level: 1

ZUCCHINI AND APPLE RISOTTO

Put the apples in a large bowl and drizzle with the lemon juice. • Sauté the onion in the oil in a large, deep frying pan over medium heat until softened, about 3 minutes. • Add the potatoes, zucchini, and carrot. Sauté for 2 minutes. • Add the rice and cook for 2 minutes, stirring constantly. • Stir in the apple mixture. • Stir the curry powder and saffron into the stock. Gradually add the stock to the rice, $1/2$ cup (125 ml) at a time. Cook and stir until each addition has been absorbed and the rice is tender, 15–18 minutes. • Remove from the heat and stir in the curry powder, dill, and saffron. • Season with salt and pepper. • Garnish with the sprigs of dill and serve hot.

2	red apples, peeled, cored, and cut into cubes
	Freshly squeezed juice of 1 lemon
1	large onion, finely chopped
2	tablespoons extra-virgin olive oil
4	potatoes, peeled and cut into small cubes
3	zucchini (courgettes), cut into small cubes
1	large carrot, cut into small cubes
2	cups (400 g) Italian risotto rice (Arborio, Carnaroli, or Vialone Nano)
4	cups (1 liter) vegetable stock, boiling
1	teaspoon curry powder
$1/8$	teaspoon saffron threads
2	tablespoons finely chopped fresh dill + extra to garnish
	Salt and freshly ground black pepper

Preparation: 10 minutes
Cooking: 20 minutes

Serves: 4
Level: 1

VEGETABLE RISOTTO WITH SMOKED CHEESE

Sauté the shallots in 2 tablespoons of the butter and oil in a large, deep frying pan over medium heat for about 3 minutes, until softened. • Add the rice and cook for 2 minutes, stirring constantly. • Pour in the wine and cook over high heat for 3 minutes. • Stir in the mixed vegetables. • Gradually add the stock, 1/2 cup (125 ml) at a time. Cook and stir until each addition has been absorbed and the rice is tender, 15–18 minutes. • Remove from the heat and stir in the cubes of provolone, the remaining butter, and parsley. Season with salt and pepper. Arrange the sliced provolone on top of the risotto and serve hot.

2 shallots, finely chopped

1/3 cup (90 g) butter

2 tablespoons extra-virgin olive oil

2 cups (400 g) Italian risotto rice (Arborio, Carnaroli, or Vialone Nano)

1/3 cup (90 ml) dry white wine

2 cups (300 g) mixed frozen vegetables

4 cups (1 liter) vegetable stock, boiling

3 ounces (90 g) smoked provolone or other mild smoked cheese, cubed

1 tablespoon finely chopped parsley

Salt and freshly ground black pepper

2 ounces (60 g) smoked provolone or other mild smoked cheese, thinly sliced

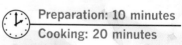

Preparation: 10 minutes
Cooking: 20 minutes

Serves: 4
Level: 1

PEA, BACON, AND SPINACH RISOTTO

Sauté the bacon, leeks, and garlic in the oil in a large, deep frying pan over medium heat until softened, about 3 minutes. • Add the rice and cook for 2 minutes, stirring constantly. • Gradually add the stock, 1/2 cup (125 ml) at a time. Cook and stir until each addition has been absorbed. • Add the peas and spinach about 5 minutes before the rice is cooked. • Cook and stir until the rice, peas, and spinach are tender. The whole process should take 15–18 minutes. • Stir in the mint and season with salt and pepper. • Sprinkle with the Parmesan and serve hot.

6   slices bacon, coarsely chopped

2   leeks, thinly sliced

2   cloves garlic, finely chopped

2   tablespoons extra-virgin olive oil

2   cups (400 g) Italian risotto rice (Arborio, Carnaroli, or Vialone Nano)

4   cups (1 liter) vegetable stock, boiling

1   cup (125 g) frozen peas, thawed

5   ounces (150 g) baby spinach leaves

2   tablespoons finely chopped fresh mint

1/2 cup (60 g) freshly grated Parmesan cheese

Salt and freshly ground black pepper

Preparation: 10 minutes

Cooking: 20 minutes

Serves: 4

Level: 1

CREAMY TROUT RISOTTO WITH CAPERS

334

Sauté the leek and garlic in 1 tablespoon of oil in a large, deep frying pan over medium-low heat until softened, about 3 minutes. • Add the rice and cook for 2 minutes, stirring constantly. • Gradually add the stock, ½ cup (125 ml) at a time. Cook and stir until each addition has been absorbed. • Meanwhile, sauté the trout in the remaining oil in a large frying pan over medium heat for 3 minutes. • Transfer to a plate and break the trout into flakes using a fork. • Add the trout and capers with the last ½ cup of stock. • Cook and stir until the rice is tender. The whole process should take 15–18 minutes. • Stir in the cream and dill. Season with pepper. • Let stand for 5 minutes. • Serve hot.

1 leek, thinly sliced

2 cloves garlic, finely chopped

2 tablespoons extra-virgin olive oil

2 cups (400 g) Italian risotto rice (Arborio, Carnaroli, or Vialone Nano)

4 cups (1 liter) fish or vegetable stock, boiling

10 ounces (300 g) trout fillets

2 tablespoons salt-cured capers, rinsed

1 cup (250 ml) light (single) cream

2 tablespoons finely chopped fresh dill

Freshly ground black pepper

Preparation: 10 minutes
Cooking: 20 minutes

Serves: 4
Level: 1

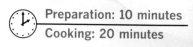

SEAFOOD PAELLA

Preheat the oven to 400°F (200°C/ gas 6). • Sauté the onion, garlic, and bell pepper in the oil in a paella pan or large frying pan over medium heat until softened, about 3 minutes. • Stir in the rice, mixed seafood, peas, and saffron. • Pour in the fish stock and bring to a boil. Season with salt and pepper. • Cook over medium-high heat until all the liquid has almost been absorbed, about 10 minutes. The rice grains should still be slightly crunchy, and there should still be liquid in the pan. • Bake in the oven, uncovered, for 10 minutes. • Add the parsley, garnish with the lemon wedges, and serve hot.

1	onion, finely chopped
2	cloves garlic, finely chopped
1	small red bell pepper (capsicum), seeded and cut into small cubes
1	tablespoon extra-virgin olive oil
2	cups (400 g) short-grain rice
1¾	pounds (750 g) fresh mixed seafood (mussels, clams, shrimp. etc.), cleaned
¾	cup (90 g) frozen peas, thawed
½	teaspoon saffron threads
4	cups (1 liter) fish stock, hot
	Salt and freshly ground black pepper
2	tablespoons finely chopped parsley
	Lemon wedges, to serve

■■■ *Paella is a classic Spanish dish. If possible, use short-grain Spanish rice, which absorbs liquid well and stays relatively firm during cooking. The rice should be dry and separate when done, not creamy like risotto.*

Preparation: 10 minutes
Cooking: 20 minutes

Serves: 4
Level: 1

CHORIZO AND CHICKEN PAELLA

Preheat the oven to 400°F (200°C/ gas 6). • Sauté the chicken and chorizo in 1 tablespoon oil in a paella pan or large frying pan over medium heat for 3 minutes until golden. • Add the onion, garlic, and bell peppers. Cook for 3 minutes. • Stir in the rice and peas. • Pour in the saffron stock and bring to a boil. Season with salt and pepper. • Cook over medium-high heat until all the liquid has almost been absorbed, about 10 minutes. The rice grains should still be slightly crunchy, and there should still be liquid in the pan. • Bake in the oven, uncovered, for 10 minutes. • Stir in the parsley and serve hot.

10	ounces (300 g) boneless, skinless chicken breasts, diced
2	dried chorizo sausages, sliced
2	tablespoons extra-virgin olive oil
1	onion, finely chopped
2	cloves garlic, finely chopped
1	small green bell pepper (capsicum), seeded and diced
1	small yellow bell pepper (capsicum), seeded and diced
2	cups (400 g) short-grain rice
1/2	cup (70 g) frozen peas, thawed
1/2	teaspoon saffron dissolved in 4 cups (1 liter) chicken stock, boiling
	Salt and freshly ground black pepper
2	tablespoons finely chopped parsley

Preparation: 10 minutes
Cooking: 20 minutes

Serves: 4
Level: 1

ALMOND AND CURRANT PILAF WITH CHICKEN

Sauté the scallions, bell pepper, and garlic in 1 tablespoon of oil in a large saucepan over medium heat until softened, about 3 minutes. • Stir in the rice, turmeric, and peas. • Pour in the stock and bring to a boil. • Cover and simmer over low heat until the rice is tender and has absorbed almost all the liquid, 12–15 minutes. • Meanwhile, toast the almonds in a large frying pan until golden, 2–3 minutes. • Remove and set aside. • Sauté the chicken in the remaining oil in the same pan over medium heat until cooked through and golden, about 5 minutes. • Remove the rice from the heat and set aside. • Stir in the currants, almonds, and parsley. • Serve the pilaf hot with the chicken.

3 scallions (spring onions), thinly sliced

1 red bell pepper (capsicum), seeded and diced

2 cloves garlic, finely chopped

2 tablespoons extra-virgin olive oil

1¹/₂ cups (300 g) basmati rice

¹/₂ teaspoon ground turmeric

²/₃ cup (110 g) frozen peas, thawed

2¹/₂ cups (625 ml) chicken stock

¹/₂ cup (75 g) slivered almonds

8 chicken tenders (tenderloins)

¹/₄ cup (45 g) currants

2 tablespoons finely chopped fresh parsley

Preparation: 10 minutes
Cooking: 20–25 minutes

Serves: 4
Level: 1

PILAF WITH CHICKEN LIVERS, CURRANTS, AND PINE NUTS

342

Sauté the chicken livers in the oil and butter in a large saucepan over medium heat until they change color, about 5 minutes . • Add the scallions and cook for 2 minutes. • Stir in the rice and stock. • Cover and simmer over low heat until the rice is tender and has absorbed almost all the liquid, 12–15 minutes. • Stir in the currants, pine nuts, parsley, and mint. Season with salt and pepper.

1   pound (500 g) chicken livers, cleaned and diced

1   tablespoon extra-virgin olive oil

2   tablespoons butter

4   scallions (spring onions), thinly sliced

1½ cups (300 g) long-grain rice

4   cups (1 liter) chicken stock, boiling

½   cup (90 g) currants

½   cup (90 g) pine nuts

2   tablespoons finely chopped fresh parsley

2   tablespoons finely chopped fresh mint

Salt and freshly ground black pepper

Preparation: 10 minutes
Cooking: 17–20 minutes

Serves: 4–6
Level: 1

CARROT, ZUCCHINI, AND CASHEW PILAF

Sauté the onion and garlic in the oil in a large saucepan over medium heat until softened, about 3 minutes. • Stir in the turmeric, cinnamon stick, and rice. • Pour in the stock. • Cover and simmer over low heat until the rice is tender and has absorbed almost all the liquid, 12–15 minutes. • Add the carrots and zucchini. Season with salt and pepper. • Discard the cinnamon stick. • Stir in the cashews. • Spoon into bowls. Garnish with the cilantro leaves and serve.

1   onion, finely chopped

2   cloves garlic, finely chopped

2   tablespoons extra-virgin olive oil

1   teaspoon ground turmeric

1   stick cinnamon

1¼ cups (250 g) basmati rice

1½ cups (375 ml) vegetable stock, boiling

2   carrots, finely grated

2   zucchini (courgettes), finely grated

Salt and freshly ground black pepper

½   cup (50 g) coarsely chopped roasted cashew nuts

4   sprigs fresh cilantro (coriander) leaves

Preparation: 10 minutes

Cooking: 14–17 minutes

Serves: 4
Level: 1

NASI GORENG

Cook the rice in a large saucepan of boiling water until tender, about 15 minutes. Drain well. • Meanwhile, place a wok over high heat. • When it is very hot, add 1 tablespoon of oil. • Lightly beat 2 of the eggs and stir-fry until scrambled and cooked, 1–2 minutes. • Remove from the wok and set aside. • Sauté the chicken in 1 tablespoon of oil in the same wok over medium heat until golden, about 3 minutes. • Add the scallions, cabbage, garlic, and carrots. Stir-fry for 2 minutes. • Stir in the cooked rice, scrambled eggs, and soy sauces. • Stir-fry for 2 minutes more. • Meanwhile, heat the remaining oil in a small frying pan. • Break the remaining 4 eggs into the pan and fry until cooked to your liking, 2–5 minutes. • Spoon the rice into 4 serving dishes and top each one with a fried egg. • Serve hot.

$1\frac{1}{2}$ cups (300 g) long-grain rice

3 tablespoons peanut oil

6 large eggs

1 pound (500 g) boneless, skinless chicken breasts, diced

3 scallions (spring onions), thinly sliced

2 cups (200 g) finely shredded cabbage

2 cloves garlic, finely chopped

1 carrot, finely grated

2 tablespoons kecap manis

1 tablespoon dark soy sauce

4 large eggs

Preparation: 10 minutes

Cooking: 20 minutes

Serves: 4

Level: 1

■■■ This dish comes from Indonesia and Malaysia where the word "nasi" means cooked rice and the word "goreng" means fried. Rice is a staple food in both countries and leftover cooked rice is often garnished with soy sauce, chiles, garlic, scallions (green onions) and other ingredients and fried up the next day. The dish often includes shrimps or chicken and is topped with a fried egg. Always use a long-grain, fragrant Asian rice for nasi goreng. Kecap manis is a sweet Indonesian type of soy sauce. It is available in the Asian foods section of most supermarkets and in specialized stores.

RICE WITH PORK AND ASIAN GREENS

Cook the rice in a large saucepan of boiling water until tender, about 15 minutes. Drain and rinse well. • Meanwhile, mix the oyster sauce, soy sauce, and sweet chili sauce in a large bowl. • Add the pork and coat well. • Place a wok over high heat. • When it is very hot, add 1 tablespoon of oil. • Add the pork and stir-fry for 4 minutes. • Add the scallions, bok choy, garlic, and ginger. • Stir-fry for 2 minutes. • Add the rice and stir-fry for 2 minutes more. • Spoon into bowls and serve hot.

2 tablespoons Chinese oyster sauce

1 tablespoon dark soy sauce

1 tablespoon Thai sweet chili sauce

1 pound (500 g) pork fillet, cut into thin strips

2 cups (400 g) long-grain rice

2 tablespoons vegetable oil

6 scallions (spring onions), thinly sliced

1 bunch baby bok choy, coarsely chopped

2 cloves garlic, finely chopped

2 teaspoons finely grated ginger

Preparation: 5 minutes
Cooking: 25 minutes

Serves: 4–6
Level: 1

RICE WITH HERB PESTO AND FETA

Cook the rice in a large saucepan of boiling water until tender, about 15 minutes. • Drain and rinse under cold water to stop the cooking process. • Meanwhile, put the herbs in the bowl of a food processor with the pine nuts, walnuts, chile, and garlic. Process for 15 seconds. • Transfer the herb pesto to a large bowl and stir in the oil. • Add the tomatoes and season with salt. • Add the rice to the tomato and pesto mixture. Stir in the feta. • Toss well and serve.

2	ounces (60 g) mixed fresh herbs (such as marjoram, parsley, thyme, chives, basil)
2	tablespoons pine nuts
12	walnuts
1	fresh red chile, seeded
1	clove garlic
1/4	cup (60 ml) extra-virgin olive oil
1	pound (500 g) cherry tomatoes, quartered
	Salt
1 1/2	cups (300 g) long-grain rice
4	ounces (125 g) feta cheese, cut into small cubes

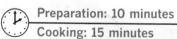

Preparation: 10 minutes
Cooking: 15 minutes

Serves: 4
Level: 1

BROWN RICE SALAD

Cook the rice in a large saucepan of boiling water, according to the instructions on the package. • Drain and rinse under ice-cold water to stop the cooking process. • Mix the rice, carrot, pea shoots, corn, scallions, and celery in a large bowl. • Mix the soy sauce, sesame oil, garlic, and ginger in a small bowl. • Pour the dressing over the rice and toss well. • Garnish with the cilantro and serve.

1½ cups (300 g) quick-cooking brown rice

1 carrot, peeled and finely grated

4 ounces (125 g) pea shoots or snow pea sprouts, trimmed and shredded

²/₃ cup (110 g) canned corn (sweet corn)

4 scallions (spring onions), thinly sliced

2 sticks celery, thinly sliced

¼ cup (60 ml) light soy sauce

2 teaspoons Asian sesame oil

2 cloves garlic, finely chopped

2 teaspoons finely grated ginger

Fresh cilantro (coriander) leaves, to serve

■■■ Brown rice usually takes 35–40 minutes to cook. Quick cooking brown rice is readily available in supermarkets and takes 10–15 minutes to cook. If preferred, replace the brown rice in this dish with the same quantity of short-grain white rice.

Preparation: 10 minutes

Cooking: 10 minutes

Serves: 4

Level: 1

MEXICAN RICE IN TORTILLA CUPS

Preheat the oven to 425°F (220°C/gas 7). • Spray the tortillas with the oil and arrange them in 1-cup (250-ml) ramekins. • Bake for about 10 minutes, until crisp. • Meanwhile, cook the rice in a large saucepan of boiling water until tender, about 15 minutes. • Drain and set aside. • Sauté the chicken in the oil in a large frying pan over medium-high heat until golden, about 5 minutes. • Stir in the Cajun spices, scallions, and bell pepper. Cook for 3 minutes. • Add the rice, red kidney beans, peas, and corn. • Cook for 2 minutes. • Spoon the mixture into the tortilla cups. Top with the lettuce and ranch dressing.

4   fajita-size flour tortillas
    Olive oil spray
1   cup (200 g) long-grain rice
1   pound (500 g) boneless, skinless chicken breasts, diced
1   tablespoon extra-virgin olive oil
2   teaspoons Cajun spices
4   scallions (spring onions), thinly sliced
1/2 red bell pepper (capsicum), seeded and cubed
1   (14-ounce/400-g) can red kidney beans, drained and rinsed
1/2 cup (75 g) frozen peas
1/2 cup (60 g) canned corn (sweet corn)
    Shredded lettuce and ranch dressing

Preparation: 10 minutes
Cooking: 20 minutes

Serves: 4
Level: 1

RICE WITH BEEF AND PINE NUTS

Sauté the onion, beef, and pine nuts in the oil in a large frying pan over medium-high heat for 4 minutes.
• Add the rice and water. • Bring to a boil. • Cover and simmer over low heat until the rice is tender and has absorbed almost all the liquid, 12–15 minutes.
• Stir in the oregano and season with salt and pepper. • Serve hot with the yogurt spooned over the top.

1   onion, finely chopped

1   pound (500 g) ground (minced) beef

1/2 cup (90 g) pine nuts

2   tablespoons extra-virgin olive oil

1 1/4 cups (250 g) basmati rice

2 1/2 cups (625 ml) water

2   tablespoons finely chopped fresh oregano

    Salt and freshly ground black pepper

1/3 cup (90 ml) plain yogurt

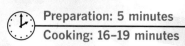

Preparation: 5 minutes

Cooking: 16–19 minutes

Serves: 2–4
Level: 1

SAUSAGE COUSCOUS WITH ARUGULA

Bring the water to a boil. • Stir in the couscous and 1 tablespoon of oil. • Cover and remove from the heat. • Let stand until the couscous has completely absorbed the liquid and is tender, about 10 minutes. • Meanwhile, sauté the sausages in 1 tablespoon of oil in a large frying pan over medium heat for 10 minutes, turning them from time to time. • Remove from the pan and slice thickly. • Transfer the couscous to a large bowl. Fluff it up with a fork. • Stir in the sausages, tomatoes, scallions, onion, and arugula. Drizzle with the remaining oil and lemon juice. Season with salt and pepper. • Toss well and serve hot.

$1^1/4$ cups (300 ml) water

$1^1/4$ cups (250 g) instant couscous

$1/4$ cup (60 ml) extra-virgin olive oil

4 good-quality pork sausages

8 ounces (250 g) cherry tomatoes, halved

4 scallions (spring onions), thinly sliced

1 small red onion, thinly sliced

4 ounces (100 g) arugula (rocket)

Freshly squeezed juice of 1 lemon

Salt and freshly ground black pepper

Preparation: 10 minutes + 10 minutes to stand

Cooking: 10 minutes

Serves: 4
Level: 1

COUSCOUS WITH ROASTED SWEET POTATOES

Preheat the oven to 450°F (230°C/ gas 8). • Arrange the sweet potatoes on a large roasting tray. Drizzle with 1 tablespoon oil. • Bake for about 20 minutes, until golden. • Meanwhile, bring the water to a boil. • Stir in the couscous and 1 tablespoon of oil. • Cover and remove from the heat. • Let stand until the couscous has completely absorbed the liquid and is tender, about 10 minutes. • Transfer the couscous to a large bowl. Fluff it up with a fork. • Stir in the onion, bell pepper, garbanzo beans, parsley, cilantro, lemon juice, and the remaining oil. • Toss well. • Add the roasted sweet potatoes and season with salt and pepper. • Serve hot.

1 **pound (500 g) sweet potatoes, peeled and cut into small cubes**

¼ **cup (60 ml) extra-virgin olive oil**

1¼ **cups (300 ml) water**

1¼ **cups (250 g) instant couscous**

1 **small red onion, thinly sliced**

1 **small red bell pepper (capsicum), seeded and thinly sliced**

1 **(14-ounce/400-g) can garbanzo beans (chick-peas), drained and rinsed**

1 **cup (60 g) finely chopped fresh parsley**

3 **tablespoons finely chopped fresh cilantro (coriander)**

Juice of 1 lemon

Salt and freshly ground black pepper

Preparation: 10 minutes
+ 10 minutes to stand
Cooking: 20 minutes

Serves: 4
Level: 1

TUNA COUSCOUS SALAD

Bring the water to a boil. • Stir in the couscous and 1 tablespoon of oil. • Cover and remove from the heat. • Let stand until the couscous has completely absorbed the liquid and is tender, about 10 minutes. • Transfer the couscous to a large bowl. • Fluff it up with a fork. • Add the onion, cucumber, tomatoes, olives, tuna, parsley, lemon juice, and the remaining oil. • Toss well and season with salt and pepper. • Serve with pita bread.

1¼ cups (300 ml) water

1¼ cups (250 g) instant couscous

¼ cup (60 ml) extra-virgin olive oil

1 small red onion, thinly sliced

1 cucumber, thinly sliced

5 ounces (150 g) cherry tomatoes, halved

1 cup (100 g) pitted kalamata olives

2 cups (400 g) canned tuna, drained

3 tablespoons finely chopped fresh parsley

Freshly squeezed juice of 1 lemon

Salt and freshly ground black pepper

Pita bread, to serve

Preparation: 10 minutes
+ 10 minutes to stand
Cooking: 5 minutes

Serves: 4
Level: 1

POLENTA AND CORN FRITTERS

Bring the water to a boil in a medium saucepan. • Gradually sprinkle in the polenta, stirring constantly with a wooden spoon to prevent lumps from forming. • Continue cooking over medium heat, stirring almost constantly, until it is thick and starts to pull away from the sides of the pan, 8–10 minutes. • Remove from the heat. • Stir in the corn, chile, scallions, garlic, and 2 tablespoons of cilantro. Season with salt and pepper. • Shape the mixture into balls about the size of a walnut and flatten slightly. Dip in the flour, shaking off the excess. • Heat the oil in a large frying pan until very hot. • Pan-fry the half fritters until golden, 2–3 minutes each side. Drain on paper towels in a warm oven while you fry the second batch. • Stir the remaining cilantro into the yogurt. Serve the fritters hot with the yogurt and arugula.

$1^{1}/_{2}$ cups (375 ml) water

$^{1}/_{2}$ cup (75 g) instant polenta

$^{3}/_{4}$ cup (90 g) canned corn (sweet corn)

1 fresh red chile, seeded and finely chopped

4 scallions (spring onions), thinly sliced

2 cloves garlic, finely chopped

4 tablespoons finely chopped fresh cilantro (coriander)

Salt and freshly ground black pepper

$^{1}/_{3}$ cup (50 g) all-purpose (plain) flour

$^{1}/_{2}$ cup (125 ml) olive oil, for frying

Arugula (rocket), to serve

1 cup (250 ml) yogurt

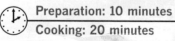

Preparation: 10 minutes

Cooking: 20 minutes

Serves: 6–8
Level: 1

SEAFOOD

SPICY MUSSEL SOUP

Scrub the mussels thoroughly, removing any beards and discarding broken shells. Rinse well. • Sauté the garlic, chiles, and scallions in the oil in a large saucepan over medium heat for 1 minute. • Pour in the stock and tomato paste. Bring to a boil. • Add the mussels and cook until they open up, 3–5 minutes. Discard any shells that do not open. • Stir in the cilantro. Serve hot.

2 pounds (1 kg) mussels

2 cloves garlic, finely chopped

2 small fresh red chiles, seeded and finely chopped

4 scallions (spring onions), thinly sliced

1 tablespoon extra-virgin olive oil

2 cups (500 ml) fish stock

2 tablespoons tomato paste

2 tablespoons finely chopped fresh cilantro (coriander)

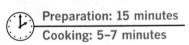

Preparation: 15 minutes
Cooking: 5–7 minutes

Serves: 4
Level: 1

SALT AND PEPPER SQUID

Cut the squid bodies in half lengthwise. Cut into squares and use a sharp knife to score the inside of the squid. • Crush the pepper in a pestle with a mortar until finely ground. • Mix the pepper, salt, and flour in a small bowl. • Heat the oil in a large frying pan until hot. Test the oil temperature by dropping a small piece of bread into the hot oil. If the bread immediately bubbles to the surface and begins to turn golden, the oil is ready.

• Dip the squid in the seasoned flour.

• Fry the squid in batches until golden and crisp, 2–3 minutes.

• Serve hot with the mixed salad greens, sweet chili sauce, and lemon wedges.

1³/4 pounds (800 g) squid, cleaned

1¹/2 tablespoons black peppercorns

1¹/2 tablespoons salt

¹/3 cup (50 g) all-purpose (plain) flour

4 cups (1 liter) olive oil, for frying

4 ounces (125 g) mixed salad greens

Thai sweet chili sauce, to serve

Lemon wedges, to serve

Preparation: 15 minutes
Cooking: 10 minutes

Serves: 4
Level: 1

MUSSELS IN GARLIC, WHITE WINE, AND TARRAGON

Heat the oil in a large saucepan over high heat. • Sauté the scallions and garlic until tender, about 3 minutes. • Add the wine, stock, and 1 tablespoon of tarragon. Bring to a boil. Reduce the heat to low and simmer for 10 minutes. • Increase the heat to high. Add the mussels. Cover with a tight-fitting lid and cook, shaking the pan from time to time, until the shells open, 3–5 minutes. • Using tongs, transfer the mussels to serving bowls. Discard any mussels that have not opened. • Drain the cooking liquid, season with pepper and pour over the mussels. Sprinkle with remaining tarragon. • Serve hot with crusty bread and a green salad.

2 tablespoons extra-virgin olive oil

3 scallions (spring onions), finely chopped

3 cloves garlic, finely chopped

1½ cups (325 ml) dry white wine

1 cup (250 ml) fish stock or clam juice

2 tablespoons coarsely chopped fresh tarragon leaves

4 pounds (2 kg) mussels, scrubbed and debearded

Freshly ground black pepper

Crusty bread and green salad, to serve

Preparation: 15 minutes

Cooking: 12 minutes

Serves: 4

Level: 1

CHILE AND CILANTRO SHRIMP

Mix the peanut oil, garlic, chiles, and cilantro in a large bowl. • Add the shrimp and toss well. • Heat 2 cups (500 ml) of the olive oil in a medium, deep frying pan until hot. Heat the remaining oil in a deep-fryer. Test the oil temperature by dropping a small piece of bread into the hot oil. If the bread immediately bubbles to the surface and begins to turn golden, the oil is ready. • Add the potatoes to the deep-fryer and fry until golden brown. Drain on paper towels. • Dip the shrimp in the flour, shaking off any excess. • Fry the shrimp in batches in the frying pan until golden and crisp, about 2 minutes. • Serve the shrimp and French fries hot with the lime wedges.

1 tablespoon peanut oil

2 cloves garlic, finely chopped

2 small red chiles, seeded and finely chopped

1 tablespoon finely chopped fresh cilantro (coriander)

2 pounds (1 kg) large shrimp (prawn), shelled and deveined

1/2 cup (75 g) all-purpose (plain) flour

6 cups (1.5 liters) olive oil, for frying

1 pound (500 g) frozen French fries (potato chips)

Lime wedges, to serve

Preparation: 10 minutes

Cooking: 10 minutes

Serves: 4
Level: 1

SEAFOOD KEBABS WITH CREAMY ANISEED SAUCE

Bring a large saucepan of salted water to a boil. • Add the rice and cook over medium heat for 10–15 minutes, until tender. • Drain well and set aside. • Preheat a broiler (grill). • Mix 2 tablespoons of oil, the lemon zest, and 1 tablespoon of lemon juice in a small bowl. Season with salt and pepper.

• Thread the shrimp and tuna onto skewers and place them on a plate. Drizzle with the oil mixture. • Mix the cream, anisette, remaining lemon juice, remaining oil, paprika, and dill in a small bowl. Season with salt and pepper.

• Broil the kebabs, turning them often, for 5 minutes, or until cooked through.

• Arrange the rice on serving dishes and top with the kebabs. • Drizzle the kebabs with the sauce and serve hot.

2	cups (400 g) basmati rice
3	tablespoons extra-virgin olive oil
	Finely grated zest and juice of 1 lemon
	Salt and freshly ground black pepper
12	large shrimp (prawn)
1	pound (500 g) tuna steak, cut into small chunks
1	cup (250 ml) heavy (double) cream
1	tablespoon anisette (aniseed liqueur)
1/2	teaspoon sweet paprika
2	tablespoons finely chopped fresh dill

Preparation: 10 minutes
Cooking: 15 minutes

Serves: 4
Level: 1

TUNA STEAKS WITH ORANGE AND CAPERS

Preheat a broiler (grill). • Use a sharp knife to cut the zest from the oranges in very fine strips. • Blanch the zest in boiling water for 2 minutes. • Drain and set aside. • Arrange the fennel, radishes, celery, tomatoes, olives, and salad greens in a large salad bowl. • Add the chervil, dill, and orange zest. Drizzle with half the oil and the vinegar. Season with salt and pepper and toss well. • Squeeze the juice from the oranges into a small bowl. Season with salt and pepper. • Gradually beat in the remaining oil until well blended. • Stir in the capers. • Grill the tuna steaks for about 5 minutes, turning them occasionally, until cooked through. • Place the salad on a large serving plate. • Arrange the tuna steaks on top and drizzle with the orange and caper dressing. • Serve hot.

2	large ripe oranges
1	bulb fennel, thinly sliced
4	radishes, thinly sliced
1	stalk celery, thinly sliced
4	cherry tomatoes, cut into wedges
1	cup (100 g) black olives
10	ounces (300 g) mixed salad greens
1	sprig chervil, finely chopped
1	sprig dill, finely chopped
1/3	cup (90 ml) extra-virgin olive oil
3	tablespoons balsamic vinegar
	Salt and freshly ground black pepper
1/3	cup (60 g) capers in brine, rinsed and drained
4	tuna steaks

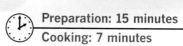

Preparation: 15 minutes
Cooking: 7 minutes

Serves: 4
Level: 1

SNAPPER FILLETS WITH AVOCADO SALSA

To prepare the snapper fillets, place a grill pan over medium-high heat. • Mix the potatoes with 1 tablespoon of oil. Season with salt and pepper. • Grill the potatoes, turning them from time to time, until cooked, about 10 minutes. • Brush the snapper fillets with the remaining oil. Season with salt and pepper. • Grill the fish until cooked, about 3 minutes on each side. • To prepare the avocado salsa, mix the avocado, cucumber, tomato, and onion in a medium bowl. • Add the lemon juice, white wine vinegar, cilantro, and sugar. Toss well. • Arrange the potatoes on individual serving plates. Top with the fish and avocado salsa.

Snapper Fillets

2 large potatoes, very thinly sliced

2 tablespoons extra-virgin olive oil

Salt and freshly ground black pepper

4 snapper fillets, each weighing about 6 ounces (180 g)

Avocado Salsa

1 avocado, peeled and diced

1 small cucumber, diced

1 tomato, diced

1/2 small red onion, finely chopped

2 tablespoons freshly squeezed lemon juice

2 tablespoons white wine vinegar

1/3 cup (20 g) fresh cilantro (coriander)

1/8 teaspoon superfine (caster) sugar

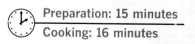

Preparation: 15 minutes
Cooking: 16 minutes

Serves: 4
Level: 1

STEAMED FISH WITH SOY AND GINGER

Mix the soy sauce, rice vinegar, mirin, oyster sauce, sesame oil, garlic, ginger, and scallions in a shallow dish. • Add the fish to the mixture and coat well. • Place a large saucepan of salted water on the heat and bring to a boil. • Add the rice and cook over medium heat until tender, 10–15 minutes. • Drain well. • While the rice is cooking, remove the fish from the marinade, reserving it. • Place the fish in a steamer and steam until tender, about 5 minutes. • Add the choy sum and steam for about 3 minutes until wilted. • Meanwhile, combine the marinade and water in a small saucepan. • Bring to a boil. Simmer over low heat for about 2 minutes, until slightly reduced. • Arrange the choy sum on serving plates and top with the fish. Drizzle with the sauce and serve hot with the rice on the side.

1/4 cup (60 ml) light soy sauce

2 tablespoons rice vinegar

2 tablespoons mirin or sweet sherry

1 tablespoon Chinese oyster sauce

2 teaspoons Asian sesame oil

2 cloves garlic, finely chopped

2 teaspoons freshly grated ginger

3 scallions (spring onions), thinly sliced

4 boneless white fish fillets, each weighing about 5 ounces (150 g)

2 cups (400 g) jasmine rice

2 bunches baby choy sum or Chinese broccoli, trimmed and halved

1/3 cup (90 ml) water

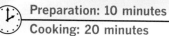

Preparation: 10 minutes
Cooking: 20 minutes

Serves: 4
Level: 1

SOLE BAKED WITH CHERRY TOMATOES

Preheat the oven to 350°F (180°C/gas 4).
• Grease a large baking dish with oil.
• Drizzle each fillet with a little oil.
• Arrange the sole in the prepared dish.
• Top with the tomatoes, garlic, and
parsley. Season with salt and pepper.
Drizzle with the remaining oil. • Bake
for 10–15 minutes, until the sole and
tomatoes are cooked. • Serve hot.

8   sole fillets

1/4   cup (60 ml) extra-virgin olive oil

1   pound (500 g) cherry tomatoes, halved

4   cloves garlic, finely chopped

2   tablespoons finely chopped fresh parsley

  Salt and freshly ground black pepper

Preparation: 10 minutes
Cooking: 10–15 minutes

Serves: 4
Level: 1

SEA BREAM WITH FENNEL AND ONIONS

Preheat a broiler (grill). • Mix the onions, fennel, celery, and parsley in a large bowl. • Mix ⅓ cup (90 ml) of the oil, the orange juice, and garlic in a small bowl. Season with salt and pepper. • Drizzle the fish fillets with the remaining oil and season with salt and pepper. • Broil for 2 minutes. Turn the fillets over and broil for about 2 minutes more, or until cooked through. • Drizzle half of the dressing over the vegetables and toss well. • Arrange the vegetables on serving plates and place the fish on top. Drizzle with the remaining dressing. • Serve hot.

1   red onion, finely sliced

4   small white onions, finely sliced

1   pound (500 g) fennel bulbs, finely sliced

2   stalks celery, finely sliced

4   tablespoons finely chopped fresh parsley

½   cup (125 ml) extra-virgin olive oil

¼   cup (60 ml) freshly squeezed orange juice

2   cloves garlic, finely chopped

    Salt and freshly ground black pepper

4   sea bream fillets (or substitute pompano, porgy, rockfish, or ocean perch)

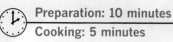

Preparation: 10 minutes
Cooking: 5 minutes

Serves: 4
Level: 1

PERCH WITH CHERRY TOMATOES AND OLIVES

Sauté the onions in the oil in a large frying pan over medium heat for about 3 minutes, until softened. • Add the perch and cook for 2 minutes. Turn the fish over and cook for 2 more minutes. • Add the tomatoes and olives. Cook for 3 minutes. • Pour in the beer and let it evaporate for 2 minutes. • Pour in the stock and cook for 5 minutes. • Season with salt and pepper and garnish with the basil. • Serve hot.

2   small onions, finely chopped

3   tablespoons extra-virgin olive oil

2   pounds (1 kg) perch fillets

1   pound (500 g) cherry tomatoes, halved

1   cup (100 g) black olives, pitted and cut in half

1/2   cup (125 ml) beer

1/3   cup (90 ml) fish or vegetable stock

Salt and freshly ground black pepper

Basil leaves, to garnish

Preparation: 10 minutes
Cooking: 17 minutes

Serves: 4–6
Level: 1

PAN-FRIED SALMON WITH GRAPES AND ZUCCHINI

Cook the zucchini in a large pot of salted, boiling water until tender, about 5 minutes. • Drain well. • Sauté the salmon and grapes in half the butter in a large frying pan over medium heat until the salmon is cooked and the grapes have softened slightly, about 5 minutes.
• Transfer the salmon and grapes to a serving dish and keep warm. • Add the wine and water to the cooking juices in the pan. Bring to a boil over high heat.
• Add the remaining butter and cook until melted. • Add the zucchini and season with salt and pepper. Sauté over high heat for 1 minute. • Add the zucchini and pan juices to the salmon and grapes. • Garnish with the parsley and serve hot.

2   large zucchini (courgettes), cut into short lengths

1   pound (500 g) salmon fillets, skinned and cut into small cubes

16 large green (white) grapes, preferably seedless, halved

1/4 cup (60 g) butter

1/4 cup (60 ml) dry white wine

1/3 cup (90 ml) water

Salt and freshly ground black pepper

2   tablespoons coarsely chopped fresh flat-leaf parsley, to garnish

Preparation: 10 minutes
Cooking: 15 minutes

Serves: 4–6
Level: 1

COD WITH POTATOES

Sauté the onion in the oil and butter in a large frying pan over medium heat until softened, about 3 minutes • Add the potatoes and sauté for 5 minutes. • Add the hake, rosemary, and lemon zest.
• Pour in the milk and enough water to cover the ingredients. Season with salt and pepper. • Simmer until the fish and potatoes are tender and the sauce has reduced to half its original volume, 5–10 minutes. • Sprinkle with the parsley and garnish with sprigs of rosemary.
• Serve hot.

1	**large onion, cut into rings**
2	**tablespoons extra-virgin olive oil**
1	**tablespoon butter**
2	**pounds (1 kg) potatoes, peeled, and cut into thin wedges**
1$^{1}/_{4}$	**pounds (600 g) cod, hake, or other white-flesh fish fillets**
1	**tablespoon finely chopped rosemary + extra sprigs, to garnish**
	Zest of $^{1}/_{2}$ lemon, very finely cut
$^{1}/_{4}$	**cup (60 ml) milk**
$^{1}/_{2}$	**cup (125 ml) water**
	Salt and freshly ground black pepper
1	**tablespoon finely chopped fresh parsley**

Preparation: 5 minutes
Cooking: 12–18 minutes

Serves: 4
Level: 1

PARMESAN-CRUMBED BAKED SALMON

Preheat the oven to 400°F (200°C/gas 6). Line a baking sheet with parchment paper. • Combine the bread crumbs, parsley, Parmesan, lemon zest, salt, and pepper in a bowl. • Drizzle with the oil. Stir until the bread crumbs are lightly coated in oil. • Press the bread crumb mixture onto the flesh-side of the fish to form an even topping. • Place the fish, skin-side down, on the prepared baking sheet. Spray liberally with oil. • Roast the fish about 12–15 minutes, until the bread crumbs are lightly golden and fish is just cooked through. • Serve hot with a leafy green salad and lemon wedges.

1/2 cup (30 g) fresh multigrain bread crumbs

1/4 cup finely chopped flat-leaf parsley leaves

2 ounces (60 g) freshly grated Parmesan cheese

1 teaspoon finely grated lemon zest

Salt and freshly ground black pepper

2 tablespoons extra-virgin olive oil

4 (8-ounce/250-g) salmon or ocean trout fillets

Olive oil cooking spray

Leafy green salad, to serve

Lemon wedges, to serve

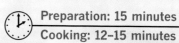

Preparation: 15 minutes
Cooking: 12–15 minutes

Serves: 4
Level: 1

CHERMOULA FISH WITH COUSCOUS

To make the chermoula, combine the cilantro, cumin, cayenne pepper, paprika, garlic, 4 tablespoons of oil, lemon juice, salt, and pepper in a food processor. Process until well combined. • Pour the mixture into a shallow dish. • Add the fish to the chermoula. Turn the fish to coat well in the chermoula. • Set aside for 10 minutes. • Meanwhile, put the couscous in a heatproof bowl. Pour the boiling water over the top. Cover and set aside until the water is absorbed, about 5 minutes. Stir with a fork to separate grains. • Stir in the remaining 3 tablespoons of oil and season with salt and pepper. • Add the tomatoes. Set aside. • Preheat a greased frying pan over medium-high heat. • Cook the fish until just tender, 3–5 minutes on each side. • Serve hot with the couscous and lemon wedges.

■■■ *Chermoula is a North African marinade used to flavor fish or seafood. It is usually made from a mixture of olive oil, lemon juice, garlic, and herbs.*

1 cup (50 g) fresh cilantro (coriander)
1 teaspoon ground cumin
1/4 teaspoon cayenne pepper
1 teaspoon paprika
2 cloves garlic, crushed
1/4 cup (60 ml) extra-virgin olive oil
3 tablespoons freshly squeezed lemon juice
Salt and freshly ground black pepper
4 firm white fish steaks, such as cod, snapper, ling, or warehou
1³/4 cups (350 g) instant couscous
2 cups (500 ml) water, boiling
8 ounces (250 g) cherry tomatoes, chopped
Lemon wedges, to serve

Preparation: 20 minutes
Cooking: 10 minutes

Serves: 4
Level: 1

GINGER, HONEY, AND SOY GLAZED FISH

To make the soy glaze, combine the honey, soy sauce, ginger, and sesame oil in a small saucepan. Stir to combine over medium heat. Bring to a boil. Remove from the heat. • Reserve 3 tablespoons of the mixture. • Pour the remaining mixture into a shallow dish. Set aside to cool. • Add the fish to the soy mixture. Turn well to coat. Set aside for 5 minutes. • Preheat a grill on medium-high heat. Line a grill tray with aluminum foil. • Place the fish on tray, draining the marinade. • Grill the fish, brushing with marinade occasionally, until just cooked through, 2–4 minutes on each side. • Meanwhile, steam the bok choy and broccolini in a steamer over simmering water until tender, about 2 minutes. • Place the greens onto serving plates. Top with the fish. Drizzle with the reserved soy mixture and serve hot.

1/3 cup (90 ml) honey

1/3 cup (90 ml) soy sauce

2 teaspoons finely grated ginger

1 teaspoon Asian sesame oil

4 8-ounce (250-g) white fish fillets such as John Dory, sea bass, hapuku, cod, ling, pollack, mahi mahi, or snapper

1 bunch bok choy, trimmed

1 bunch broccolini, trimmed

Preparation: 20 minutes

Cooking: 10 minutes

Serves: 4
Level: 1

LIME AND LEMON GRASS SHRIMP SALAD

Combine the lemon grass, lime juice, oil, sugar, fish sauce, and chiles in a large bowl. Whisk until the sugar dissolves.
• Reserve 1/4 cup (60 ml) of the lemon grass mixture. • Add the shrimp to the remaining mixture. Toss well to coat the shrimp. Set aside to marinate for 10 minutes. • Heat a lightly oiled grill or nonstick frying pan over high heat.
• Cook the shrimp in batches, tossing often, until they change color and are just cooked through, about 2 minutes. Transfer to a plate. Keep warm. • Combine the cucumbers, scallions, cilantro, and mint in a large bowl. • Pour in the reserved lemon grass mixture. Gently toss to combine. • Arrange the shrimp and cucumber salad on serving plates. Sprinkle with roasted peanuts and serve hot.

2   stems lemon grass, finely sliced

1/2 cup (125 ml) freshly squeezed lime juice

3   tablespoons peanut oil

1 1/2 tablespoons brown or palm sugar

2   teaspoons Asian fish sauce

2   small fresh red chiles, thinly sliced

2   pounds (1 kg) large shrimp (king prawns), peeled, and deveined

2   cucumbers, thinly sliced lengthwise

2   scallions (green onions), thinly sliced

1/2 cup fresh cilantro (coriander) leaves

1/3 cup fresh mint leaves

1/4 cup (40 g) roasted peanuts, chopped

Salt and freshly ground black pepper

Preparation: 20 minutes
Cooking: 6 minutes

Serves: 4
Level: 1

FISH, BELL PEPPER, AND RED ONION SKEWERS

Place the fish in a shallow dish. Combine the oil, lemon juice, oregano, salt, and pepper in a screw-top jar. Shake until well combined. • Pour the oil and lemon mixture over the fish. Toss to coat well. Set aside for 5 minutes. • Thread the fish, bell pepper, and onion alternately onto pre-soaked bamboo skewers. • Preheat a lightly oiled grill on medium-high heat. • Grill the skewers, turning frequently and brushing with the remaining marinade, until the fish is cooked through, 5–8 minutes. • Serve the skewers hot with the tartar sauce and lemon wedges.

$1^1/2$ pounds (750 g) firm white fish fillets, skinned and cut into into 1-inch (2.5-cm) cubes

$^1/3$ cup (90 ml) extra-virgin olive oil

Freshly squeezed juice of 2 lemons

2 teaspoons dried oregano

Salt and freshly ground black pepper

1 red bell pepper (capsicum), trimmed, seeded and cut into 1-inch (2.5-cm) pieces

2 small red onions, cut into thin wedges

Tartar sauce and lemon wedges, to serve

■■■ *You will need 12 pre-soaked bamboo skewers to prepare this dish.*

Preparation: 20 minutes
Cooking: 5–8 minutes

Serves: 4
Level: 1

FISH, FENNEL, AND MUSSEL STEW

Heat the oil in a large deep frying pan over medium-high heat. • Sauté the garlic and fennel until softened, about 3 minutes. • Add the stock and wine to the pan. Simmer over medium-low heat until reduced by half. • Stir in the tomato sauce, sugar, bay leaves, and saffron. Season with salt and pepper. Cover and bring to a boil. Stir in the fish. • Cover and cook for 2 minutes. Add the mussels and cook until opened and the fish is just tender, 2–3 minutes. • Discard any unopened mussels. • Sprinkle with the reserved chopped fennel leaves. • Serve hot with mashed potatoes and lemon wedges.

1	tablespoon extra-virgin olive oil
3	cloves garlic, crushed
1	fennel bulb, halved and thinly sliced (reserve leaves)
1/2	cup (125 ml) fish stock or clam juice
1/3	cup (90 ml) dry white wine
3	cups (750 ml) tomato pasta sauce
1/2	teaspoon superfine (caster) sugar
2	bay leaves
1/4	teaspoon saffron threads soaked in 1 tablespoon water
	Salt and freshly ground black pepper
1 1/2	pounds (750 g) firm white fish fillets, skinned and cubed
12	mussels, scrubbed and beards removed
	Mashed potatoes, to serve

Preparation: 15 minutes

Cooking: 6 minutes

Serves: 4

Level: 1

SHRIMP WITH MIRIN AND MUSHROOMS

Combine the soy sauce, sugar, mirin, and 1 tablespoon oil in a small bowl. • Add the shrimp. Set aside to marinate for 10 minutes. • Drain the shrimp, reserving the marinade. • Heat a wok over high heat. Add 2 teaspoons of oil and the shrimp. Stir-fry until the shrimp are pink, 1–2 minutes. Remove and set aside. • Add the remaining oil and shiitake mushrooms. Stir-fry for 1 minute. • Add the reserved marinade and stir-fry for 1 minute. • Add the enoki mushrooms, scallions, and shrimp. • Stir-fry for 1 minute, or until heated through. • Serve hot with steamed rice.

1/4 **cup (60 ml) soy sauce**

2 **tablespoons superfine (caster) sugar**

3 **tablespoons mirin**

3 **tablespoons peanut oil**

1 1/2 **pounds (750 g) large shrimp (green king prawns), peeled and deveined**

5 **ounces (150 g) shiitake mushrooms, sliced**

4 **ounces (125 g) enoki mushrooms, trimmed**

4 **scallions (green onions), trimmed and cut into short lengths**

Steamed short-grain rice, to serve

■■■ *Enoki mushrooms, also known as golden mushrooms, are used in Japanese and many other Asian cuisines. If you can't find them, substitute with the same quantity of white mushrooms.*

Preparation: 15 minutes
Cooking: 8 minutes

Serves: 4
Level: 1

SPICY BABY OCTOPUS

Preheat a lightly oiled grill pan on high.
• Combine the oil, lime juice, garlic, and chiles in a bowl. Add the octopus. Toss to coat. Set aside to marinate for 10 minutes. • Grill the octopus, tossing until tender, about 2–3 minutes. • To make the sweet chili dressing, combine the sweet chili sauce, fish sauce, and sesame oil in a bowl. Stir to combine. • Arrange the baby Asian salad greens and cilantro on serving plates. Top with the octopus. • Drizzle with the sweet chili dressing and serve hot.

3 tablespoons extra-virgin olive oil

1 tablespoon freshly squeezed lime or lemon juice

2 cloves garlic, crushed

2 small fresh red chiles, finely chopped

1¼ pounds (750 g) cleaned baby octopus or squid, halved

1/3 cup (90 ml) Thai sweet chili sauce

1 tablespoon Asian fish sauce

1 teaspoon Asian sesame oil

4 ounces (125 g) baby Asian salad greens

1 cup fresh cilantro (coriander) leaves

Preparation: 20 minutes
Cooking: 3 minutes

Serves: 4
Level: 1

SPICY LIME AND CILANTRO FISH PACKAGES

Preheat the oven to 400°F (200°C/gas 6). • Spray four 12 x 16-inch (30 x 40-cm) sheets of parchment paper with nonstick cooking spray. • Score the thickest part of the fish twice. Place a fillet in the center of each sheet of parchment paper. • Combine the cilantro, sugar, fish sauce, lime juice, and sweet chili sauce in a small bowl. • Drizzle over the fish. Top the fish with the scallions. • Fold the paper and wrap the fish to form secure packages. • Place the packages folded side up on a baking sheet. • Bake for 10–15 minutes (timing will depend on the thickness of the packages), until the fish is just cooked through when tested with a skewer. • Open the packages and top with cilantro. Serve with the lime wedges and steamed jasmine rice.

4 (8-ounce/250-g) salmon or ocean trout fillets

1/4 cup coarsely chopped cilantro (coriander) leaves + extra leaves, to garnish

1 tablespoon light brown sugar

1 teaspoon Asian fish sauce

1/4 cup (60 ml) freshly squeezed lime juice

3 tablespoons Thai sweet chili sauce

3 scallions (green onions), thinly sliced diagonally

Lime wedges, to serve

Steamed jasmine rice, to serve

Preparation: 15 minutes
Cooking: 10–15 minutes

Serves: 4
Level: 1

CRISP BATTERED FISH WITH LEMON AND DILL MAYONNAISE

Combine the mayonnaise, lemon zest and juice, and dill in a bowl. Season with salt and pepper. Stir to combine. Chill until ready to serve. • To make the batter, place the flour in a bowl. Gradually whisk in enough beer to form a smooth batter. Set aside. • Heat the oil in deep-fryer until hot. Test the oil temperature by dropping a small piece of bread into the hot oil. If the bread immediately bubbles to the surface and begins to trun golden, the oil is ready. • Dust the fish in cornstarch and dip in the batter, draining off any excess. • Deep-fry the fish in batches until golden brown and just cooked through, 2–3 minutes. Drain on paper towels. • Serve hot with the lemon wedges and lemon and dill mayonnaise.

1 cup (250 ml) mayonnaise

2 teaspoons finely grated lemon zest

1 tablespoon freshly squeezed lemon juice

1 tablespoon finely chopped fresh dill leaves

Salt and freshly ground black pepper

1 cup (150 g) all-purpose (plain) flour

About ³/₄ cup (180 ml) chilled beer

4 cups (1 liter) vegetable oil, for frying

8 (5-ounce/150-g) skinless firm white fish fillets such as whiting, snapper, or hake

1 tablespoon cornstarch (cornflour)

Lemon wedges, to serve

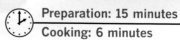

Preparation: 15 minutes

Cooking: 6 minutes

Serves: 4

Level: 1

THAI FISH CAKES

To make the fish cakes, combine the fish, egg, curry paste, fish sauce, and cornstarch in a food processor. Process until just combined. • Stir in the scallions, cilantro, and lime leaves, if using. • Shape the mixture into 12 patties. • Heat 1/2 inch (1 cm) of oil in a large frying pan. • Fry the fish cakes in batches, turning once, until golden and cooked through, 3–4 minutes on each side. • Drain on paper towel and place in a 200°F (100°C) oven to keep warm.

Fish Cakes

1   **pound (500 g) boneless skinned white fish fillets**

1   **large egg, lightly beaten**

3   **tablespoons Thai red curry paste**

1   **tablespoon Asian fish sauce**

1   **tablespoon cornflour (cornstarch)**

2   **scallions (green onions), trimmed and thinly sliced**

2   **tablespoons finely chopped fresh cilantro (coriander)**

2   **Kaffir lime leaves, finely shredded (optional)**

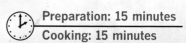

Preparation: 15 minutes
Cooking: 15 minutes

Serves: 4
Level: 1

ASIAN SALAD

Asian Salad

5 ounces (150 g) baby Asian salad greens

1 Lebanese (or normal) cucumber, halved lengthwise and thinly sliced diagonally

1 cup (30 g) fresh cilantro (coriander) leaves

1 tablespoon Thai sweet chili sauce

1 tablespoon Asian fish sauce

1 tablespoon rice vinegar

1 tablespoon peanut oil

Freshly ground black pepper

To make the salad, combine the Asian salad greens, cucumber, and cilantro in a salad bowl. • Combine the sweet chili sauce, fish sauce, rice vinegar, and peanut oil in a small bowl. Whisk to combine. • Drizzle over the salad. Toss gently to combine. • Serve the fish cakes with the Asian salad on the side.

■■■ *Fish cakes are a delicious way to serve fish, especially to children or people who are not generally enthusiastic about seafood. Fish cakes are a common item in British fish and chip shops and were generally made of cod, until cod stocks became depleted; nowadays other varieties of white fish are used, such as whiting, haddock, or snapper. Our recipe has a spicy Asian flavor given by the Thai red curry paste. If you don't like spicy dishes, you may prefer to replace the curry paste with the same quantity of tomato paste.*

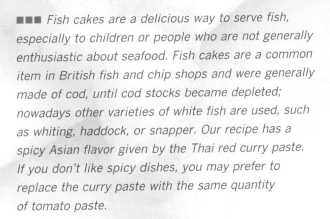

GRILLED TUNA WITH TOMATO AND MOZZARELLA SALAD

To make the salad, combine the tomatoes, olives, onion, bocconcini, and parsley in a bowl. Season with salt and pepper. • Drizzle with 2 tablespoons of the oil and the balsamic vinegar. Toss to combine. Set aside. • Preheat a grill on high. • Brush both sides of the tuna steaks with the remaining oil. Season with salt and pepper. • Grill the tuna until half cooked through, 2–3 minutes on each side (tuna can be served slightly raw in the center). • Place the tuna on serving plates. Top with the tomato salad and arugula leaves and serve hot.

8 ounces (250 g) cherry tomatoes, chopped

2 ounces (60 g) pitted black olives, chopped

1/2 small red onion, halved and very thinly sliced

4 mozzarella balls (bocconcini), chopped

2 tablespoons coarsely chopped flat-leaf parsley

Salt and freshly ground black pepper

1/4 cup (60 ml) extra-virgin olive oil

2 tablespoons balsamic vinegar

4 6-ounce (180-g) tuna steaks

Arugula (rocket) leaves, to serve

Preparation: 15 minutes

Cooking: 4–6 minutes

Serves: 4

Level: 1

FLOUNDER WITH LEMON AND CHIVE BUTTER

Preheat a broiler (grill) on medium-high. • Line a shallow baking dish with aluminum foil. Brush with a little melted butter. • Combine the remaining butter, chives, and lemon juice and zest in a bowl. • Season with salt and pepper. • Place the fish on in the baking dish. Drizzle with the lemon and chive butter. • Broil the fish, turning once, until just cooked through, 3–4 minutes on each side. • Place the fish on serving plates. Drizzle with the lemon and chive butter in the baking dish. • Serve hot with lemon wedges and a green salad.

1/3 cup (90 g) butter, melted

2 tablespoons finely chopped fresh chives

2 tablespoons freshly squeezed lemon juice

1 teaspoon finely grated lemon zest

Salt and freshly ground black pepper

4 whole flounder, cleaned

Lemon wedges, to serve

Green salad, to serve

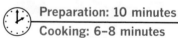

Preparation: 10 minutes
Cooking: 6–8 minutes

Serves: 4
Level: 1

POULTRY

CHICKEN, LEEK, AND MUSHROOM PIES

Preheat the oven to 425°F (220°C/gas 7).
• Sauté the chicken in the oil in a large,
deep frying pan over medium-high heat
until cooked, about 3 minutes. • Add the
leeks and mushrooms. Cover and simmer
for 3 minutes. • Stir in the sour cream,
mustard, and thyme. Season with salt
and pepper. • Spoon the mixture evenly
into four 1-cup (250-ml) ramekins. • Cut
the pastry into four squares and place
over the tops of the ramekins. • Brush
the pastry with the beaten egg. • Bake
for 8–10 minutes until puffed and golden.
• Serve hot.

$1^1/2$ pounds (750 g) boneless, skinless chicken breasts, cut into small cubes

2 tablespoons extra-virgin olive oil

2 leeks, halved lengthwise and thinly sliced

8 ounces (250 g) mushrooms, quartered

1 cup (250 ml) sour cream

1 tablespoon Dijon mustard

2 tablespoons finely chopped fresh thyme

Salt and freshly ground black pepper

8 ounces (250 g) frozen puff pastry, thawed

1 large egg, lightly beaten

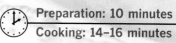

Preparation: 10 minutes
Cooking: 14–16 minutes

Serves: 4
Level: 1

CHICKEN WITH ASPARAGUS AND PROSCIUTTO

Preheat the oven to 425°F (220°C/gas 7). • Flatten the chicken with a meat tenderizer. • Spread each piece of chicken with 2 teaspoons of mustard. • Top evenly with the asparagus and roll up. Secure with toothpicks. • Cook the chicken in the oil in a large frying pan over medium-high heat, turning frequently, until browned, about 5 minutes. • Remove from the pan and set aside. • Wrap the prosciutto around each piece of chicken. • Arrange on a baking sheet in a single layer. • Bake for about 15 minutes, until cooked. • Meanwhile, cook the potatoes in a large saucepan of boiling water until tender, 10–15 minutes. • Drain well. • Serve the chicken with the potatoes and salad greens.

2 boneless, skinless chicken breasts, halved lengthwise

2 tablespoons whole-grain mustard

8 ounces (250 g) asparagus, halved

2 tablespoons extra-virgin olive oil

4 slices prosciutto (Parma ham)

1¼ pounds (600 g) new potatoes, halved

Mixed salad greens, to serve

Preparation: 15 minutes
Cooking: 30 minutes

Serves: 4
Level: 1

CHICKEN WITH TOMATOES AND MOZZARELLA

Cook the pasta in a large pot of salted boiling water until al dente. • Drain well. • Meanwhile, sauté the chicken in the oil in a large frying pan over medium-high heat until cooked, about 3 minutes on each side. • Remove from the pan and set aside. • Add the onion and garlic. Sauté until softened, about 3 minutes. • Stir in the tomatoes and stock. Season with salt and pepper. • Return the chicken to the pan. Top with the mozzarella and sprinkle with the basil. • Bring to a boil. • Decrease the heat to low. • Cover and simmer for about 5 minutes, until the chicken is tender and the cheese has melted. • Serve the chicken with the pasta on the side.

1	pound (500 g) (risoni) pasta
2	boneless, skinless chicken breasts, halved lengthwise
2	tablespoons extra-virgin olive oil
1	red onion, finely chopped
2	cloves garlic, finely chopped
1	(14-ounce/400-g) can tomatoes, with juice
1/4	cup (60 ml) chicken stock
	Salt and freshly ground black pepper
4	slices mozzarella cheese
4	tablespoons torn basil

Preparation: 10 minutes
Cooking: 20 minutes

Serves: 4
Level: 1

GRILLED CHICKEN WITH GARLIC, LEMON, AND PARSLEY

Mix the oil, lemon zest and juice, garlic, and parsley in a small dish. • Add the chicken and coat well. Season with salt and pepper. • Place a grill pan over medium-high heat. • Grill the chicken until cooked through, about 5 minutes on each side. • Serve the chicken hot with the arugula and tomatoes.

2 tablespoons extra-virgin olive oil

Finely grated zest and juice of 1 lemon

2 cloves garlic, finely chopped

2 tablespoons finely chopped fresh parsley

3 boneless, skinless chicken breasts, halved lengthwise

Salt and freshly ground black pepper

8 ounces (250 g) arugula (rocket)

4 tomatoes, cut into wedges

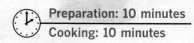

Preparation: 10 minutes

Cooking: 10 minutes

Serves: 4

Level: 1

GREEK CHICKEN KEBABS WITH TZATZIKI

To prepare the chicken kebabs, thread the chicken onto bamboo skewers. • Mix the oil, lemon juice, garlic, and oregano in a small dish. Season with salt and pepper. • Add the chicken skewers and coat well. • To prepare the tzatziki, mix the yogurt, lemon juice, cucumber, and mint in a small bowl. • Place a grill pan over medium-high heat. • Grill the kebabs, turning them from time to time, until cooked through. 6–8 minutes. • Serve the chicken kebabs with the tzatziki, tomatoes, lettuce, and pita bread.

Preparation: 15 minutes
Cooking: 6–8 minutes

Serves: 4
Level: 1

Chicken Kebabs

1³/4 pounds (800 g) boneless, skinless chicken, cut into small cubes

¹/4 cup (60 ml) extra-virgin olive oil

2 tablespoons freshly squeezed lemon juice

2 cloves garlic, finely chopped

2 teaspoons dried oregano

Salt and freshly ground black pepper

Tzatziki

³/4 cup (180 ml) plain yogurt

2 tablespoons freshly squeezed lemon juice

1 small cucumber, finely grated

2 tablespoons finely chopped fresh mint

To Serve

2 tomatoes, diced

Finely shredded lettuce, to serve

Pita bread, to serve

LIME AND CILANTRO CHICKEN KEBABS

Bring a large saucepan of salted water to a boil. • Add the rice and cook over medium heat until tender, 10–15 minutes. Drain well. • Thread the chicken onto bamboo skewers. • Mix the sweet chili sauce, lime juice, soy sauce, and cilantro in a small bowl. • Add the chicken skewers and coat well. • Place a grill pan over medium-high heat. • Grill the chicken until cooked, about 3 minutes on each side. • Serve the kebabs with the rice and Asian salad greens.

2 cups (400 g) jasmine rice

3 boneless, skinless chicken breasts, trimmed

2 tablespoons Thai sweet chili sauce

2 tablespoons freshly squeezed lime juice

1 tablespoon light soy sauce

1 tablespoon finely chopped fresh cilantro (coriander)

4 ounces (125 g) baby Asian greens

Preparation: 10 minutes

Cooking: 16–21 minutes

Serves: 4
Level: 1

CHICKEN WITH FETA AND BASIL

Cut a pocket in each chicken breast.
• Stuff the chicken evenly with the feta, basil, and sun-dried tomatoes. Secure with toothpicks. • Sauté the chicken in the oil in a large, deep frying pan over medium-high heat until cooked, about 3 minutes on each side. • Pour in the spicy tomato sauce and water. • Bring to a boil. Cover and simmer over low heat until the chicken is tender, about 4 minutes. • Meanwhile, cook the potatoes in a large saucepan of salted boiling water until tender, 10–15 minutes. • Drain well and return to the pan. • Add the butter and mash until smooth.
• Serve the chicken hot with the mashed potato.

4 small boneless, skinless chicken breasts

4 ounces (125 g) feta cheese, crumbled

12 large fresh basil leaves

8 sun-dried tomatoes

2 tablespoons extra-virgin olive oil

1²/₃ cups (400 ml) store-bought tomato sauce, such as enchilada sauce, pasta sauce, or salsa

¹/₄ cup (60 ml) water

1¹/₂ pounds (750 g) new potatoes, peeled and diced

2 tablespoons butter

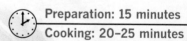

Preparation: 15 minutes
Cooking: 20–25 minutes

Serves: 4
Level: 1

JAPANESE-STYLE CHICKEN WITH RICE

Bring a large saucepan of salted water to a boil. • Add the rice and cook over medium heat until tender, 12–15 minutes. • Drain and rinse under ice-cold water to stop the cooking process. • Mix 2 tablespoons of peanut oil, the soy sauce, mirin, ginger, and half the garlic in a small dish. • Add the chicken and coat well. • Place a grill pan over medium-high heat. • Grill the chicken until cooked, about 3 minutes on each side. • Meanwhile, heat 2 teaspoons of oil in a wok or large frying pan over medium heat. • Add the eggs and stir-fry until scrambled, about 1 minute. • Remove from the pan and set aside. • Sauté the scallions and remaining garlic in the remaining oil in the same pan for about 1 minute until softened. • Add the rice and return the eggs to the wok. • Stir-fry for 1 minute. • Serve the chicken hot with rice.

1¹⁄₄ cups (250 g) long-grain rice

¹⁄₄ cup (60 ml) peanut oil

¹⁄₄ cup (60 ml) light soy sauce

¹⁄₄ cup (60 ml) mirin or sweet sherry

2 teaspoons freshly grated ginger

4 cloves garlic, finely chopped

3 boneless, skinless chicken breasts, halved

2 large eggs, lightly beaten

4 scallions (green onions), thinly sliced

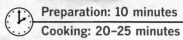

Preparation: 10 minutes
Cooking: 20–25 minutes

Serves: 4
Level: 1

MOROCCAN CHICKEN WITH CORN SALSA

Mix the ras el hanout with the oil in a small bowl. • Brush the chicken with the mixture. • Place a grill pan over medium-high heat. • Grill the chicken until cooked, about 3 minutes on each side. • To prepare the salsa, mix the corn, tomatoes, cucumber, onion, lemon juice, cilantro, and oil in a small bowl. • Season with salt and pepper. • Serve the chicken hot with the salsa.

2 teaspoons ras el hanout (mixed Moroccan spices)

2 tablespoons extra-virgin olive oil

4 small boneless, skinless chicken breasts, halved

Salsa

2 cups (250 g) canned corn (sweet corn), drained

2 tomatoes, diced

1 cucumber, diced

1 small red onion, finely chopped

2 tablespoons freshly squeezed lemon juice

2 tablespoons finely chopped fresh cilantro (coriander)

2 tablespoons extra-virgin olive oil

Salt and freshly ground black pepper

■■■ *Ras el hanout is a blend of up to 30 different Moroccan spices. It has a subtle yet fiery kick and is used to add nuance and flavor to many different dishes. It is available at African foodstores and on line.*

Preparation: 10 minutes
Cooking: 6 minutes

Serves: 4
Level: 1

HERB-CRUMBED CHICKEN

Flatten the chicken with a meat tenderizer. • Mix the bread crumbs, parsley, and chives in a small bowl. Season with salt and pepper. • Dip the chicken first in the flour, then in the beaten eggs, followed by the herbed bread crumbs. • Fry the chicken in batches in the oil in a large frying pan over medium heat until golden and crisp, about 2 minutes on each side. • Serve the chicken with the lemon wedges and French fries.

4   small boneless, skinless chicken breasts

2   cups (120 g) fresh bread crumbs

2   tablespoons finely chopped fresh parsley

2   tablespoons finely chopped fresh chives

Salt and freshly ground black pepper

1/4 cup (30 g) all-purpose (plain) flour

2   large eggs, lightly beaten

2   tablespoons extra-virgin olive oil

Lemon wedges and chips, to serve

French fries (potato chips), to serve

 Preparation: 15 minutes
Cooking: 8 minutes

Serves: 4
Level: 1

CHICKEN ROLLS WITH PANCETTA AND PARMESAN

446

Cook the rice in a large saucepan of salted boiling water until tender, about 15 minutes. • Drain and rinse well. • Meanwhile, lay the chicken out on a clean surface. • Place a slice of pancetta, some Parmesan, and a sage leaf on top of each chicken breast. Season with salt and nutmeg. • Roll up the slices and secure with toothpicks. • Sauté the chicken in the oil in a large frying pan over medium heat for 3 minutes. • Drizzle with the wine. • Cook, turning often, until cooked and golden, about 12 minutes. • Serve hot with the rice.

2	cups (400 g) short-grain rice
2	large boneless, skinned chicken breasts, cut into 8 fillets
8	slices pancetta or bacon
3	ounces (90 g) Parmesan cheese, cut into small cubes
8	leaves fresh sage
	Salt
1/4	teaspoon freshly grated nutmeg
1/4	cup (60 ml) extra-virgin olive oil
1/3	cup (90 ml) dry white wine

 Preparation: 10 minutes
Cooking: 30 minutes

Serves: 4
Level: 1

CHICKEN BURGERS WITH OLIVE BUTTER

Process 1/2 cup (60 g) of olives in a food processor until smooth. • Mix the butter, olive paste, and garlic in a small bowl. • Place the mixture on a sheet of aluminum foil and shape into a log. Wrap in the foil and place in the freezer. • Meanwhile, place the chicken in a medium bowl. Stir in the shallot and thyme. Season with salt and pepper. • Divide the chicken mixture into 6–8 portions and shape into burgers. • Fry the burgers in the oil in a large frying pan over medium-high heat until cooked, about 4 minutes on each side. • Arrange the burgers on a bed of arugula and garnish with the remaining olives. • Slice the frozen butter and place on top of the burgers. • Serve hot.

3/4 cup (90 g) pitted black olives

1/2 cup (125 g) butter at room temperature

1 clove garlic, finely chopped

2 pounds (1 kg) ground (minced) chicken

1 shallot, finely chopped

3 tablespoons finely chopped fresh thyme

Salt and freshly ground black pepper

1/4 cup (60 ml) extra-virgin olive oil

1 bunch arugula (rocket), to serve

Preparation: 15 minutes
Cooking: 8 minutes

Serves: 4–6
Level: 1

SPICED DUCK WITH WINTER SQUASH

Preheat the oven to 425°F (220°C/gas 7). • Line a baking sheet with parchment paper. • Place the squash on the baking sheet and brush with 1 tablespoon of oil. Season with salt and pepper. • Roast the squash, turning once, until tender, about 15 minutes. • Meanwhile, combine the soy sauce, honey, and Chinese five-spice powder in a bowl. • Brush the duck with this mixture. • Heat a frying pan over medium-high heat. Sauté the duck, skin-side down, until golden brown and crisp, about 5 minutes. • Turn and sauté for 3–5 minutes, until cooked to your liking. • Transfer to a plate, cover, and let rest for 5 minutes. • Slice the duck. • To make the dressing, combine the remaining oil, vinegar, sugar, salt, and pepper in a small bowl. Whisk to combine. • Arrange the squash on serving plates. Top with the sliced duck. • Drizzle with the dressing and serve with the Asian salad greens.

1/2 medium butternut squash (pumpkin), seeded and cut into (1/2-inch/1-cm) thick slices

1/3 cup (90 ml) extra-virgin olive oil

1 tablespoon soy sauce

1 tablespoon honey

1 teaspoon Chinese five-spice powder

4 duck breasts, with skin

3 tablespoons red wine vinegar

1 teaspoon caster sugar

Asian baby salad greens, to serve

Preparation: 10 minutes
Cooking: 20 minutes

Serves: 4
Level: 1

451

CITRUS CHICKEN WITH FETA AND ARUGULA

Heat the oil in a large frying pan over medium-high heat. Sauté the chicken, turning once, until golden, about 10 minutes. • Add the onion and sauté until just tender, about 3 minutes. • Add the orange and lemon juice. Cover and bring to a boil. Sprinkle with the olives and feta. Cover and cook for 1 minute. • Arrange the chicken on serving plates, drizzle with the pan juices and serve hot with the arugula.

3 tablespoons extra-virgin olive oil

6 boneless chicken thighs, with skin, halved

2 red onions, thinly sliced

Freshly squeezed juice of 1 orange

Freshly squeezed juice of 1 lemon

3/4 cup (90 g) pitted black olives

3 ounces (90 g) feta cheese, crumbled

1 bunch arugula (rocket), trimmed

 Preparation: 10 minutes

Cooking: 12 minutes

Serves: 4
Level: 1

CHICKEN, AVOCADO, AND ONION SANDWICHES

Preheat a grill pan on medium-high heat. • Place the onions in a dish and toss with half the oil. Season with salt and pepper. • Grill the onions, tossing from time to time, until tender, about 3 minutes. • Brush the chicken with the remaining oil. Season with salt and pepper. Grill the chicken until just cooked through, 3–4 minutes each side. Set aside on a plate. • Split the bread rolls in half and toast until just crisp. • Spread the bottom half of the rolls with mango chutney. Top with chicken, onion, avocado, and snow pea shoots. Season with salt and pepper. • Cover with the tops of the rolls and serve hot.

2 **medium red onions,** thinly sliced

4 **small boneless, skinless chicken breast fillets**

3 **tablespoons extra-virgin olive oil**

Salt and freshly ground black pepper

1 **large ripe avocado, peeled, pitted, and thinly sliced**

4 **crusty bread rolls or sandwich buns**

1/3 **cup (90 g) mango chutney**

3 **ounces (90 g) snow pea shoots**

Preparation: 15 minutes
Cooking: 10 minutes

Serves: 4
Level: 1

VIETNAMESE CHICKEN STICKS

Trim six lemon grass stems. Cut each one in half lengthwise and set aside.
• Finely chop the remaining lemon grass stem. • Combine the finely chopped lemon grass, chicken, scallions, chiles, cilantro, mint, egg, and bread crumbs in a medium bowl. Mix until well combined.
• Divide the mixture into 12 equal portions. • Shape each portion into a sausage shape around each of the lemon grass stems. • Place on a baking sheet lined with parchment paper. Cover and refrigerate for 10 minutes. • Heat a lightly oiled grill on medium heat. • Cook the chicken sticks, turning frequently, until cooked through, about 10 minutes.
• Serve immediately with steamed jasmine rice and sweet chili sauce.

7   stems lemon grass
1   pound (500 g) ground (minced) chicken
4   scallions (green onions), thinly sliced
2   small fresh red chiles, seeded and finely chopped
$1/4$ cup finely chopped cilantro (coriander) leaves
2   tablespoons finely chopped Vietnamese (or regular) mint leaves
1   large egg, lightly beaten
1   cup (60 g) fresh bread crumbs
    Steamed jasmine rice, to serve
    Thai sweet chili sauce, to serve

Preparation: 15 minutes
Cooking: 10 minutes

Serves: 4
Level: 1

DUCK WITH SNOW PEAS

Heat 1 tablespoon of oil in a wok over high heat. • Add half the duck. Stir-fry until golden and the skin is crisp, 3–4 minutes. Using a slotted spoon, transfer the duck to a plate. Repeat to cook the remaining duck. • Heat the remaining oil in a wok over high heat. Add the onion and garlic. Stir-fry until tender, about 2 minutes. • Add the soy sauce, sesame oil, and sugar. Stir-fry for 1 minute. • Add the snow peas and duck. Stir-fry until the snow peas are bright green, 1–2 minutes. • Serve hot with the noodles.

3 **tablespoons peanut oil**

3 **duck breasts, with skin, thinly sliced**

1 **red onion, cut into thin wedges**

2 **cloves garlic, crushed**

3 **tablespoons light soy sauce**

1 **tablespoon Asian sesame oil**

2 **teaspoons superfine (caster) sugar**

5 **ounces (150 g) snow peas, trimmed**

Preparation: 10 minutes
Cooking: 12 minutes

Serves: 4
Level: 1

GLAZED CHICKEN WINGS WITH POTATO WEDGES

Preheat the oven to 450°F (230°C/gas 8).
• Line two large baking sheets with parchment paper. • Combine the tomato, barbecue, and Worcestershire sauces, brown sugar, and paprika in a large bowl. Season with salt and pepper. • Add the chicken. Toss to coat in the mixture.
• Place the chicken in a single layer on one baking sheet. Place the potato wedges on the other baking sheet.
• Roast the chicken and potato wedges for about 20 minutes, turning once, until crisp and golden. • Serve hot with the green salad.

12	large chicken wings, cut in three pieces (discard wing tips)
1/3	cup (90 ml) tomato sauce
1/3	cup (90 ml) barbecue sauce
1	tablespoon Worcestershire sauce
1/3	cup (70 g) firmly packed brown sugar
1/2	teaspoon ground paprika
	Salt and freshly ground black pepper
1	pound (500 g) frozen potato wedges
	Leafy green salad, to serve

Preparation: 10 minutes

Cooking: 20 minutes

Serves: 4
Level: 1

DUCK AND GREEN ONION YAKITORI

Presoak 12 bamboo skewers. • To make the yakitori sauce, combine the soy sauce, stock, mirin, and sugar in a saucepan. Bring to a boil, stirring from time to time, over high heat. • Reduce the heat and simmer until the sauce is reduced by about one-third, about 5 minutes. • Set aside to cool slightly. Pour into a shallow ceramic dish. • Divide the ingredients evenly, and thread the duck and scallion (crosswise) onto the skewers. • Place the skewers in the yakitori sauce. Turn to coat in the sauce. • Preheat a lightly oiled grill on medium-high heat. • Grill the skewers, basting with the yakitori sauce from time to time, until just cooked through, 8–10 minutes. • Serve hot with the rice.

$1/2$ cup (125 ml) reduced salt soy sauce

$1/3$ cup (90 ml) chicken stock

$1/4$ cup (60 ml) mirin

$1/4$ cup (50 g) superfine (caster) sugar

$13/4$ pounds (800 g) boneless duck breasts, trimmed and cut into 1-inch (2.5-cm) pieces

8 scallions (green onions), trimmed and cut into 2-inch (5-cm) lengths

Steamed short grain rice, to serve

Preparation: 15 minutes
Cooking: 8–15 minutes

Serves: 4
Level: 1

CHINESE CHICKEN FRIED RICE

Heat a wok over high heat until hot. Add 2 teaspoons of oil. • Pour in the eggs and cook, stirring constantly, until set, about 2 minutes. Transfer to a cutting board and chop. • Heat the remaining oil in a wok over high heat. Add the onion, garlic, and bacon. Stir-fry until tender, 2–3 minutes. • Add the wine and sugar. Stir-fry for 1 minute. • Add the chicken and peas. Stir-fry for 1 minute. • Add the rice, soy sauce, oyster sauce, scallions and half the eggs to the wok. Stir-fry until the rice is hot, 2–3 minutes. • Spoon into serving bowls. Sprinkle with the remaining egg and serve hot.

3	tablespoons peanut oil
2	eggs, lightly beaten
1	onion, finely chopped
2	cloves garlic, finely chopped
4	ounces (125 g) bacon slices, chopped
3	tablespoons Shaoxing wine or dry sherry
2	teaspoons caster sugar
4	cups (400 g) cooked shredded chicken
1/2	cup (60 g) frozen green peas
4	cups cooked long-grain rice

Preparation: 15 minutes

Cooking: 12 minutes

Serves: 4
Level: 1

■ ■ ■ *You will need about 1¹/₂ cups (300 g) of uncooked rice to make about 4 cups of cooked rice.*

3 **tablespoons soy sauce**

1 **tablespoon Chinese oyster sauce**

4 **scallions (green onions), thinly sliced diagonally**

■ ■ ■ *Garlic is a member of the onion family. Its use in cooking dates from the earliest times; it has been found in Egyptian tombs, where it was placed as a food offering, and is even mentioned in the Bible (Numbers 11:5). Its health benefits have also been lauded for thousands of years, although only in recent times has modern medical science confirmed its medicinal properties as an antibacterial, antifungal, and antithrombotic (preventing blood from clotting). It is rich in sulfur and vitamins B1 and C and contains trace minerals such as phosphorus, iron, and calcium.*

465

BARBECUED PLUM-SPICED QUAILS

Cut along each side of the quails' or cornish hens' backbones and discard the backbones and necks. Press the pieces to flatten. • Combine the plum sauce and Chinese five-spice powder in a ceramic dish. • Add the quail or cornish hens and turn to coat in mixture. • Heat a lightly oiled grill pan on medium-high heat. • Cook the quails, turning and basting with plum sauce from time to time, until just cooked through, about 20 minutes. • Meanwhile, steam the snow peas and bok choy in a steamer over simmering water until just tender, 2–3 minutes. • Serve the quails hot with steamed vegetables and rice.

6 quails or 4 cornish hens, halved

1 cup (250 ml) Chinese plum sauce

1 teaspoon Chinese five-spice powder

5 ounces (150 g) snow peas, trimmed

1 bunch baby bok choy, trimmed

Steamed rice, to serve

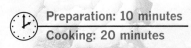

Preparation: 10 minutes

Cooking: 20 minutes

Serves: 4
Level: 1

SPICY LAO TURKEY SALAD

Combine the stock, lime juice, lemon grass, and garlic in a frying pan. Bring to a boil over high heat. • Add the turkey. Reduce the heat to low and sauté, breaking up the meat with a wooden spoon, until cooked through, about 5 minutes. • Remove from the heat. Stir in the fish sauce and sugar. Set aside to cool slightly. • Stir in the chiles, scallions, mint, and cilantro. • Serve hot with the lettuce and rice.

$1/3$ cup (90 ml) chicken stock

3 tablespoons freshly squeezed lime juice

1 stem lemon grass, trimmed, crushed, and finely sliced

2 cloves garlic, crushed

1 pound (500 g) ground (minced) turkey

1 tablespoon Asian fish sauce

1 tablespoon superfine (caster) sugar

2 small fresh red chiles, seeded and finely chopped

3 scallions (green onions), trimmed and finely sliced

$1/4$ cup finely chopped fresh cilantro (coriander)

2 tablespoons finely chopped fresh mint

Crisp lettuce leaves, to serve

Steamed jasmine rice, to serve

 Preparation: 20 minutes

Cooking: 10 minutes

Serves: 4
Level: 1

SMOKED CHICKEN SALAD WITH CRANBERRY DRESSING

Shred the smoked chicken flesh, discarding the skin and bones. Place in a large bowl. • Add the celery, scallions, and snow pea shoots. Gently toss to combine. • To make the cranberry dressing, heat the cranberry sauce in a saucepan over medium heat until warm. Pour into a small bowl. Add the vinegar and oil. Season with salt and pepper. Whisk until combined. • Arrange the avocados on serving plates. Top with smoked chicken mixture. • Drizzle with the cranberry dressing and serve.

1   smoked chicken (about 2 pounds/ 1 kg)

3   stalks celery, thinly sliced

2   scallions (green onions), trimmed and finely sliced

3   ounces (60 g) snow pea shoots, trimmed

1/3   cup (90 ml) extra-virgin olive or grape seed oil

1/3   cup (90 ml) whole berry cranberry sauce

3   tablespoons red wine vinegar

2   medium avocados, peeled, pitted, and sliced lengthwise

Preparation: 20 minutes
Cooking: 2 minutes

Serves: 4
Level: 1

TURKEY WITH MARMALADE GLAZE

Heat the oil and butter in a large frying pan over medium-high heat. • Sauté the turkey in batches until golden and just cooked through, 5–8 minutes. Transfer to a plate, cover, and keep warm. • Add the marmalade, orange juice, and chicken stock to the pan. Season with salt and pepper. • Simmer over medium heat, stirring from time to time, until slightly thickened, about 5 minutes.

• Meanwhile, steam the asparagus in a steamer over simmering water until just tender, 2–3 minutes. • Arrange the asparagus and turkey on serving plates. Spoon the marmalade glaze over the top and serve hot.

1 tablespoon extra-virgin olive oil

3 tablespoons butter

8 turkey cutlets (about 1³/₄ pounds/800 g)

¹/₂ cup (125 ml) orange marmalade

3 tablespoons freshly squeezed orange juice

¹/₄ cup (60 ml) chicken stock

Salt and freshly ground black pepper

2 bunches asparagus, trimmed

Preparation: 10 minutes
Cooking: 15 minutes

Serves: 4
Level: 1

CHICKEN, BROCCOLI, AND CASHEW STIR-FRY

Heat a wok over high heat. • Add 1 tablespoon of oil and the cashews. Stir-fry until golden, 2–3 minutes. Transfer to a plate using a slotted spoon. • Heat 1 tablespoon of oil in a wok over high heat. Stir-fry half the chicken until golden and almost cooked through, 3–4 minutes. Transfer to a plate. Repeat with the remaining chicken. • Add the remaining 1 tablespoon of oil to a wok. Add the onion and stir-fry until tender, about 2 minutes. • Add the broccoli and garlic. Stir-fry until bright green, about 2 minutes. • Add the oyster sauce, soy sauce, and chicken to the wok. Stir-fry until hot. • Add the cashews and toss well. • Serve hot with the rice.

3 tablespoons peanut oil

1/2 cup (80 g) cashew nuts

1³/4 pounds (800 g) boneless, skinless chicken thighs

1 brown onion, cut into thin wedges

8 ounces (250 g) broccoli florets

3 cloves garlic, crushed

1/2 cup (125 ml) Chinese oyster sauce

3 tablespoons soy sauce

Steamed jasmine rice, to serve

Preparation: 15 minutes
Cooking: 10 minutes

Serves: 4
Level: 1

SAGE-CRUMBED TURKEY WITH SWEET POTATOES

Combine the bread crumbs and sage in a shallow dish. Season with salt and pepper. • Lightly coat the turkey with flour and egg. Lightly press the crumb mixture over the turkey. • Cook the sweet potatoes in a saucepan of boiling water until tender, about 10 minutes. • Drain and return to the saucepan. Mash briefly. Add the milk, butter, and nutmeg. Season with salt and pepper. Mash until smooth. • Meanwhile, heat the oil in a frying pan over medium heat. Cook the turkey in batches until golden and crisp, about 2 minutes on each side. Drain on paper towels. • Serve the turkey with the sweet potatoes.

1^1/$_2$ cups (120 g) fresh bread crumbs

^{1}/$_4$ cup finely chopped fresh sage leaves

Salt and freshly ground black pepper

4 turkey breast fillets

2 tablespoons all-purpose (plain) flour

2 large eggs, lightly beaten

1^3/$_4$ pounds (800 g) sweet potatoes, peeled and cut into large chunks

^{1}/$_3$ cup (90 ml) milk, hot

2 tablespoons butter, diced

Pinch ground nutmeg

2 tablespoons extra-virgin olive oil

Preparation: 15 minutes
Cooking: 10 minutes

Serves: 4
Level: 1

CHICKEN SALAD WITH YOGURT DRESSING

Combine the chicken, oil, 3 tablespoons of lime juice, salt and pepper in a bowl. • Heat a grill over medium-high heat. Grill the chicken until golden and just cooked through, about 5 minutes each side. • Transfer to a plate, cover with aluminum foil, and let stand for 5 minutes. • Meanwhile, combine the mayonnaise, yogurt, and remaining lime juice in a bowl. Whisk until combined. • Slice the chicken. Arrange the lettuce, cucumber, and chicken on serving plates. Drizzle with the dressing and serve.

4 **boneless, skinless chicken breasts**

3 **tablespoons extra-virgin olive oil**

¹/₄ **cup (60 ml) freshly squeezed lime juice**

Salt and freshly ground black pepper

¹/₃ **cup (90 ml) mayonnaise**

¹/₄ **cup (60 ml) Greek-style yogurt**

2 **teaspoons honey**

2 **cucumbers, very thinly sliced lengthwise**

1 **small Iceberg lettuce, halved and cut into in thin wedges**

Preparation: 10 minutes

Cooking: 20 minutes

Serves: 4
Level: 1

GRUYÈRE ROAST CHICKEN WITH SPINACH

Preheat the oven to 400°F (200°C/gas 6). • Line a baking sheet with parchment paper. • Make a slit lengthwise through each chicken breast to form a pocket (do not cut all the way through). • Stuff the cheese and chives inside each pocket. • Heat the oil in a frying pan over medium-high heat. • Sauté the chicken in batches until golden, about 2 minutes each side. • Transfer the chicken to the baking sheet. Roast for 6–8 minutes, until just cooked through. Cover and let rest for 5 minutes. • Meanwhile, heat the butter in the frying pan over medium heat. Sauté the spinach until just wilted, 2–3 minutes. Season with salt, pepper, and nutmeg. • Serve the chicken hot with the spinach.

4 boneless, skinless chicken breast fillets

5 ounces (150 g) Gruyère cheese, thinly sliced

2 tablespoons finely chopped fresh chives

1 tablespoon extra-virgin olive oil

1/3 cup (90 g) butter

1 bunch spinach, trimmed

Salt and freshly ground black pepper

Pinch ground nutmeg

Preparation: 15 minutes
Cooking: 12 minutes

Serves: 4
Level: 1

INDIAN-STYLE CHICKEN CURRY

Heat 1 tablespoon of oil in a large saucepan over medium-high heat. Sauté the chicken in batches until browned, about 3–4 minutes per batch. Transfer to a plate. • Add the remaining 2 tablespoons of oil to the saucepan over medium-high heat. • Sauté the onion, garlic, and ginger until tender, about 3 minutes. • Add the cumin, coriander, and mustard and fennel seeds. Sauté until fragrant, about 1 minute. • Stir in the tomatoes and chicken. Reduce the heat to low. Simmer, stirring from time to time, until the chicken is tender, 10–12 minutes. • Spoon into serving bowls and top with the cilantro. Serve hot with the yogurt, rice, and mango chutney.

Preparation: 10 minutes
Cooking: 20 minutes

Serves: 4
Level: 1

3	tablespoons peanut oil
1¹/₂	pounds (750 g) boneless, skinless chicken thighs, cut into small pieces
1	onion, thinly sliced
2	cloves garlic, crushed
2	teaspoons grated fresh ginger
1	tablespoon ground cumin
2	teaspoons ground coriander
2	teaspoons mustard seeds
2	teaspoons fennel seeds
1	(14-ounce/400-g) can tomatoes, with juice
¹/₃	cup (90 ml) Greek-style yogurt
¹/₄	cup fresh cilantro (coriander) leaves, to serve
	Freshly cooked basmati rice, to serve
	Mango chutney, to serve

MEAT

BEEF FILLETS WITH TOMATO PESTO AND PROSCIUTTO

Cook the potatoes in a large saucepan of boiling water until tender, 10–15 minutes. Drain well. • Meanwhile, place the beef on a clean work surface. Spread evenly with the sun-dried tomato pesto.

• Wrap a slice of prosciutto around the edges of the beef fillets. • Secure with toothpicks. • Cook the green beans in a small saucepan of boiling water until just tender 3 minutes. • Place a grill pan over medium-high heat.

• Grill the beef for about 4 minutes on each side, or until cooked to your liking.

• Serve the beef hot with the potatoes and green beans.

$1^1/4$ pounds (550 g) new potatoes, halved

4   thick beef fillets

$1^1/2$ tablespoons sun-dried tomato pesto

4   thin slices prosciutto (Parma ham)

8   ounces (250 g) green beans

Preparation: 10 minutes

Cooking: 20 minutes

Serves: 4
Level: 1

BEEF FAJITAS

Mix the beef, paprika, cumin, coriander, chili powder, and lime juice in a large bowl. • Cover with plastic wrap (cling film) and let marinate for 5 minutes. • Meanwhile, sauté the onions and bell pepper in 2 tablespoons of oil in a large frying pan over medium-high heat until softened, about 5 minutes. Remove and set aside. • Add the remaining oil to the pan. • Add the beef and sauté until cooked, about 3 minutes. • Add the onions and bell pepper. Cook for 1 minute. • Warm the tortillas by placing them over the mixture in the pan, one at a time. • Serve the tortillas warm with the beef mixture, cilantro, and sour cream.

1	pound (500 g) lean beef strips, cut from the rump
1	teaspoon sweet paprika
1	teaspoon ground cumin
1	teaspoon ground coriander
1/2	teaspoon chili powder
1/4	cup (60 ml) freshly squeezed lime juice
2	onions, thinly sliced
1	red bell pepper (capsicum), seeded and thinly sliced
1/4	cup (60 ml) extra-virgin olive oil
8	fajita-size flour tortillas
	Cilantro (coriander) leaves
	Sour cream, to serve

Preparation: 15 minutes
Cooking: 10 minutes

Serves: 4
Level: 1

GROUND BEEF WITH VEGETABLES AND MASHED POTATO

Cook the potatoes in a large saucepan of boiling water until tender, 10 minutes. • Drain well and return to the pan. • Add the butter and milk. Mash until smooth. Season with salt and pepper. • Meanwhile, sauté the onion and garlic in the oil in a large frying pan over medium-low heat until softened, about 3 minutes. • Add the beef and sauté until browned, about 5 minutes. • Stir in the tomatoes. Bring to a boil. • Cover and simmer over low heat until thickened, about 5 minutes. • Add the vegetables and simmer for 5 minutes. • Season with salt and pepper. • Serve the beef hot with the mashed potato. Garnish with the parsley.

- 1 **pound (500 g) potatoes, peeled and diced**
- 2 **tablespoons butter**
- 2 **tablespoons milk**
- **Salt and freshly ground black pepper**
- 1 **onion, finely chopped**
- 2 **cloves garlic, finely chopped**
- 1 **tablespoon extra-virgin olive oil**
- 1 **pound (500 g) ground (minced) beef**
- 2 **cups (500 ml) chopped tomatoes**
- 1 **cup (150 g) frozen mixed peas, carrots, and corn**
- **Sprigs of parsley, to garnish**

Preparation: 10 minutes

Cooking: 20 minutes

Serves: 4
Level: 1

BEEF SIRLOIN WITH TOMATO AND OLIVE SAUCE

494

Cook the potatoes in a large saucepan of boiling water until tender, 10–15 minutes. • Drain well. • Meanwhile, sauté the onion and garlic in 1 tablespoon of oil in a large frying pan over medium-low heat until softened, about 3 minutes. • Stir in the tomatoes, olives, and sugar. Simmer over low heat until thickened, about 4 minutes. • Add the oregano and season with salt and pepper. • Heat the remaining oil in a large frying pan over medium-high heat. • Sauté the steaks for about 4 minutes on each side, or until cooked to your liking. • Serve the steaks hot with the sauce and potatoes.

1½ pounds (750 g) new potatoes, halved

1 red onion, thinly sliced

2 cloves garlic, finely chopped

2 tablespoons extra-virgin olive oil

1½ cups (375 ml) chopped tomatoes

2/3 cup (60 g) pitted kalamata olives

1 teaspoon sugar

2 tablespoons finely chopped fresh oregano

Salt and freshly ground black pepper

4 sirloin steaks

Preparation: 10 minutes
Cooking: 20 minutes

Serves: 4
Level: 1

BEEF STEAKS WITH MUSHROOMS AND SWEET POTATOES

Cook the sweet potatoes in a large saucepan of boiling water until tender, 10–15 minutes. • Drain well and return to the pan. • Add the butter and milk. Mash until smooth. Season with salt and pepper. • Meanwhile, sauté the mushrooms, scallions, and garlic in 2 tablespoons of oil in a large frying pan over medium heat until softened, about 3 minutes. • Stir in the cream, lemon juice, and thyme. • Bring to a boil. Simmer over low heat until thickened, about 1 minute. • Heat the remaining oil in a large frying pan over medium-high heat. • Sauté the steaks for about 4 minutes on each side, or until cooked to your liking. • Serve the steaks hot with the mushroom sauce and sweet potatoes.

$1^1/_2$ pounds (750 g) sweet potatoes, peeled and diced

2 tablespoons butter

$^1/_4$ cup (60 ml) milk

Salt and freshly ground black pepper

8 ounces (250 g) mushrooms, thinly sliced

4 scallions (spring onions), thinly sliced

2 cloves garlic, finely chopped

$^1/_4$ cup (60 ml) extra-virgin olive oil

1 cup (250 ml) light (single) cream

3 tablespoons freshly squeezed lemon juice

1 tablespoon fresh thyme leaves

4 beef fillet steaks

Preparation: 15 minutes

Cooking: 15 minutes

Serves: 4

Level: 1

GREEK BEEF KEBABS

Mix the beef, bread crumbs, egg, feta, garlic, onion, cumin, lemon zest, parsley, and oregano in a large bowl. • Shape the mixture into eight long sausages. • Thread the sausages onto metal skewers. • Place a grill pan over medium-high heat. • Grill the kebabs until cooked to your liking, turning from time to time, 6–8 minutes. • Serve the kebabs hot with the tomatoes and salad.

1¹/₂ pounds (750 g) ground (minced) beef

1 cup (60 g) fresh bread crumbs

1 large egg, lightly beaten

4 ounces (125 g) feta cheese, crumbled

2 cloves garlic, finely chopped

2 tablespoons grated red onion

2 teaspoons ground cumin

Finely grated zest of 1 lemon

2 tablespoons finely chopped fresh parsley

2 tablespoons finely chopped fresh oregano

4 tomatoes, cut into wedges

Mixed salad greens, to serve

Preparation: 15 minutes

Cooking: 6–8 minutes

Serves: 4–6
Level: 1

FILLET STEAK
WITH SPICY VEGETABLES

Cook the potatoes in a large saucepan of boiling water until tender, 10–15 minutes. • After 7 minutes, add the green beans and sugar snap peas. • Cook until tender, about 3–5 minutes. • Drain well. • Sauté the steaks in 1 tablespoon of oil for about 4 minutes on each side, or until cooked to your liking. • Season with salt and pepper. • Slice the steak into thin strips. • Mix the remaining oil, red wine vinegar, garlic, mustard, and sugar in a small bowl. • Arrange the steak, potatoes, green beans, sugar snap peas, olives, chile, parsley, and tomatoes in a large salad bowl. Drizzle with the dressing and toss gently. • Serve hot.

1	pound (500 g) new potatoes, quartered
4	ounces (125 g) green beans
4	ounces (125 g) sugar snap peas (mangetout)
1	pound (500 g) fillet steak
1/2	cup (125 ml) extra-virgin olive oil
	Salt and freshly ground black pepper
1/4	cup (60 ml) red wine vinegar
1	clove garlic, finely chopped
2	teaspoons mustard
1	teaspoon sugar
3/4	cup (75 g) stuffed green olives
1/2	fresh red chile, seeded and finely chopped
1	tablespoon finely chopped parsley
2	tomatoes, diced

Preparation: 10 minutes
Cooking: 20 minutes

Serves: 4
Level: 1

CLASSIC BEEF BURGERS

Mix the bread crumbs, beef, tomato ketchup, mixed herbs, and egg in a large bowl. • Season with salt and pepper. • Divide the mixture into four and shape into patties. • Place a grill pan over medium-high heat. • Drizzle with oil. Grill the onions until golden, about 10 minutes. • Set aside. • Grill the burgers until cooked, about 5 minutes on each side. • Lightly toast the buns on the grill. • Fill the buns with the lettuce, tomato, burgers, and onion. • Top with tomato ketchup and sandwich together. • Serve hot.

1 cup (60 g) fresh white bread crumbs

1 pound (500 g) ground (minced) beef

2 tablespoons tomato ketchup + extra, to serve

2 teaspoons dried mixed herbs

1 large egg, lightly beaten

Salt and freshly ground black pepper

2 tablespoons extra-virgin olive oil

2 onions, thinly sliced

4 hamburger buns, cut in half

1 small lettuce

1 large tomato, thinly sliced

 Preparation: 10 minutes
Cooking: 20 minutes

Serves: 4
Level: 1

GARLIC STEAK BAGUETTES

Sauté the onions in 1 tablespoon of oil in a large frying pan over medium-high heat until softened, about 3 minutes. • Set aside. • Heat the remaining oil in the same pan. • Sauté the steak with the garlic for about 4 minutes on each side, or until cooked to your liking. • Cut each steak in half lengthwise. • Fill the baguettes with the arugula, tomatoes, steak, and onions. Season with salt and pepper. • Drizzle with the barbeque sauce. • Cut each baguette in half and serve warm.

2	red onions, thinly sliced
2	tablespoons extra-virgin olive oil
4	thick beef fillet steaks
2	cloves garlic, finely chopped
2	baguettes, halved lengthwise
2	ounces (60 g) arugula (rocket)
2	tomatoes, thickly sliced
	Salt and freshly ground black pepper
	Barbeque sauce, to serve

Preparation: 15 minutes
Cooking: 11 minutes

Serves: 4
Level: 1

TANDOORI KEBABS WITH SALAD

Mix the tandoori paste and yogurt in a small bowl. • Thread the beef onto metal skewers and place in a shallow dish. • Coat the beef with the tandoori yogurt. • Chill for 10 minutes. • Meanwhile, mix the cucumbers, tomatoes, onion, lemon juice, and oil in a salad bowl. Season with salt and pepper. Toss well. • Place a grill pan over medium-high heat. • Grill the kebabs, turning from time to time, until cooked, 8–10 minutes. • Serve the kebabs with the salad and lemon wedges.

1/2 cup (125 ml) tandoori curry paste

1/3 cup (90 ml) plain yogurt

1³/4 pounds (800 g) beef rump steak, cut into small pieces

2 cucumbers, halved and diced

3 vine tomatoes, coarsely chopped

1/2 small red onion, finely sliced

Juice of 1 lemon

2 tablespoons extra-virgin olive oil

Salt and freshly ground black pepper

Lemon wedges, to serve

Preparation: 20 minutes

Cooking: 8–10 minutes

Serves: 4

Level: 1

■■■ *Tandoori curry paste is available wherever Indian foods are sold and online.*

PORK BURGERS WITH POTATO SALAD

Cook the potatoes in a large saucepan of boiling water until tender, 10–15 minutes. • Drain well and let cool. • Meanwhile, mix the onion, ground pork, eggs, flour, and milk in a large bowl. Season with salt and pepper. • Form the mixture into 12 patties. • Sauté the pork burgers in the oil and butter in a large frying pan over medium-high heat until golden, about 8 minutes, turning from time to time. • Mix the potatoes with the scallions, mayonnaise, lemon juice, and mustard in a large bowl. • Serve the pork burgers hot with the potato salad and beets.

1 **pound (500 g) new potatoes, quartered**

1 **onion, finely chopped**

1 **pound (500 g) ground (minced) pork**

2 **large eggs, lightly beaten**

1/4 **cup (30 g) all-purpose (plain) flour**

1/4 **cup (60 ml) milk**

Salt and freshly ground black pepper

2 **tablespoons extra-virgin olive oil**

2 **tablespoons butter**

2 **scallions (spring onions), thinly sliced**

1/3 **cup (90 ml) mayonnaise**

1 **tablespoon freshly squeezed lemon juice**

2 **teaspoons mustard**

1 **(15-ounce/450-g) can beets (beetroot), drained and sliced**

Preparation: 15 minutes
Cooking: 15 minutes

Serves: 4–6
Level: 1

GRILLED PORK
WITH BEAN SALAD

Mix the beans, tomatoes, feta, oregano, and 1 tablespoon of oil in a large bowl. Season with salt and pepper. • Place a grill pan over medium-high heat. • Drizzle the pork with the remaining oil. Season with salt and pepper. • Grill the pork until cooked, 4–5 minutes each side. • Arrange the pork on serving plates. • Top with the bean salad. • Serve hot with the lemon wedges and tzatziki.

1	(14-ounce/400-g) can cannellini beans, drained and rinsed
2	tomatoes, diced
4	ounces (125 g) feta cheese, crumbled
1	tablespoon dried oregano
2	tablespoons extra-virgin olive oil
	Salt and freshly ground black pepper
4	pork loin steaks
1	lemon, cut into wedges, to serve
	Tzatziki, to serve

Preparation: 15 minutes
Cooking: 6–8 minutes

Serves: 4
Level: 1

■■■ *Tzatziki is a yogurt-based Greek sauce. It is available in some Greek delicatessens or can easily be made at home. See our recipe on page 434).*

PORK WITH SAGE AND LEMON

Sauté the sage in the oil in a large frying pan over medium-high heat for about 2 minutes, until crisp. • Remove the sage from the pan and drain on paper towels. • Sauté the pork in the oil in the same pan until cooked, about 4 minutes on each side. • Remove from the pan and set aside. • Decrease the heat to low. • Add the butter, garlic, chicken stock, and asparagus. • Bring to a boil and simmer until the asparagus is tender, about 3 minutes. • Stir in the lemon juice and season with salt and pepper. • Remove the asparagus with a slotted spoon and arrange on serving plates. • Top with the pork and drizzle with the pan juices. • Garnish with the lemon zest and sage leaves. • Serve hot.

6	leaves fresh sage
2	tablespoons extra-virgin olive oil
4	pork loin steaks
2	tablespoons butter
2	cloves garlic, finely chopped
1/4	cup (60 ml) chicken stock
1	pound (500 g) asparagus, trimmed
	Finely grated zest and juice of 1 lemon
	Salt and freshly ground black pepper

Preparation: 10 minutes
Cooking: 13 minutes

Serves: 4
Level: 1

PORK MARSALA

Cook the potatoes in a large saucepan of boiling water until tender, 10–15 minutes. • Drain well and return to the pan. • Add 2 tablespoons of butter and the milk. Mash until smooth. Season with salt and pepper. • Meanwhile, dust the pork steaks with the flour. • Sauté the pork in 1 tablespoon of oil and the remaining butter in a large frying pan over medium heat until cooked, about 4 minutes on each side. • Remove from the pan and set aside. • Sauté the leek in the remaining oil in the same pan over medium heat until softened, about 3 minutes. • Add the Marsala. Simmer for about 2 minutes until slightly reduced. • Decrease the heat to low. Stir in the cream. Season with salt and pepper. • Return the pork to the pan and cook for 2 minutes. • Serve the pork hot with the mashed potato and broccoli.

1	pound (500 g) potatoes, peeled and diced
1/4	cup (60 g) butter
1/4	cup (60 ml) milk
	Salt and freshly ground black pepper
1 1/2	pounds (750 g) pork loin steaks
1/4	cup (30 g) all-purpose (plain) flour
1/4	cup (60 ml) extra-virgin olive oil
1	leek, halved lengthwise and thinly sliced
1/2	cup (125 ml) Marsala wine or dry sherry
1/2	cup (125 ml) light (single) cream
	Steamed broccoli, to serve

Preparation: 10 minutes
Cooking: 25–30 minutes

Serves: 4
Level: 1

MUSTARD-CRUMB PORK CUTLETS

Mix the flour and mustard powder in a small bowl. • Coat the pork in the flour mixture, shaking off the excess. Dip into the beaten egg and coat in the bread crumbs. • Heat the oil in a large, deep frying pan until very hot. • Fry the pork in batches until golden, about 3 minutes each side. • Serve the pork with the salad.

1/4 cup (30 g) all-purpose (plain) flour

2 teaspoons dry mustard powder

4 pork cutlets, cut in half lengthwise

1 large egg, lightly beaten

1 cup (125 g) fine dry bread crumbs

1/4 cup (60 ml) extra-virgin olive oil

Green salad, to serve

 Preparation: 15 minutes
Cooking: 5 minutes

Serves: 4
Level: 1

PORK AND LIME KEBABS WITH AVOCADO SALSA

Mix the juice of 2 limes, $\frac{1}{4}$ cup (60 ml) of oil, and cilantro in a large bowl. Season with salt and pepper. • Cut the remaining limes lengthwise into wedges. • Thread the pork, onions, and lime wedges onto bamboo skewers. • Place the kebabs in the lime mixture, coating them well. • Let marinate for 10 minutes. • Meanwhile, mix the avocados, chile pepper, lemon juice, and the remaining oil in a small bowl. Season with salt and chile. • Place a grill pan over medium-high heat. • Grill the kebabs, turning them from time to time, until cooked, 8–10 minutes. • Serve the kebabs with the avocado salsa.

Freshly squeezed juice of 4 limes

$\frac{1}{3}$ cup (90 ml) extra-virgin olive oil

2 tablespoons finely chopped fresh cilantro (coriander)

Salt and freshly ground black pepper

$1\frac{3}{4}$ pounds (800 g) pork fillets, cut in small cubes

2 small red onions, cut into thick wedges

2 firm-ripe avocados, peeled, pitted, and coarsely chopped

1 small fresh red chile, seeded and finely chopped

2 tablespoons freshly squeezed lemon juice

Preparation: 20 minutes

Cooking: 8–10 minutes

Serves: 4

Level: 1

LAMB BURGERS WITH COUSCOUS

Bring the water to a boil. • Stir in the couscous and 1 tablespoon of oil. • Cover and remove from the heat. • Let stand until the couscous has completely absorbed the liquid, about 10 minutes. • Mix the lamb, bread crumbs, onion, lemon zest, parsley, ras el hanout, tomato paste, and egg in a large bowl. Season with salt and pepper. • Shape the mixture into 12 patties. • Fry the burgers in the remaining oil in a large frying pan over medium-high heat until golden, about 5 minutes on each side. • Serve the burgers hot with the couscous, spinach, pita bread, and lemon wedges.

$1^{1}/_{2}$ cups (375 ml) water

$1^{1}/_{2}$ cups (300 g) instant couscous

$^{1}/_{4}$ cup (60 ml) extra-virgin olive oil

$1^{3}/_{4}$ pounds (800 g) ground (minced) lamb

1 cup (60 g) fresh bread crumbs

1 onion, finely grated

Finely grated zest of 1 lemon

3 tablespoons finely chopped fresh parsley

2 teaspoons ras el hanout (mixed Moroccan spices)

$^{1}/_{4}$ cup (60 ml) tomato paste

1 large egg

Salt and freshly ground black pepper

4 ounces (125 g) spinach

Pita bread, to serve

Preparation: 20 minutes

Cooking: 10 minutes

Serves: 4
Level: 1

LAMB NOISETTES WITH SUN-DRIED TOMATOES

Preheat the oven to 475°F (250°C/gas 9). • Arrange the potatoes in a single layer in a large roasting dish. • Drizzle with 1 tablespoon of oil and toss well. Season with salt and pepper. • Bake for about 20 minutes until golden and tender. • Meanwhile, place the lamb noisettes down on a clean surface. • Use a sharp knife to open up a pocket in each of the noisettes. Stuff with the garlic, tomatoes, and some of the arugula. • Sauté the lamb in the remaining oil in a large frying pan until cooked, about 3 minutes on each side. • Serve the lamb with the roasted potatoes and the remaining arugula.

1¼ pounds (600 g) new potatoes, quartered

2 tablespoons extra-virgin olive oil

Salt and freshly ground black pepper

4 lamb noisettes, about 1½ pounds (750 g) total

1 clove garlic, finely chopped

¾ cup (150 g) sun-dried tomatoes, packed in oil, drained

1 bunch arugula (rocket)

Preparation: 10 minutes
Cooking: 20 minutes

Serves: 4
Level: 2

LAMB STEAKS WITH ROSEMARY AND LEMON POTATOES

Preheat the oven to 475°F (250°C/gas 9). • Arrange the sweet potatoes, potatoes, 1¹/₂ tablespoons of oil, and rosemary in a single layer in a large roasting pan. Season with salt and pepper. • Toss well. • Bake for about 20 minutes until golden and tender. • Meanwhile, mix the remaining oil, garlic, and 2 tablespoons of lemon juice in a small bowl. • Coat the lamb in the mixture. • Place a grill pan over medium-high heat. • Grill the lamb until cooked to your liking, about 4 minutes on each side. • Drizzle the potatoes with remaining lemon juice. • Serve the steaks with the roasted potatoes and salad.

12 ounces (350 g) sweet potatoes, peeled and thinly sliced

12 ounces (350 g) white potatoes, thinly sliced

3 tablespoons extra-virgin olive oil

1 tablespoon finely chopped fresh rosemary

Salt and freshly ground black pepper

2 cloves garlic, finely chopped

Freshly squeezed juice of 1 lemon

4 lamb steaks, trimmed

Mixed salad greens, to serve

Preparation: 10 minutes
Cooking: 20 minutes

Serves: 4
Level: 1

LAMB CHOPS WITH MINT AND PEA PUREE

Mix the oil, white wine vinegar, and mint in a small bowl. • Add the lamb and coat well. Season with salt and pepper.
• Place a grill pan over medium-high heat. • Grill the lamb until cooked to your liking, about 4 minutes on each side.
• Meanwhile, place the peas in a microwaveable dish with a little water.
• Cover with plastic wrap (cling film) and microwave on high power for about 4 minutes, until softened. • Drain well and . mash the peas coarsely. • Stir in the sour cream and Parmesan. Season with salt and pepper. • Serve the lamb hot with the pea puree and baby carrots.

1/4 cup (60 ml) extra-virgin olive oil

2 tablespoons white wine vinegar

2 tablespoons finely chopped fresh mint

12 lamb chops

Salt and freshly ground black pepper

3 cups (375 g) frozen peas, thawed

1/4 cup (60 ml) sour cream

2 tablespoons freshly grated Parmesan cheese

Steamed baby carrots, to serve

Preparation: 15 minutes
Cooking: 5–7 minutes

Serves: 4
Level: 1

GREEK LAMB CHOPS

Mix $1/4$ cup (60 g) of oil, 2 tablespoons of lemon juice, garlic, and oregano in a small bowl. Season with salt and pepper.
• Add the lamb to the mixture and coat well. • Mix the cucumber, tomatoes, onion, feta, and olives in a bowl.
• Season with salt and pepper. Drizzle with the remaining oil and lemon juice.
• Toss well. • Place a grill pan over medium-high heat. • Grill the lamb until cooked to your liking, about 4 minutes on each side. • Serve the lamb hot with the salad and pita bread.

$1/3$ cup (90 ml) extra-virgin olive oil

$1/4$ cup (60 ml) freshly squeezed lemon juice

2 cloves garlic, finely chopped

2 teaspoons dried oregano

Salt and freshly ground black pepper

12 lamb chops, trimmed

1 small cucumber, diced

2 tomatoes, diced

$1/2$ small onion, finely chopped

2 ounces (60 g) feta cheese, crumbled

$1/3$ cup (30 g) kalamata olives

Pita bread, to serve

Preparation: 15 minutes
Cooking: 8 minutes

Serves: 4
Level: 1

LAMB RACK
WITH HERB CRUST

Preheat the oven to 400°F (200°C/ gas 6). • Mix the bread crumbs, lemon zest, parsley, oregano, and butter in a small bowl. Season with salt and pepper. • Place the racks of lamb in a large roasting dish. • Press the bread crumb mixture over the lamb and drizzle with 1 tablespoon of oil. • Bake for about 20 minutes until cooked to your liking. Cover the lamb with aluminum foil if it starts to burn. • Meanwhile, place the sweet potatoes on a baking sheet. Drizzle with the remaining oil and season with salt and pepper. • Bake for about 20 minutes until golden. • Cut the racks in half. • Serve the lamb with the roasted sweet potatoes and green beans.

2   cups (120 g) fresh bread crumbs

Finely grated zest of 1 lemon

1/2 cup (50 g) finely chopped fresh parsley

2   tablespoons finely chopped fresh oregano

1/4 cup (60 ml) butter, melted

Salt and freshly ground black pepper

2   racks of lamb, cut in half (6 chops per rack)

2   tablespoons extra-virgin olive oil

1   pound (500 g) sweet potatoes, cut into thin slices

Steamed green beans, to serve

Preparation: 10 minutes
Cooking: 20 minutes

Serves: 4
Level: 1

VEAL WITH ROASTED VEGETABLES

Preheat the oven to 425°F (220°C/gas 7). • Arrange the eggplants, bell peppers, and potatoes in a single layer in a large roasting dish. Drizzle with ¼ cup (60 ml) of oil. • Roast for 10–15 minutes, or until the vegetables are tender. • Dust the veal with the flour, shaking over the excess. Top with a piece of pancetta and a sage leaf. Secure with toothpicks. • Fry the veal, starting with the pancetta-side down, in the remaining oil in a large frying pan over medium-high heat for about 4 minutes on each side. • Add the vinegar and season with salt. • Cook until the veal is tender, about 5 minutes.

• Transfer the vegetables to a serving dish and sprinkle with the mint.

• Arrange the veal on top of the vegetables and serve hot.

2	eggplants (aubergines), diced
2	red bell peppers (capsicums), seeded and diced
2	potatoes, peeled and diced
⅓	cup (90 ml) extra-virgin olive oil
4	veal scallops (escalopes)
½	cup (75 g) all-purpose (plain) flour
8	slices pancetta or bacon
8	leaves fresh sage
2	tablespoons balsamic vinegar
	Salt
1	tablespoon coarsely chopped fresh mint

Preparation: 10 minutes

Cooking: 20 minutes

Serves: 4

Level: 1

VEAL WITH BEAN SALAD

Mix the lemon juice, chives, garlic, and ¹/₄ cup (60 ml) of oil in a small bowl. Season with salt. • Combine the arugula, beans, tomatoes, and basil in a large bowl. • Drizzle with the dressing and toss well. • Dust the veal with the flour, shaking off the excess. • Fry the veal in the remaining oil in a large frying pan over medium-high heat for about 4 minutes on each side. • Transfer the veal to a serving plate and keep warm. • Add the stock to the cooking juices in the pan. Cook over high heat for 2 minutes. • Stir in the butter. • Cook over medium heat until slightly thickened, about 2 minutes. • Pour the sauce over the veal and serve with the bean salad.

¹/₄ **cup (60 ml) freshly squeezed lemon juice**

1 **tablespoon finely chopped fresh chives**

2 **cloves garlic, finely chopped**

¹/₃ **cup (90 ml) extra-virgin olive oil**

Salt

4 **ounces (125 g) arugula (rocket)**

1 **(14-ounce/400-g) can white kidney beans, drained and rinsed**

8 **large tomatoes, finely chopped**

4 **tablespoons torn fresh basil**

4 **veal scallops (escalopes)**

¹/₂ **cup (75 g) all-purpose (plain) flour**

¹/₂ **cup (125 ml) vegetable stock**

¹/₄ **cup (60 g) butter, diced**

Preparation: 10 minutes
Cooking: 12 minutes

Serves: 4
Level: 1

VEAL WITH TOMATO AND EGGPLANT

Mix 2 tablespoons of oil and 2 tablespoons of lemon juice in a small bowl. • Add the veal and coat well. • Place a grill pan over medium-high heat. • Drizzle the eggplant and tomatoes with the remaining oil. Season with salt and pepper. • Grill the eggplant and tomatoes until tender, about 2 minutes on each side. • Set aside. • Grill the veal until cooked, about 4 minutes on each side. • Mix the parsley, mint, and lemon zest in a small bowl. • Arrange the veal on serving plates. Top with the tomatoes and eggplant. • Sprinkle with the herbs and drizzle with the remaining lemon juice.

1/4 cup (60 ml) extra-virgin olive oil

Finely grated zest and juice of 1 lemon

4 veal scallops (escalopes)

1 eggplant, cut into 8 slices

2 tomatoes, cut into 8 slices

Salt and freshly ground black pepper

2 tablespoons finely chopped fresh parsley

2 tablespoons finely chopped fresh mint

Preparation: 15 minutes
Cooking: 12 minutes

Serves: 4
Level: 1

VEAL SALTIMBOCCA

Sauté the potatoes in 2 tablespoons of oil in a large frying pan over medium heat until tender and golden, about 10 minutes. • Season with salt and pepper. • Fry the veal in 2 tablespoons of butter and the remaining oil in a large frying pan over medium-high heat for about 2 minutes on each side. • Preheat the broiler (grill). • Transfer the veal to a large roasting pan. Top each scallop with the fontina, prosciutto, and sage leaves. Secure with toothpicks. • Broil for about 2 minutes, until the cheese melts. • Melt the remaining butter in the frying pan in which you cooked the veal. • Add the stock and wine. Bring to a boil. • Simmer over low heat until the sauce reduces slightly, about 2 minutes. • Stir in the chopped sage. • Serve the veal with the potatoes and pan juices.

1¼ pounds (600 g) potatoes, thinly sliced

¼ cup (60 ml) extra-virgin olive oil

Salt and freshly ground black pepper

4 veal scallops (escalopes)

¼ cup (60 g) butter

1 cup (125 g) freshly grated fontina cheese

8 slices prosciutto (Parma ham)

12 leaves fresh sage + 1 tablespoon coarsely chopped

¼ cup (60 ml) beef stock

¼ cup (60 ml) dry white wine

Preparation: 15 minutes
Cooking: 15 minutes

Serves: 4
Level: 1

VEAL CUTLETS WITH GREMOLATA

Preheat the oven to 475°F (250°C/gas 9).
• Place the potatoes in a large roasting
dish. Drizzle with 1 tablespoon of oil and
toss well. • Season with salt and pepper.
• Bake for about 20 minutes until golden.
• Meanwhile, mix the lemon zest, parsley,
and garlic in a small bowl. • Fry the veal
in the remaining oil in a large frying pan
over medium-high heat for about 4
minutes on each side. • Drizzle with the
lemon juice and cook for 30 seconds.
• Top the veal with the gremolata.
• Serve hot with the roasted potatoes.

1¼ pounds (600 g) baby potatoes, cut in half

2 tablespoons extra-virgin olive oil

Salt and freshly ground black pepper

Finely grated zest and juice of 1 lemon

2 tablespoons finely chopped fresh parsley

1 clove garlic, finely chopped

4 veal or pork cutlets, bone in

Preparation: 15 minutes

Cooking: 5–7 minutes

Serves: 4
Level: 1

SAUSAGES WITH LENTILS AND TOMATOES

Cook the lentils in a saucepan of salted boiling water until just tender, 15–20 minutes. • Drain and set aside. • Meanwhile, fry the sausages in 1 tablespoon of oil in a large frying pan over medium heat until cooked, about 8 minutes. • Cut each sausage into three pieces. • Mix the lentils, onion, tomatoes, parsley, mint, and mizuna in a large bowl. • Season with salt and pepper. • Drizzle with the remaining oil and vinegar. • Toss well. • Arrange the salad on serving plates, topped with the sliced sausage. • Serve at once.

2 cups (300 g) puy lentils, rinsed

8 Italian sausages

2 tablespoons extra-virgin olive oil

1 red onion, thinly sliced

4 tomatoes, cut into wedges

2 tablespoons finely chopped fresh parsley

2 tablespoons finely chopped fresh mint

4 ounces (125 g) mizuna or mesclun

2 tablespoons white wine vinegar

Preparation: 10 minutes
Cooking: 20 minutes

Serves: 4
Level: 1

BEAN AND HOT DOG HOTPOT

Sauté the onion and bell pepper in the oil in a large frying pan until softened, about 3 minutes. • Add the cannellini beans, hot dogs, and tomatoes and bring to a boil. • Cover and simmer over low heat for 10 minutes. • Stir in the basil and season with salt and pepper. • Spoon into bowls and serve hot with the crusty bread.

1 onion, thinly sliced

1 yellow bell pepper (capsicum), seeded and thinly sliced

1 tablespoon extra-virgin olive oil

1 (14-ounce/400-g) can cannellini beans, drained and rinsed

6 hot dogs, sliced

1 (14-ounce/400-g) can tomatoes, with juice

2 tablespoons torn fresh basil

Salt and freshly ground black pepper

Crusty bread, to serve

Preparation: 10 minutes
Cooking: 13 minutes

Serves: 4
Level: 1

CHILE CON CARNE WITH ROASTED BELL PEPPERS

Preheat the oven to 400°F (200°C/ gas 6). • Arrange the bell peppers skin-side down in a roasting pan. • Bake for 20 minutes, or until just softened. • Meanwhile, sauté the beef and onion in the oil in a large frying pan over medium heat for 5 minutes. • Stir in the chili powder, beans and tomato sauce. • Bring to a boil. • Simmer over low heat until it thickens slightly, about 10 minutes. • Spoon the beef mixture into the bell peppers. • Top with sour cream and garnish with the cilantro. • Serve hot.

4   red bell peppers (capsicums), halved and seeded

1   pound (500 g) ground (minced) beef

1   onion, finely chopped

2   tablespoons extra-virgin olive oil

2   teaspoons chili powder

1   (14-ounce/400-g) can white kidney beans

1   (8-ounce/250-g) can tomato sauce

Sour cream, to serve

Fresh cilantro (coriander) leaves, to garnish

Preparation: 10 minutes
Cooking: 20 minutes

Serves: 4
Level: 1

EGGS AND CHEESE

PAN-FRIED EGGS WITH POTATOES AND TOMATOES

Sauté the potatoes in the oil in a large frying pan over medium heat until almost tender, about 5 minutes. • Add the scallions and tomatoes. Sauté until softened, about 2 minutes. • Stir in the parsley and season with salt and pepper. • Break the eggs gently over the mixture and sprinkle with the Parmesan. • Decrease the heat to low. • Cover and simmer until the eggs have just set, about 5 minutes. • Cut into quarters and serve hot with the arugula on the side.

2	potatoes, halved and thinly sliced
2	tablespoons extra-virgin olive oil
4	scallions (spring onions), thinly sliced
2	tomatoes, coarsely chopped
1	tablespoon finely chopped fresh parsley
	Salt and freshly ground black pepper
4	large eggs
1	cup (125 g) freshly grated Parmesan cheese
	Arugula (rocket), to serve

Preparation: 10 minutes
Cooking: 12 minutes

Serves: 4
Level: 1

RICOTTA, FETA, AND SPINACH BAKE

Preheat the oven to 400°F (200°C/ gas 6). • Butter an 8-inch (20-cm) springform pan. • Cook the spinach in a medium saucepan of salted boiling water for 1 minute. • Drain and rinse well. • Squeeze the spinach to remove any excess water. Chop it coarsely. • Mix the ricotta, feta, scallions, dill, chives, nutmeg, eggs, and spinach in a large bowl. Season with salt and pepper. • Spoon the mixture into the prepared pan. • Bake for about 20 minutes, until firm and cooked through. • Cut into slices. • Serve with the salad and crusty bread.

8	ounces (250 g) spinach
1	cup (250 g) ricotta cheese
4	ounces (125 g) feta cheese, crumbled
4	scallions (spring onions), thinly sliced
2	tablespoons finely chopped fresh dill
2	tablespoons finely chopped fresh chives
1/8	teaspoon freshly grated nutmeg
2	large eggs, lightly beaten
	Salt and freshly ground black pepper
	Green salad, to serve
	Crusty bread, to serve

Preparation: 10 minutes
Cooking: 20 minutes

Serves: 4
Level: 1

MEXICAN-STYLE EGGS

Heat the tortillas in 1 teaspoon of oil in a large frying pan over medium-high heat until golden and crisp, about 1 minute on each side. • Fry the eggs in the remaining oil in a large frying pan for about 2 minutes, or until cooked to your liking. • Meanwhile, spread the tortillas evenly with the refried beans. • Top with the tomato salsa and cheese. Preheat the broiler (grill). • Broil the tortillas for about 1 minute, until the cheese melts. • Top each tortilla with a fried egg, avocado, sour cream, and cilantro. Season with salt and pepper. • Serve hot with the lime wedges.

4   corn tortillas
1   tablespoon extra-virgin olive oil
4   large eggs
2/3 cup (150 ml) refried beans
2/3 cup (150 ml) tomato salsa
1   cup (125 g) freshly grated Monterey Jack or cheddar cheese
1   avocado, mashed
1/3 cup (90 ml) sour cream
2   tablespoons finely chopped fresh cilantro (coriander)
    Salt and freshly ground black pepper
    Lime wedges, to serve

Preparation: 15 minutes
Cooking: 10 minutes

Serves: 2–4
Level: 1

BREAKFAST SANDWICHES

Fry the bacon in batches in a large frying pan over medium heat until crisp, about 4 minutes. • Remove from the pan and drain on paper towels. • Fry the eggs in 1 tablespoon of oil in a large frying pan for about 2 minutes, or until cooked to your liking. • Meanwhile, spread each half of the hamburger buns with butter. • Top one half with the bacon and a fried egg. • Sandwich them together. • Heat the remaining oil in a large frying pan. • Fry the buns in the pan, pressing down with a spatula, until golden, about 3 minutes. • Serve at once, with the ketchup on the side.

8   slices bacon
2   tablespoons extra-virgin olive oil
4   large eggs
4   hamburger buns, halved
2   tablespoons butter
    Tomato ketchup, to serve

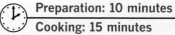
Preparation: 10 minutes
Cooking: 15 minutes

Serves: 4
Level: 1

FLORENTINE PIZZAS

Preheat the oven to 450°F (230°C/ gas 8). • Cook the spinach in a medium saucepan of salted boiling water for 1 minute. • Drain and rinse well. • Squeeze the spinach to remove any excess water. Chop it coarsely. • Mix the spinach, ricotta, scallions, basil, and sun-dried tomatoes in a large bowl. • Place the pizza crusts in pizza pans or on a large baking sheet. • Top evenly with the spinach mixture. • Crack three eggs in the center of each pizza. • Season with salt and pepper. • Bake for 12–15 minutes, or until the eggs are cooked and the crusts are crisp. • Serve hot.

8	ounces (250 g) spinach
1	cup (250 g) ricotta salata cheese, crumbled
4	scallions (spring onions), thinly sliced
3	tablespoons torn basil
1/2	cup (125 g) sun-dried tomatoes, packed in oil, drained and coarsely chopped
2	large store-bought pizza crusts
6	large eggs
	Salt and freshly ground black pepper

Preparation: 10 minutes
Cooking: 13–16 minutes

Serves: 4
Level: 1

GRILLED HALLOUMI ON TOAST

Place a grill pan over medium-high heat.
• Drizzle both sides of the bread with
1 tablespoon of oil and rub with the
garlic. • Grill the bread until golden,
about 2 minutes on each side. Set aside.
• Grill the halloumi until golden, 1–2
minutes on each side. • Arrange the
grilled bread on serving plates. • Top
with the watercress, bell peppers, and
halloumi. • Drizzle with the remaining oil.
• Season with pepper and serve hot.

4   ($^3/_4$-inch/2-cm)
    thick slices of
    ciabatta or
    sourdough bread

2   tablespoons extra-
    virgin olive oil

1   clove garlic,
    halved

8   ounces (250 g)
    halloumi or
    mozzarella cheese,
    drained and thinly
    sliced

1   cup (60 g) fresh
    watercress

$^1/_2$ cup (60 g) roasted
    bell peppers
    (capsicums), thinly
    sliced

    Freshly ground black
    pepper

Preparation: 10 minutes
Cooking: 10 minutes

Serves: 4
Level: 1

ASIAN-STYLE MUSHROOM OMELETS

Sauté the mushrooms with the ginger in half the oil in a wok or large frying pan over medium-high heat until softened, about 2 minutes. • Stir in the hoisin sauce. Cook for 2 minutes. • Set aside. • Beat the eggs in a large bowl. Season with salt and pepper. • Add the scallions and mix well. • Heat the remaining oil in a wok or large frying pan over medium heat. • Add half the beaten egg mixture. • Slide a wooden spatula under the eggs to loosen them from the pan. Shake the pan with a rotating movement to spread. • Cook until nicely browned on the underside. • Place half the mushroom filling on top. Fold the omelet over and cook for 1 minute. • Transfer to a serving plate. • Repeat using the remaining egg and mushroom mixture. • Serve hot.

4   ounces (100 g) enoki mushrooms
1   tablespoon freshly grated ginger
1   tablespoon Asian sesame oil
1/4 cup (60 ml) Chinese hoisin sauce
6   large eggs
    Salt and freshly ground black pepper
2   scallions (spring onions), finely sliced

Preparation: 10 minutes
Cooking: 12 minutes

Serves: 2
Level: 1

■■■ Enoki mushrooms are long, thin white mushrooms used in many Asian cuisines. They are also known as golden needle mushrooms.

EGG AND BACON PIES

Preheat the oven to 350°F (180°C/ gas 4). • Grease six ³/₄-cup (180-ml) ramekins with oil. • Sauté the leeks and bacon in the oil in a large frying pan over medium-high heat until the leeks have softened, about 3 minutes. • Let cool slightly. • Meanwhile, beat 4 eggs with the cream and mustard in a medium bowl. Season with salt and pepper. • Stir in the leek mixture. Mix well. • Spoon the mixture into the prepared ramekins. • Crack one egg into each ramekin. • Bake for 15–20 minutes, until golden and set. • Let cool in the ramekins for 5 minutes. • Turn out onto racks. Serve at once.

2	leeks, thinly sliced
8	ounces (250 g) bacon slices, chopped
2	tablespoons extra-virgin olive oil
10	large eggs
¹/₂	cup (125 ml) light (single) cream
1	tablespoon whole-grain mustard
	Salt and freshly ground black pepper

Preparation: 10 minutes
Cooking: 18–23 minutes

Serves: 4–6
Level: 1

CORN AND CHIVE MINI FRITTATAS

Preheat the oven to 400°F (200°C/ gas 6). • Grease eight ¹/₂-cup (125-ml) muffin cups with oil. • Beat the eggs and milk in a large bowl. • Stir in the corn, chives, and cheddar. Season with salt and pepper. • Spoon the corn mixture into the prepared muffin cups. • Bake for about 15 minutes, until puffed and golden brown. • Let cool in the pans for 5 minutes. • Turn out onto racks. • Serve the frittatas hot with the salad.

6　large eggs

¹/₂　cup (125 ml) milk

3　cups (375 g) canned corn (sweet corn)

2　tablespoons finely chopped fresh chives

¹/₂　cup (60 g) freshly grated cheddar cheese

Salt and freshly ground black pepper

Leafy green salad, to serve

Preparation: 10 minutes
Cooking: 15 minutes

Serves: 4
Level: 1

POACHED EGGS WITH SMOKED SALMON

Bring a small saucepan of water to a boil. • Add the vinegar. Decrease the heat to low and use a spoon to create a whirlpool. • Crack the eggs, one at a time, into the center of the whirlpool. • Poach until the egg whites are slightly firm, about 3 minutes. • Use a slotted spoon to remove the eggs from the pan. Drain off any excess water. • Toast the muffins until golden. • Place on serving plates. Top with the spinach, smoked salmon, and poached eggs. Season with salt and pepper. • Serve hot.

1   tablespoon white wine vinegar

2   large eggs

2   English muffins, halved

1   ounce (30 g) baby spinach leaves

8   ounces (250 g) smoked salmon, thinly sliced

Salt and freshly ground black pepper

Preparation: 10 minutes
Cooking: 10 minutes

Serves: 2
Level: 1

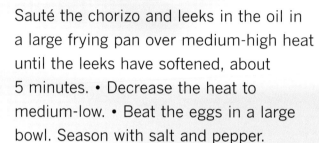

CHORIZO, LEEK, AND FETA FRITTATA

Sauté the chorizo and leeks in the oil in a large frying pan over medium-high heat until the leeks have softened, about 5 minutes. • Decrease the heat to medium-low. • Beat the eggs in a large bowl. Season with salt and pepper. • Pour the beaten eggs into the pan. Sprinkle with the feta. • Cook over low heat until almost set, about 15 minutes. • Preheat a broiler (grill). • Broil (grill) the frittata for about 2 minutes, until golden. • Cut into slices and serve hot with the arugula.

2   cured Spanish chorizo sausages, finely chopped

2   leeks, thinly sliced

2   tablespoons extra-virgin olive oil

10 large eggs

    Salt and freshly ground black pepper

4   ounces (125 g) feta cheese, crumbled

    Arugula (rocket) leaves, to serve

Preparation: 5 minutes

Cooking: 22 minutes

Serves: 4

Level: 1

WARM GOAT CHEESE WITH TOMATOES

Preheat a broiler (grill). • Place the goat cheese and tomatoes on a broiler pan (grill tray). Drizzle with 1 tablespoon of oil. • Broil for 2–3 minutes. • Arrange the spinach and tomatoes on serving plates. • Top with the warm goat cheese. • Drizzle with the remaining oil and sprinkle with pine nuts. Season with salt and pepper. • Serve warm with the crusty bread.

5	ounces (150 g) goat cheese, cut into thick slices
2	tomatoes, thickly sliced
2	tablespoons extra-virgin olive oil
1	ounce (30 g) baby spinach leaves
2	tablespoons pine nuts, toasted
	Salt and freshly ground black pepper
	Crusty bread, to serve

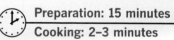

Preparation: 15 minutes

Cooking: 2–3 minutes

Serves: 2

Level: 1

PESTO SCRAMBLED EGGS

Beat the eggs and cream in a large bowl.
• Melt the butter in a large frying pan
over medium heat. • Add the egg mixture
and cook, stirring often, until the eggs
form large chunks, about 5 minutes.
• Stir in the pesto. • Spoon the
scrambled eggs onto the toast. • Sprinkle
with the pecorino. Season with salt and
pepper. • Sauté the mushrooms and
parsley in the oil in a large frying pan
until softened, about 5 minutes. • Serve
the eggs hot with the mushrooms,
sprinkled with the extra pecorino.

10 large eggs

1/2 cup (125 ml) light
(single) cream

3 tablespoons butter

2 tablespoons
basil pesto

4 thick slices bread,
toasted

1/2 cup (60 g)
freshly grated
pecorino cheese,
+ extra, to serve

   Salt and freshly
ground black pepper

8 ounces (250 g)
button mushrooms,
finely sliced

1 tablespoon finely
chopped fresh
parsley

1 tablespoon extra-
virgin olive oil

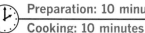

Preparation: 10 minutes

Cooking: 10 minutes

Serves: 4
Level: 1

AROMATIC EGG CURRY

Bring a large saucepan of salted water to a boil over high heat. • Add the rice and cook over medium heat until tender, 10–15 minutes. Drain well. • Meanwhile, sauté the whole eggs in the oil in a large, deep frying pan over medium-high heat for 2 minutes. • Drain the eggs on paper towels. • Sauté the onion in the same pan until softened, about 3 minutes. • Stir in the curry paste. • Cook until aromatic, about 1 minute. • Stir in the tomatoes. • Bring to a boil, stirring from time to time. • Add the coconut milk, peas, fish sauce, sugar, and eggs. • Simmer on low heat until the sauce is slightly thickened, about 5 minutes. • Stir in the cilantro. Serve hot with the jasmine rice.

2 cups (400 g) jasmine rice

8 hard-boiled eggs, shelled

2 tablespoons peanut oil

1 onion, finely chopped

3 tablespoons Thai red curry paste

$1^1/_2$ cups (375 ml) chopped tomatoes

$^2/_3$ cup (150 ml) coconut milk

1 cup (150 g) frozen peas

1 tablespoon Asian fish sauce

2 teaspoons sugar

1 cup (60 g) fresh cilantro (coriander) leaves

Preparation: 15 minutes

Cooking: 21–26 minutes

Serves: 4
Level: 1

HERB FRITTATA WITH CREAM CHEESE FILLING

Beat the cream cheese, Parmesan, garlic, basil, and Worcestershire sauce in a small bowl. • Beat the eggs and milk in a large bowl. Season with salt and pepper. • Stir in the Gruyère, thyme, and marjoram. • Heat half the oil in a large frying pan over medium heat. Pour in half the beaten eggs. • Slide a wooden spatula under the eggs to loosen them from the pan. Shake the pan with a rotating movement to spread. • Cook until nicely browned on the underside. • Transfer the frittata to a serving plate and keep warm. • Add the remaining oil to the pan. • Pour the remaining egg mixture into the pan and repeat the cooking process. • Spread the cream cheese mixture over the first frittata. Top with the second frittata. • Slice into wedges and serve hot.

2/3 cup (150 ml) cream cheese, softened

1/2 cup (60 g) freshly grated Parmesan cheese

1/2 clove garlic, finely chopped

2 tablespoons torn basil

1/4 teaspoon Worcestershire sauce

6 large eggs

2 tablespoons milk

Salt and freshly ground black pepper

1/2 cup (60 g) freshly grated Gruyère cheese

1 tablespoon finely chopped fresh thyme

1/2 teaspoon dried marjoram

1/4 cup (60 ml) extra-virgin olive oil

Preparation: 10 minutes
Cooking: 15 minutes

Serves: 4
Level: 1

SCRAMBLED EGGS WITH BROCCOLI AND PANCETTA

Cook the broccoli in a large pot of salted, boiling water until just tender, 6–8 minutes. Drain well and set aside. • Beat the eggs and cheese in a large bowl. Season with salt and pepper. • Sauté the pancetta and garlic in the oil in a large frying pan over medium heat until the garlic turns pale gold, about 1 minute. • Add the broccoli and mix well. • Pour in the egg mixture. • Cook over low heat for about 5 minutes, stirring often, until the eggs form large chunks. • Serve hot.

8   ounces (250 g) broccoli, cut into florets

4   large eggs, lightly beaten

1/2   cup (60 g) freshly grated pecorino or Parmesan cheese

Salt and freshly ground black pepper

1/2   cup (60 g) diced pancetta or bacon

1   clove garlic, finely chopped

2   tablespoons extra-virgin olive oil

Preparation: 10 minutes
Cooking: 12–14 minutes

Serves: 4
Level: 1

SCRAMBLED EGGS WITH ROASTED TOMATOES

Preheat the oven to 350°F (180°C/gas 4).
• Arrange the tomatoes in a single layer in a large roasting pan. Drizzle with the oil and season with salt and pepper.
• Bake for about 20 minutes, until the tomatoes start to soften. • Meanwhile, beat the eggs with the cream in a large bowl until frothy. • Heat the butter in a large frying pan over medium heat. • Add the egg mixture and cook, stirring often, until the eggs form large chunks, about 5 minutes. • Sprinkle with the chives and season with salt and pepper. • Serve the eggs on the toasted bread with the cherry tomatoes on the side.

12 ounces (350 g) cherry tomatoes

1 tablespoon extra-virgin olive oil

Salt and freshly ground black pepper

8 large eggs

1/2 cup (125 ml) light (single) cream

1/4 cup (60 g) butter

2 tablespoons finely chopped fresh chives

Toasted bread, to serve

Preparation: 10 minutes
Cooking: 20 minutes

Serves: 4
Level: 1

RICOTTA FRITTATA

Beat the flour and milk in a large bowl.
• Beat in the eggs and half the butter.
Season with salt and pepper. • Mix the
ricotta, Parmesan, parsley, and water in
a medium bowl. Season with salt and
pepper. • Melt half the remaining butter
in a large frying pan over medium heat.
Pour in half the beaten egg mixture.
• Slide a wooden spatula under the eggs
to loosen them from the pan. Shake the
pan with a rotating movement to spread.
• Cook until nicely browned on the
underside. • Transfer the frittata to a
serving plate and keep warm. • Add the
remaining butter to the pan. • Pour the
remaining egg mixture into the pan
and repeat. • Spread the ricotta
mixture over the frittatas. • Loosely
roll up the frittatas. • Garnish with
the parsley and serve hot.

1   cup (150 g) all-
    purpose (plain) flour
2   cups (500 ml) milk
4   large eggs
1/4 cup (60 ml) butter,
    melted
    Salt and freshly
    ground black pepper
3/4 cup (180 g) fresh
    ricotta cheese,
    drained
1/2 cup (60 g)
    freshly grated
    Parmesan cheese
1   tablespoon finely
    chopped fresh
    parsley, + extra
    sprigs, to garnish
2   tablespoons
    warm water

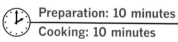

Preparation: 10 minutes
Cooking: 10 minutes

Serves: 2–4
Level: 1

VEGETABLES

POTATO, EGGPLANT, AND SPINACH CURRY

Bring a large saucepan of salted water to a boil. • Add the rice and cook over medium heat until tender, 10–15 minutes. • Drain well and set aside. • Meanwhile, sauté the onion and garlic in the oil in a large saucepan over medium-low heat for about 3 minutes, until softened. • Stir in the curry paste, tomatoes, vegetable stock, potatoes, and eggplant. • Bring to a boil. • Cover and simmer over low heat until the vegetables are tender, about 15 minutes. • Add the spinach. Cook until wilted, about 2 minutes. • Stir in the cilantro and season with salt and pepper. • Serve the curry hot with the rice.

■■■ *Korma curry paste is available wherever Indian foods are sold and online.*

2	cups (400 g) basmati rice
1	onion, thinly sliced
2	cloves garlic, finely chopped
1	tablespoon canola oil
1/4	cup (60 ml) korma curry paste
1 1/2	cups (375 ml) chopped tomatoes
1/2	cup (125 ml) vegetable stock
3	potatoes, peeled and diced
1	large eggplant (aubergine), diced
5	ounces (150 g) baby spinach leaves
2	tablespoons finely chopped fresh cilantro
	Salt and freshly ground black pepper

Preparation: 10 minutes
Cooking: 20 minutes

Serves: 4
Level: 1

ROASTED ZUCCHINI AND EGGPLANT

Preheat the oven to 475°F (250°C/gas 9).
• Arrange the zucchini, eggplants, and
onions in a single layer on a large baking
sheet. Place the zucchini and eggplants
cut-side up. • Drizzle with half the oil.
Season with salt and pepper. • Bake for
15–20 minutes, turning from time to
time, until softened. • Mix the zucchini,
eggplants, onions, and arugula in a large
serving dish. • Drizzle with the remaining
oil and the balsamic vinegar. • Sprinkle
with the Parmesan.

8   small zucchini (courgettes), halved

8   small eggplants (aubergines), halved

2   red onions, cut into wedges

2   tablespoons extra-virgin olive oil

    Salt and freshly ground black pepper

1   bunch arugula (rocket)

1   tablespoon balsamic vinegar

1/2   cup (60 g) freshly grated Parmesan cheese

Preparation: 10 minutes
Cooking: 15–20 minutes

Serves: 4
Level: 1

STIR-FRIED ASIAN GREENS

Bring a large saucepan of salted water to a boil. • Add the rice and cook over medium heat until tender, 10–15 minutes. • Drain well. • Meanwhile, place a wok over high heat. • When it is very hot, toast the sesame seeds in the wok until golden, 1–2 minutes. • Remove from the wok and set aside. • Stir-fry the garlic, ginger, and onion in the oil in the wok over medium heat until softened, about 2 minutes. • Add the bok choy, broccoli, mushrooms, soy sauce, and water. • Stir-fry until the vegetables are tender, about 3 minutes. • Serve the vegetables hot with the rice and sprinkle with sesame seeds.

2	cups (400 g) jasmine rice
1	tablespoon sesame seeds
2	cloves garlic, finely chopped
2	teaspoons freshly grated ginger
1	onion, thinly sliced
1	tablespoon peanut oil
1	bunch baby bok choy, trimmed and leaves separated
1	bunch Chinese broccoli, trimmed and stems halved
10	ounces (300 g) oyster mushrooms
2	tablespoons kecap manis
2	tablespoons water

Preparation: 10 minutes
Cooking: 15 minutes

Serves: 4
Level: 1

THAI VEGETABLE GREEN CURRY

Bring a large saucepan of salted water to a boil. • Add the rice and cook over medium heat until tender, 10–15 minutes. • Drain well. • Meanwhile, place a wok over high heat. • When it is very hot, stir-fry the garlic and onion in the oil until softened, about 2 minutes. • Stir in the curry paste. • Cook until aromatic, about 30 seconds. • Add the zucchini, squash, mushrooms, coconut milk, vegetable stock, brown sugar, and fish sauce. • Decrease the heat to low. • Cover and simmer until the vegetables are tender, about 10 minutes. • Garnish with the cilantro. • Serve the curry hot with the rice.

2	cups (400 g) jasmine rice
2	cloves garlic, finely chopped
1	onion, thinly sliced
1	tablespoons peanut oil
1/4	cup (60 ml) Thai green curry paste
2	zucchini (courgettes), thinly sliced
12	baby yellow summer squash, quartered
8	ounces (250 g) mushrooms, thinly sliced
1	cup (250 ml) coconut milk
1/4	cup (60 ml) vegetable stock
2	teaspoons brown sugar
1	tablespoon Asian fish sauce
3	tablespoons fresh cilantro (coriander)

Preparation: 10 minutes

Cooking: 15 minutes

Serves: 4
Level: 1

ASPARAGUS AND LEEK TART

Preheat the oven to 425°F (220°C/gas 8). • Line two baking sheets with parchment paper. • Sauté the leeks and garlic in 2 tablespoons of oil in a large frying pan over medium heat until softened, about 3 minutes. • Set aside. • Place the pastry sheets one on top of the other and cut in half. Arrange on the prepared baking sheets. • Use a sharp knife to make a 3/4-inch (2-cm) border around the edge of the pastry. • Spoon the leeks in the pastry bases and top with the asparagus. • Sprinkle with the thyme and drizzle with the remaining oil. • Season with salt and pepper. • Bake for about 15 minutes, until golden and puffed. • Serve hot or at room temperature.

2	leeks, trimmed, halved lengthwise, and thinly sliced
2	cloves garlic, finely chopped
3	tablespoons extra-virgin olive oil
2	sheets puff pastry, thawed
1	pound (500 g) thin asparagus
12	sprigs fresh thyme
	Salt and freshly ground black pepper

Preparation: 10 minutes
Cooking: 20 minutes

Serves: 4
Level: 1

TOMATO, GARBANZO BEAN, AND OLIVE PILAF

Heat the oil in a large saucepan over medium-high heat. • Sauté the onion and garlic until softened, about 3 minutes. • Add the tomatoes, tomato paste, sugar, salt, and pepper. Stir to combine and bring to a boil. • Reduce the heat to low. Cover and simmer until the tomatoes are broken down, about 10 minutes. • Add the rice, stock, and garbanzo beans. Stir to combine. • Cover and simmer until the rice is tender and liquid is absorbed, about 12 minutes. • Stir in the olives and parsley. Check the seasoning and serve hot.

1 tablespoon extra-virgin olive oil

1 onion, finely chopped

2 cloves garlic, finely chopped

1 pound (500 g) ripe tomatoes, finely chopped

3 tablespoons tomato paste

1/2 teaspoon sugar

Salt and freshly ground black pepper

1 1/4 cups (250 g) long grain rice

3/4 cup (180 ml) chicken or vegetable stock

1 (14-ounce/400-g) can garbanzo beans (chick-peas), drained and rinsed

1/3 cup (30 g) black olives

1/3 cup coarsely chopped flat-leaf parsley

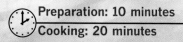

Preparation: 10 minutes
Cooking: 20 minutes

Serves: 4
Level: 1

SPICY BEAN STEW

Bring a large saucepan of salted water to a boil. • Add the rice and cook over medium heat until tender, 10–15 minutes. • Drain well. • Meanwhile, sauté the onion, bell peppers, garlic, and chiles in the oil in a large frying pan over medium heat until softened, about 3 minutes. • Add the cumin and paprika. Cook until aromatic, about 30 seconds. • Stir in the carrot, tomatoes, and the bean mix. Season with salt and pepper. • Bring to a boil. • Cover and simmer over low heat until the sauce reduces slightly, 10–12 minutes. • Stir in the cilantro. • Garnish with the cilantro and serve hot with the rice.

Preparation: 10 minutes
Cooking: 15 minutes

Serves: 4–6
Level: 1

- **2** cups (400 g) jasmine rice
- **1** onion, thinly sliced
- **1** small red bell pepper (capsicum), seeded and thinly sliced
- **1** small green bell pepper (capsicum), seeded and thinly sliced
- **2** cloves garlic, finely chopped
- **1–2** green chiles, seeded and finely chopped
- **1** tablespoon extra-virgin olive oil
- **1** teaspoon ground cumin
- **1** teaspoon paprika
- **1** carrot, diced
- **2** (14-ounce/400-g) cans tomatoes, with juice
- **1** (14-ounce/400-g) can white kidney beans
- **1** (14-ounce/400-g) can red kidney beans
- Salt and freshly ground black pepper
- Cilantro (coriander) to garnish

GARBANZO BEANS WITH TOMATOES AND ARUGULA

Sauté the onion and garlic in 1 tablespoon of oil in a large frying pan over medium-low heat until softened, about 3 minutes. • Add the cumin. Cook until aromatic, about 30 seconds. • Stir in the tomatoes. Cook for about 2 minutes, until softened. • Add the garbanzo beans and arugula. Toss gently. • Spoon the mixture into a serving bowl. • Drizzle with the remaining oil and balsamic vinegar. Season with salt and pepper. • Toss well and serve.

1   red onion, thinly sliced

2   cloves garlic, finely chopped

3   tablespoons extra-virgin olive oil

2   teaspoons ground cumin

8   ounces (250 g) cherry tomatoes, halved

1   (14-ounce/400-g) garbanzo beans (chick-peas), drained and rinsed

8   ounces (250 g) arugula (rocket)

1   tablespoon balsamic vinegar

    Salt and freshly ground black pepper

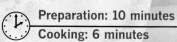

Preparation: 10 minutes
Cooking: 6 minutes

Serves: 4
Level: 1

POTATOES STUFFED WITH BEANS

Pierce the potatoes four times with a skewer. • Microwave on high power for 4 minutes. • Turn the potatoes over and microwave for 4 minutes more. • Remove the potatoes from the microwave and wrap in aluminum foil. • Let stand for 5 minutes. • Cut each potato in half. • Carefully scoop out the flesh and coarsely mash it. • Meanwhile, sauté the onion, garlic, and bacon in the oil in a large frying pan over medium heat until softened, about 3 minutes. • Mix the onion mixture into the mashed potato. Stir in the tomatoes and beans. • Spoon the mixture into the potato shells. • Place the potatoes on a baking sheet. • Sprinkle with the cheddar. • Preheat the broiler (grill). • Broil the potatoes for about 3 minutes, until the cheese melts. • Serve hot.

8	medium potatoes
1	red onion, finely chopped
2	cloves garlic, finely chopped
3	slices bacon, coarsely chopped
2	tablespoons extra-virgin olive oil
2	tomatoes, coarsely chopped
1	(14-ounce/400-g) cannellini beans, drained and rinsed
1	cup (125 g) freshly grated cheddar cheese

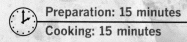

Preparation: 15 minutes
Cooking: 15 minutes

Serves: 4
Level: 1

MUSHROOMS WITH BORLOTTI BEANS

Preheat the oven to 400°F (200°C/gas 6) • Drizzle the mushrooms with half the oil. Sprinkle with the garlic. Season with salt and pepper. • Place the mushrooms in a large baking dish cut-side up. • Bake for about 15 minutes until just cooked. • Meanwhile, mix the beans, onion, bell pepper, parsley, mint, lemon juice, and the remaining oil in a large bowl. • Serve the mushrooms topped with he beans.

8	large flat mushrooms, stems removed
1/3	cup (90 ml) extra-virgin olive oil
3	cloves garlic, finely chopped
	Salt and freshly ground black pepper
1	(14-ounce/400-g) can borlotti or red kidney beans, drained and rinsed
1	small red onion, thinly sliced
1	small red bell pepper (capsicum), seeded and thinly sliced
3	tablespoons finely chopped fresh parsley
3	tablespoons finely chopped fresh mint
1	tablespoon freshly squeezed lemon juice

Preparation: 10 minutes
Cooking: 15 minutes

Serves: 4
Level: 1

SPICY LENTILS WITH SPINACH

Cook the lentils in a saucepan of salted boiling water until just tender, 15–20 minutes. • Drain and set aside.
• Meanwhile, sauté the scallions and garlic in the oil in a large frying pan until softened, about 2 minutes. • Stir in the cumin seeds, coriander, and turmeric. Cook until aromatic, about 1 minute.
• Add the lentils and stock. Cook until heated through, about 2 minutes.
• Stir in the lemon juice, mint, parsley, and spinach. • Serve hot.

2   cups (200 g) red lentils

4   scallions (spring onions), thinly sliced

2   cloves garlic, finely chopped

2   tablespoons extra-virgin olive oil

2   teaspoons cumin seeds

1   teaspoon ground coriander

1/2 teaspoon ground turmeric

1/2 cup (125 ml) chicken stock

3   tablespoons freshly squeezed lemon juice

2   tablespoons finely chopped fresh mint

2   tablespoons finely chopped fresh parsley

4   ounces (125 g) baby spinach leaves

Preparation: 10 minutes

Cooking: 20 minutes

Serves: 4

Level: 1

FAVA BEANS
WITH PANCETTA

Cook the fava beans in a saucepan of boiling water for 1 minute. • Use a slotted spoon to remove the fava beans and rinse them under cold water to stop the cooking process. • Add the green beans. Cook for 3 minutes. • Drain and rinse under cold water. • Preheat a broiler (grill). • Broil the pancetta for 1–2 minutes until crisp. • Break into pieces. • Mix the fava beans, green beans, pancetta, and onion in a large salad bowl. • Drizzle with the oil and vinegar. • Sprinkle with the sugar, cilantro, and parsley. • Toss well and season with salt and pepper. • Serve at once.

3   cups (100 g) shelled fava (broad) beans
8   ounces (250 g) baby green beans
8   slices pancetta
1   small red onion, thinly sliced
2   tablespoons extra-virgin olive oil
1   tablespoon red wine vinegar
1/4 teaspoon sugar
2   tablespoons finely chopped fresh cilantro (coriander)
1   tablespoon finely chopped fresh parsley
    Salt and freshly ground black pepper

Preparation: 10 minutes
Cooking: 6 minutes

Serves: 4
Level: 1

INDEX

INDEX

701

SPICY GARBANZO BEANS WITH EGGPLANT

Cook the rice in a large saucepan of boiling water until tender, about 15 minutes. • Drain and rinse well. • Sauté the onion in the oil in a large frying pan over medium heat until softened, about 3 minutes. • Stir in the curry paste, tomatoes, bell pepper, and eggplant. Cook for 5 minutes. • Add the garbanzo beans. Cook until heated through, about 2 minutes. • Season with salt and pepper. • Serve hot with the rice.

2	cups (400 g) basmati rice
1	onion, thinly sliced
2	tablespoons extra-virgin olive oil
2	tablespoons mild curry paste
4	tomatoes, coarsely chopped
1	red bell pepper (capsicum), seeded and thinly sliced
1	eggplant (aubergine), diced
1	(14-ounce/400-g) can garbanzo beans (chick-peas), drained and rinsed
	Salt and freshly ground black pepper

Preparation: 10 minutes
Cooking: 25 minutes

Serves: 4
Level: 1

■■■ *Curry paste is available wherever Indian foods are sold and online.*

GADO GADO

Combine the satay sauce, coconut milk, lime juice, and kecap manis in a small saucepan. Heat over medium heat until simmering. • Cover and keep warm. • Meanwhile, boil the eggs in a small saucepan of boiling water for 4 minutes. Drain. • Cool the eggs in cold water and peel. • Place the potatoes in a steamer basket over a pan of simmering water. Cover and steam until almost tender, about 5 minutes. • Add the beans and carrots. Cover and steam for 2 minutes. • Add cabbage and bean sprouts. Cover and steam until cabbage just begins to wilt, about 1 minute. • Arrange the steamed vegetables and tomatoes on serving plates. Halve the eggs lengthwise and place on the plates. • Drizzle the vegetables with warm satay mixture. Garnish with the chiles and serve.

1/3 cup (90 ml) Thai satay sauce

1/3 cup (90 ml) coconut milk

1 tablespoon freshly squeezed lime juice

2 teaspoons kecap manis (see page 286)

4 large eggs

8 small new potatoes, halved

5 ounces (150 g) green beans, topped

2 carrots, thickly sliced on the diagonal

1/2 small medium Chinese cabbage, thickly sliced lengthwise

1 cup (100 g) bean sprouts

2 medium tomatoes, cut into thick wedges

Sliced fresh red chiles, to serve

Preparation: 15 minutes
Cooking: 15 minutes

Serves: 4
Level: 1

ASPARAGUS WITH EGGS AND BACON

Bring a large frying pan of water to a boil over high heat. • Add asparagus and cook until just tender, 2–3 minutes. Drain well and set aside. • Wipe the pan with paper towels and set aside. • Heat 1 tablespoon of oil in the pan over medium-high heat. • Sauté the bacon until crisp, about 5 minutes. • Drain on paper towels. • Add the remaining 2 tablespoons of oil to the pan. Fry the eggs until the whites set, about 5 minutes. • Place the asparagus on four serving plates. Top each plate with an egg. Top with bacon and season with salt and pepper. Serve hot.

2	bunches asparagus, trimmed
3	tablespoons extra-virgin olive oil
8	ounces (250 g) bacon, thinly sliced
4	large free-range eggs
	Salt and freshly ground black pepper

Preparation: 10 minutes
Cooking: 12–15 minutes

Serves: 4
Level: 1

GRILLED VEGETABLES WITH CHEESE

Brush the eggplant, zucchini, bell pepper, onion, tomatoes, and cheese with 3–4 tablespoons of the oil. • Season with salt and pepper. • Preheat a large grill pan on medium-high heat. • Grill the vegetables in batches until tender, 2–3 minutes each side per batch. Transfer to a plate. • Grill the cheese until golden, about 1 minute on each side. • Arrange the arugula and vegetables on serving plates. Top with the olives and cheese. Drizzle with the remaining oil and serve hot.

8 **baby eggplants (aubergine), trimmed and halved lengthwise**

2 **medium zucchini (courgettes), thinly sliced lengthwise**

1 **large yellow bell pepper (capsicum), halved, seeded, and thickly sliced lengthwise**

1 **red onion, cut into wedges**

3 **tomatoes, cut into wedges**

8 **ounces (250 g) haloumi or mozzarella cheese, drained and sliced**

5 **tablespoons extra-virgin olive oil**

Salt and freshly ground black pepper

1 **bunch arugula (rocket)**

1/2 **cup (60 g) black olives, pitted**

Preparation: 15 minutes

Cooking: 15 minutes

Serves: 4
Level: 1

SNOW PEA, ASPARAGUS, AND CASHEW STIR-FRY

Heat a wok over high heat. Add both the oils and heat until hot. • Add scallions and stir-fry for 1 minute. • Add the garlic, chiles, snow peas, bell pepper, and asparagus. Stir-fry for 1 minute. • Add the stock, cover, and cook until the vegetables are vibrant, about 2 minutes. • Add the basil, lime leaves, and cashews and toss well. • Serve hot.

3 **tablespoons peanut oil**

1 **teaspoon Asian sesame oil**

6 **scallions (green onions), cut into 2-inch (5-cm) pieces**

2 **cloves garlic, finely chopped**

2 **small fresh red chiles, finely sliced**

8 **ounces (250 g) snow peas (mangetout)**

1 **small red bell pepper (capsicum), seeded and thinly sliced**

1 **bunch asparagus, trimmed and cut into 2-inch (5-cm) lengths**

1/3 **cup (90 ml) chicken or vegetable stock**

1 **cup Thai or regular basil leaves**

3 **kaffir lime leaves, (see page 174)**

1/3 **cup (50 g) roasted salted cashews, chopped**

Preparation: 10 minutes

Cooking: 15 minutes

Serves: 4
Level: 1

ROAST BUTTERNUT SQUASH WITH SWEET ORANGE DRESSING

Preheat the oven to 450°F (230°C/gas 8).
• Place the squash on a large nonstick baking sheet. Drizzle with the olive oil and season with salt and pepper. • Roast for 15–20 minutes, or until tender.
• Meanwhile, to make the dressing, combine the grape seed oil, vinegar, orange juice, honey, cayenne pepper, salt, and pepper in a saucepan. Stir to combine. • Heat over low heat until warm. • Arrange the spinach, roast squash, and fennel on serving plates. Drizzle with the warm dressing and serve hot.

1³/₄ pounds (800 g) butternut squash or pumpkin, seeded and cut into ¹/₂-inch (1-cm) thick wedges

3 tablespoons extra-virgin olive oil

Salt and freshly ground black pepper

1 tablespoon grape seed oil

1 tablespoon red wine vinegar

1 tablespoon freshly squeezed orange juice

3 tablespoons honey

Pinch cayenne pepper

1 cup (50 g) baby spinach leaves

2 baby fennel bulbs, trimmed and very thinly sliced

 Preparation: 10 minutes
Cooking: 15–20 minutes

Serves: 4
Level: 1

POTATO, GREEN BEAN, AND FETA SALAD

626

Bring a saucepan of water to a boil over high heat. • Add the beans and cook until just crisp, 2–3 minutes. Remove with a slotted spoon. Refresh in cold water and drain well. Place in a large bowl. • Add the potatoes to the pan. Boil until just tender, about 10 minutes. Drain. Refresh in cold water. Add the potatoes to the beans in the bowl. • Heat a small frying pan over medium heat. • Add 2 teaspoons of oil and heat until hot. • Add the walnuts and cook, stirring from time to time, until golden, about 2 minutes. • Add the walnuts and feta to the beans and potatoes in the bowl. • To make the dressing, combine the remaining oil, balsamic vinegar, salt, and pepper in a screw-top jar. Shake well to combine. • Pour the dressing over potato mixture and gently toss to combine.

8	ounces (250 g) green beans, topped
1	pound (500 g) new potatoes, scrubbed and halved
1/4	cup (60 ml) extra-virgin olive oil
1/2	cup (80 g) walnuts, roughly chopped
4	ounces (125 g) feta cheese, sliced
1	tablespoon balsamic vinegar
	Salt and freshly ground black pepper

Preparation: 15 minutes
Cooking: 15 minutes

Serves: 4
Level: 1

SWEET AND SOUR MUSHROOMS

Heat a wok over high heat. • Add the oil and heat until hot. • Add onion and stir-fry for 1 minute. • Add celery and bell pepper. Stir-fry for 1 minute. • Add the mushrooms and stir-fry for 2 minutes. • Add the sweet and sour sauce and soy sauce. Stir-fry until the sauce is hot, 1–2 minutes. • Add the tomatoes and toss well. • Serve hot with the jasmine rice and scallions.

2 tablespoons peanut oil

1 red onion, cut into thin wedges

2 stalks celery, thinly sliced diagonally

1 red bell pepper (capsicum), halved, seeded and coarsely chopped

12 ounces (350 g) button mushrooms, halved

1 cup (250 ml) sweet and sour sauce

2 teaspoons soy sauce

4 ounces (125 g) cherry tomatoes, halved lengthwise

Steamed jasmine rice, to serve

Shredded scallions (green onions), to serve

 Preparation: 15 minutes
Cooking: 5 minutes

Serves: 4
Level: 1

SPICED CRUMBED EGGPLANT WITH FETA

Combine the bread crumbs with the cumin and coriander in a small bowl. Season with salt and freshly ground black pepper. • Dip the eggplant into the egg. Coat evenly in spiced bread crumbs, pressing the crumbs onto the eggplant. • Heat the oil in a large frying pan over medium-high heat. • Fry the eggplant in batches, until golden, 2–3 minutes per side. • Arrange the arugula on serving plates. Top with eggplant and feta. Serve hot with the hummus, if preferred.

1	cup (150 g) fine dry bread crumbs
1	teaspoon ground cumin
1	teaspoon ground coriander
	Salt and freshly ground black pepper
10	baby eggplants (aubergine), halved lengthwise
1	large egg, lightly beaten
1	bunch arugula (rocket)
4	ounces (125 g) feta cheese, very thinly sliced
	Hummus, to serve (optional)

Preparation: 15 minutes
Cooking: 12 minutes

Serves: 4
Level: 1

SWEET POTATO, ZUCCHINI, AND GARBANZO BEAN STEW

Heat the oil in a large deep frying pan over medium-high heat. • Sauté the onion and garlic until softened, about 3 minutes. • Add the cumin. Cook for 1 minute, until fragrant. • Add the cinnamon stick, saffron, tomatoes, and vegetable stock. Cover and bring to a boil. • Add the sweet potato, zucchini, and garbanzo beans. Reduce the heat to medium-low and simmer until tender, 15–20 minutes. • Stir in the parsley and season with salt and pepper. • Remove the cinnamon stick. Serve hot with the couscous.

3	tablespoons extra-virgin olive oil
1	onion, finely chopped
2	cloves garlic, finely chopped
2	teaspoons ground cumin
1	cinnamon stick
1/4	teaspoon saffron threads, soaked in 1 tablespoon water
2	(14-ounce/400-g) cans diced tomatoes, with juice
1/2	cup (125 ml) vegetable stock
1	pounds (800 g) orange sweet potato (kumara), peeled and diced
2	zucchini (courgettes), sliced
1	(14-ounce/400-g) can garbanzo beans (chick-peas), drained and rinsed
1/3	cup coarsely chopped flat leaf parsley
	Salt and freshly ground black pepper
	Couscous, to serve

Preparation: 10 minutes
Cooking: 20 minutes

Serves: 4
Level: 1

HONEY, VEGETABLE, AND ALMOND COUSCOUS

634

Heat the oil in a large frying pan over medium-high heat. • Sauté the onion and garlic until softened, about 3 minutes. • Add the parsnips, zucchini, carrots, and cumin. Sauté until tender, about 10 minutes. • Stir in the honey. • Meanwhile, place the couscous in a heatproof bowl. Pour in the boiling water. • Cover and let stand until the water is absorbed, about 5 minutes. • Break the couscous up with a fork to separate the grains. • Stir in the butter and vegetable mixture. Season with salt and pepper. Add the almonds and spinach, toss well, and serve hot.

Preparation: 15 minutes
Cooking: 15 minutes

Serves: 4
Level: 1

3 tablespoons extra-virgin olive oil

2 red onions, cut into thin wedges

2 cloves garlic, finely chopped

2 parsnips, peeled and cut into thin sticks

2 zucchini (courgettes), cut into thin sticks

2 carrots, cut into thin sticks

2 teaspoons ground cumin

3 tablespoons honey

2 cups (280 g) instant couscous

2 cups (500 ml) boiling water

2 tablespoons butter, softened

Salt and freshly ground black pepper

1/4 cup (30 g) slivered almonds, toasted

1 cup (60 g) baby spinach leaves

CABBAGE, BROCCOLI, AND BABY CORN STIR-FRY

636

Heat a wok over high heat. Add the oil.
• Add the onion and stir-fry until tender, about 2 minutes. • Add the curry paste and stir-fry until fragrant, about 1 minute.
• Add the coconut milk. Stir until the oil separates. • Add the broccoli, corn, and fish sauce. Cover and bring to a boil.
• Add the cabbage and tofu. • Stir-fry until the cabbage just wilts, 1–2 minutes.
• Add the lime juice and toss gently.
• Spoon into serving bowls. Top with the cucumber and cilantro. • Serve hot with the rice.

1	tablespoon peanut oil
1	onion, cut into thin wedges
1/4	cup (60 ml) Thai green curry paste
1	cup (250 ml) coconut milk
8	ounces (250 g) broccoli, cut into small florets
8	ounces (250 g) baby corn, halved
1	tablespoon Asian fish sauce
1/4	Chinese cabbage, trimmed and shredded
12	ounces (350 g) firm bean curd, cut into 1-inch (2.5-cm) cubes
1	tablespoon freshly squeezed lime juice
1	small cucumber, cut into matchsticks
1/2	cup cilantro (coriander) sprigs
	Steamed jasmine rice, to serve

Preparation: 15 minutes
Cooking: 12 minutes

Serves: 4
Level: 1

SWEET CORN FRITTERS WITH AVOCADO SALSA

To prepare the salsa, combine the avocados, lime juice, 1 tablespoon of cilantro, and Tabasco sauce in a bowl. Season with salt and pepper. Stir to combine. Set aside. • To prepare the corn fritters, put the flour in a large bowl. • Beat the egg and milk in small bowl • Whisk the egg mixture into the flour until smooth. Set aside for 5 minutes. • Add the corn, scallions, and cilantro to the egg batter. Season with salt and pepper. Stir to combine. • Heat the oil in a large nonstick frying pan over medium-high heat. • Add 1/3 cup of batter for each fritter and fry until golden and cooked through, about for 2–3 minutes per side. Drain on paper towels while you cook the remaining batter. • Serve the fritters hot with the avocado salsa and garnished with lime wedges.

Salsa

- **2** ripe avocados, peeled, halved, pitted, and chopped
- **3** tablespoons freshly squeezed lime juice
- **1** tablespoon chopped cilantro (coriander)
- **Dash of Tabasco**
- **Salt and freshly ground black pepper**

Corn Fritters

- **2/3** cup (100 g) self-rising flour
- **1** large egg, lightly beaten
- **2/3** cup (150 ml) milk
- **1** (14-ounce/400-g) can corn, drained
- **4** scallions (green onions), thinly sliced
- **1** tablespoon chopped cilantro (coriander)
- **1** cup (250 ml) vegetable oil, to fry
- **Lime wedges, to serve**

 Preparation: 15 minutes
Cooking: 15 minutes

Serves: 4
Level: 1

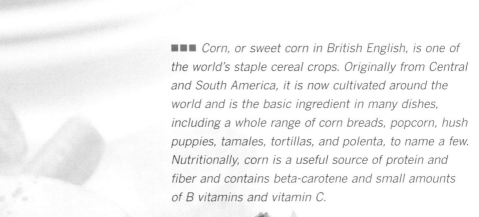 *Corn, or sweet corn in British English, is one of the world's staple cereal crops. Originally from Central and South America, it is now cultivated around the world and is the basic ingredient in many dishes, including a whole range of corn breads, popcorn, hush puppies, tamales, tortillas, and polenta, to name a few. Nutritionally, corn is a useful source of protein and fiber and contains beta-carotene and small amounts of B vitamins and vitamin C.*

639

DESSERTS

CHOCOLATE CHIP PUDDINGS

To prepare the puddings, preheat the oven to 350°F (180°C/gas 4). • Butter four 3/4-cup (180-ml) ramekins or mini soufflé dishes. Arrange on a baking sheet. • Sift the flour, cocoa, and salt into a large bowl. • Stir in the brown sugar. • Mix in the butter, milk, and egg until well combined. • Stir in 1/4 cup (30 g) of chocolate chips. • Spoon the mixture evenly into the ramekins and sprinkle with the remaining chocolate chips. • To prepare the sauce: Mix the brown sugar and cocoa in a small bowl. • Sprinkle the mixture evenly over the ramekins. • Gently pour over the boiling water over the back of a spoon, dividing it evenly among the ramekins. • Bake for about 20 minutes, until set. • Serve warm.

Puddings
- 1 cup (150 g) self-rising flour
- 1 tablespoon unsweetened cocoa powder
- 1/8 teaspoon salt
- 1/3 cup (50 g) firmly packed dark brown sugar
- 1/4 cup (60 g) butter, melted
- 1/3 cup (90 ml) milk
- 1 large egg, lightly beaten
- 1/3 cup (50 g) dark chocolate chips

Sauce
- 1/4 cup (50 g) firmly packed dark brown sugar
- 2 teaspoons unsweetened cocoa powder
- 3/4 cup (180 ml) water, boiling

Preparation: 10 minutes
Cooking: 20 minutes

Serves: 4
Level: 1

PASSIONFRUIT AND APRICOT SOUFFLÉS

Preheat the oven to 350°F (180°C/gas 4).
• Butter four 3/4-cup (180-ml) ramekins
or mini soufflé dishes. Dust each ramekin
with 1 teaspoon of superfine sugar.
Arrange on a baking sheet. • Drain the
apricots, reserving the liquid. • Put the
apricots in a food processor and process
until smooth. • Mix 1/2 cup (125 ml) of
the apricot purée with the passionfruit
pulp. • Mix the remaining apricot
purée with 1/4 cup (60 ml) of the
reserved liquid. • Set aside. • Beat the
egg whites and salt in a large bowl with
an electric mixer at high speed until soft
peaks form. • Gradually add the
remaining superfine sugar, beating until
stiff peaks form. • Use a large rubber
spatula to gently fold in the apricot and
passionfruit mixture. • Spoon the mixture
evenly into the ramekins. • Bake for
10–12 minutes, until risen. • Dust with
the confectioners' sugar. Serve with the
apricot sauce on the side.

1/2 cup (100 g)
   superfine (caster)
   sugar
1 (14-ounce/400-g)
   can apricot halves
   Pulp of 2
   passionfruit
3 large egg whites
1/8 teaspoon salt
   Confectioners'
   (icing) sugar, to dust

Preparation: 15 minutes
Cooking: 10–12 minutes

Serves: 4
Level: 1

NECTARINE PARCELS

Preheat the oven to 425°F (220°C/gas 7).
• Line a baking sheet with parchment
paper. • Cut the pastry into four squares.
• Turn pastry over so that the corners are
facing you. • Sprinkle evenly with the
almonds and cinnamon sugar. • Place
two nectarine halves on top. • Fold the
edges over. • Arrange the parcels on the
prepared tray. • Bake for about 15
minutes until golden. • Dust with the
confectioners' sugar. Serve with the
ice cream.

1   **sheet frozen or chilled shortcrust pastry, thawed if frozen**

2   **tablespoons ground almonds**

2   **teaspoons cinnamon sugar**

4   **firm-ripe nectarines, halved and pitted**

Confectioners' sugar (icing), to dust

Vanilla ice cream, to serve

 Preparation: 10 minutes
Cooking: 15 minutes

Serves: 4
Level: 1

APPLE PASTRIES

Preheat the oven to 400°F (200°C/ gas 6). • Line a baking sheet with parchment paper. • Cut each pastry sheet into 4 squares. • Arrange 4 squares of pastry on the prepared sheet. • Brush lightly with water. • Top with the remaining pastry squares and press together lightly. • Use a sharp knife to cut a $^1/_2$-inch (1 cm) border around the edge. • Arrange the apple slices on top of the pastry. • Brush with the melted butter and sprinkle evenly with the superfine sugar. • Bake for 15–20 minutes, until golden and puffed.
• Dust with the confectioners' sugar.

2 sheets frozen puff pastry, thawed

3 apples, peeled, cored, and thinly sliced

2 tablespoons butter, melted

1 tablespoon superfine (caster) sugar

Confectioners' (icing) sugar, to dust

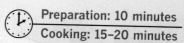

Preparation: 10 minutes
Cooking: 15–20 minutes

Serves: 4
Level: 1

RASPBERRY STAR PASTRIES

Preheat the oven to 425°F (220°C/gas 7).
• Line a baking sheet with parchment
paper. • Use a 2½-inch (6-cm) star
cutter to cut 16 stars from the pastry.
• Transfer to the prepared sheet and
lightly brush with the egg. • Bake for
about 5 minutes, until puffed and golden.
• Mix the sour cream and brown sugar in
a bowl. • Mash half the raspberries with
a fork. • Mix the mashed raspberries
into the sour cream mixture.
• Arrange 2 pastries on each serving
plate. • Top with the berry cream. •
Sprinkle with the remaining raspberries.
• Top with the remaining pastries. • Dust
with the confectioners' sugar and serve.

2   sheets frozen puff
    pastry, thawed
1   large egg,
    lightly beaten
½   cup (125 ml)
    sour cream
2   tablespoons
    dark brown sugar
1   cup (250 g) fresh
    raspberries (or
    frozen berries,
    thawed)
    Confectioners'
    (icing) sugar, to dust

Preparation: 15 minutes
Cooking: 5 minutes

Serves: 4
Level: 1

GRILLED PINEAPPLE WITH MINT

654

Cut the pineapple halves into quarters and cut the quarters into thirds. • Thread the pineapple onto metal skewers. • Mix the honey, orange zest and juice, lemon juice, and orange liqueur in a small bowl. • Add the pineapple skewers and coat well. • Preheat a grill over medium heat. • Grill the pineapple for 3 minutes on each side. • Drizzle with any remaining juice and sprinkle with the mint. • Serve at once.

1   **pineapple, halved lengthwise and peeled**

1/3 **cup (90 ml) honey**

Finely grated zest and freshly squeezed juice of 1 orange

2   **tablespoons freshly squeezed lemon juice**

1/4 **cup (60 ml) orange liqueur**

2   **tablespoons finely chopped fresh mint**

Preparation: 10 minutes

Cooking: 9 minutes

Serves: 4

Level: 1

655

BROILED FIGS WITH MARSALA AND ALMONDS

Preheat the broiler. • Toast the almonds for about 2 minutes until golden. • Set aside. • Cut two slits in the top of each fig and open them gently. • Arrange the figs in a shallow baking dish. • Sprinkle evenly with 2 tablespoons of brown sugar. • Broil for about 5 minutes, until the sugar melts and bubbles.
• Meanwhile, mix the remaining brown sugar and Marsala in a small saucepan. • Simmer over low heat until the mixture thickens and resembles syrup, about 3 minutes. • Drizzle the syrup over the figs. • Sprinkle with the almonds and serve with the mascarpone cheese.

1/4 cup (40 g)
    flaked almonds

8 fresh figs

5 tablespoons
    firmly packed dark
    brown sugar

1/3 cup (90 ml) Marsala
    or sweet sherry

1/3 cup (90 ml)
    mascarpone cheese

Preparation: 7 minutes

Cooking: 10 minutes

Serves: 4
Level: 1

WARM ORANGE FRUIT SALAD

Mix the superfine sugar, water, lemon grass, and ginger in a small saucepan over medium-high heat. • Cook, stirring, until the sugar dissolves, about 3 minutes. • Bring to a boil over high heat. • Decrease the heat to medium. • Add the oranges and simmer, stirring from time to time, for 5 minutes. • Spoon the oranges into serving bowls. • Drizzle with the syrup and serve at once.

$^1/_2$ **cup (100 g) superfine (caster) sugar**

$^1/_2$ **cup (125 ml) water**

1 **stem lemon grass, trimmed and thinly sliced**

2 **teaspoons freshly grated ginger**

6 **large oranges, peeled, zest removed, and thinly sliced**

Preparation: 15 minutes
Cooking: 8 minutes ·

Serves: 4
Level: 1

SUMMER FRUIT KEBABS WITH CHOCOLATE

Cut the fruit in halves and remove the pits. • Cut the fruit into bite-size pieces. Thread onto metal skewers. • Set aside. • Melt the chocolate in a double boiler over barely simmering water. • Arrange the fruit kebabs on individual serving plates. • Drizzle with the melted chocolate. • Let stand at room temperature for 5 minutes. • Serve at once.

2 **firm-ripe peaches**
2 **firm-ripe nectarines**
4 **firm-ripe apricots**
5 **ounces (150 g) milk chocolate, coarsely chopped**

Preparation: 15 minutes
Cooking: 5 minutes

Serves: 4
Level: 1

BOOZY STRAWBERRIES

Mix the sugar, orange zest and juice, and liqueur in a small saucepan over medium heat. • Cook, stirring, until the sugar dissolves, about 3 minutes. • Let cool completely. • Arrange the strawberries in individual serving bowls. • Drizzle with the syrup and sprinkle with the almonds. • Serve with the cream on the side.

1/4 cup (50 g) superfine (caster) sugar

Finely grated zest and freshly squeezed juice of 1 orange

2 tablespoons orange liqueur

1 pound (500 g) strawberries, quartered

1/4 cup (40 g) slivered almonds, toasted

Heavy (double) cream, to serve

Preparation: 10 minutes
Cooking: 4 minutes

Serves: 4
Level: 1

TROPICAL FRUIT SALAD

Mix the orange juice and superfine sugar in a small saucepan over high heat. • Cook, stirring, until the sugar dissolves, about 3 minutes. • Cover and bring to a boil. • Simmer until the syrup thickens slightly, about 5 minutes. • Remove from the heat. • Stir in the passionfruit pulp. • Let cool for 10 minutes. • Meanwhile, arrange the papaya, bananas, and pineapple on individual serving plates. • Pour the syrup over the fruit and serve.

1 cup (250 ml) freshly squeezed orange juice

1/2 cup (100 g) superfine (caster) sugar

Pulp of 2 passionfruit

1 pound (500 g) papaya (pawpaw), peeled, seeded, and thinly sliced

2 bananas, sliced diagonally lengthwise

1/2 small pineapple, peeled and cut into wedges

Preparation: 15 minutes
Cooking: 8 minutes

Serves: 4
Level: 1

SPICED POACHED PEARS

Mix the water, superfine sugar, lemon juice, orange zest, and cinnamon stick in a large saucepan over high heat. • Use a teaspoon to scrape seeds from the vanilla pod into the pan. • Add the scraped pod to the pan. • Bring to a boil, stirring from time to time. • Decrease the heat to medium. • Cook, uncovered, until the volume has reduced by one-third, 8–10 minutes. • Add the pears to the syrup. • Cover and simmer until tender, 5–8 minutes. • Arrange the warm pears in individual serving bowls. • Spoon over the syrup and serve with the cream.

2 cups (500 ml) water

1 cup (200 g) superfine (caster) sugar

1 tablespoon freshly squeezed lemon juice

1 piece orange zest

1 cinnamon stick

1 vanilla pod, halved lengthwise

4 large firm-ripe pears, quartered lengthwise and cored

Heavy (double) cream, to serve

Preparation: 10 minutes
Cooking: 13–18 minutes

Serves: 4
Level: 1

BERRIES WITH YOGURT AND TOFFEE

668

Combine the strawberries, blueberries, and raspberries in a shallow serving dish. • Top with the yogurt. • Set aside. • Put the superfine sugar in a medium frying pan over medium heat. • Cook, stirring occasionally, until golden and caramelized, 8–10 minutes. • Drizzle the toffee syrup over the yogurt and berries. • Serve at once.

2   **cups (300 g) strawberries, halved lengthwise**

1   **cup (150 g) blueberries**

2   **cups (300 g) raspberries**

2   **cups (500 ml) plain yogurt**

1/2 **cup (100 g) superfine (caster) sugar**

Preparation: 10 minutes
Cooking: 8–10 minutes

Serves: 4
Level: 1

APPLE AND RHUBARB CRISP

Preheat the oven to 400°F (200°C/ gas 6). • Butter four 1-cup (250-ml) ramekins or mini soufflé dishes. Arrange on a baking sheet. • Mix the apples, water, and superfine sugar in a large saucepan. • Bring to a boil. • Cover and simmer over low heat for 3 minutes. • Stir in the rhubarb. • Cook until tender, 2–3 minutes. • Meanwhile, mix the granola, flour, brown sugar, and butter in a small bowl. • Spoon the fruit into the prepared ramekins. • Sprinkle the crumble evenly over the tops. • Bake for about 15 minutes, until golden and crisp. • Serve the crisp hot with ice cream.

3 apples, peeled, cored, and diced

2 tablespoons water

3 tablespoons superfine (caster) sugar

1 pound (500 g) rhubarb, trimmed, washed, and cut into short lengths

1/2 cup (125 g) granola (muesli)

1/3 cup (50 g) self-rising flour

1/4 cup (50 g) firmly packed dark brown sugar

1/4 cup (60 g) butter, softened

Ice cream, to serve

Preparation: 10 minutes
Cooking: 20 minutes

Serves: 4
Level: 1

CHOCOLATE MOUSSE

Melt the chocolate with the cream in a double boiler over barely simmering water. • Meanwhile, beat the egg yolk in a small bowl with an electric mixer at high speed until light and creamy. • Stir the beaten yolk into the chocolate mixture. Cook until the mixture registers 160°F (80°C) on an instant-read thermometer. • Set aside. • With a mixer at high speed, beat the egg white in a small bowl placed over a pan of barely simmering water until soft peaks form. • Gradually add the superfine sugar, beating until stiff peaks form. • Use a large rubber spatula to fold the beaten white into the chocolate mixture. • Spoon the mixture into four 1/2-cup (125-ml) ramekins. • Freeze for about 20 minutes, until just set. • Sprinkle with the chopped peanut candy and serve.

8 ounces (250 g) semisweet (dark) chocolate, coarsely chopped

3/4 cup (180 ml) single (light) cream

1 tablespoon superfine (caster) sugar

2 tablespoons coffee liqueur

1 large egg, separated

1/2 cup (90 g) chocolate coated peanuts, coarsely chopped

Preparation: 10 minutes
+ 20 minutes to freeze

Serves: 4
Level: 1

QUICK TIRAMISU

Mix the coffee and Marsala in a shallow dish. • Beat the cream cheese and confectioners' sugar with an electric mixer at high speed in a large bowl until creamy. • Use a large rubber spatula to fold the mascarpone cheese into the cream cheese mixture. • Dip the ladyfingers in the coffee mixture and arrange them standing upright in four individual serving glasses. • Spoon the cream cheese mixture into the dishes and sprinkle with the chocolate. • Chill for 15 minutes, or until ready to serve.

½   cup (125 ml) strong black coffee, cooled

2   tablespoons Marsala or sweet sherry

1   cup (250 g) cream cheese, softened

3   tablespoons confectioners' (icing) sugar

1   cup (250 ml) mascarpone cheese

12 small ladyfingers (sponge fingers)

Finely grated chocolate, to garnish

Preparation: 10 minutes + 15 minutes to chill

Serves: 4
Level: 1

CHOCOLATE RICOTTA WITH ITALIAN COOKIES

676

Mix the ricotta and confectioners' sugar in a medium bowl until smooth.
• Reserve 2 tablespoons of chocolate.
• Stir the remaining chocolate, ginger, and orange zest and juice into the ricotta mixture. • Arrange the cookies on serving plates. • Top with the chocolate ricotta.
• Sprinkle with the remaining grated chocolate and serve.

1   cup (250 ml) ricotta cheese

2   tablespoons confectioners' (icing) sugar

4   ounces (125 g) semisweet (dark) chocolate, finely grated

1   ounce (30 g) preserved ginger, finely chopped

1   teaspoon finely grated orange zest

2   tablespoons freshly squeezed orange juice

8   large Italian crostoli cookies or ladyfingers

 Preparation: 15 minutes

Serves: 4
Level: 1

TOASTED SPONGE CAKE WITH HONEYCOMB CREAM

Mix the cream, vanilla, yogurt, and honeycomb or milk chocolate bars in a medium bowl. • Let stand for 10 minutes. • Drizzle the cake on both sides with the melted butter. • Lightly dip the cake in the sugar. • Heat a large nonstick frying pan over high heat. • Fry the cake until golden, about 2 minutes on each side. • Place on serving plates. • Top with the honeycomb cream and serve at once.

1 cup (250 ml) heavy (double) cream

1 teaspoon vanilla extract (essence)

1/2 cup (125 ml) plain yogurt

5 ounces (150 g) honeycomb or milk chocolate bars, coarsely chopped

8 1-inch- (2.5-cm)- thick slices sponge cake

3 tablespoons butter, melted

2 tablespoons superfine (caster) sugar

Preparation: 15 minutes
Cooking: 4 minutes

Serves: 4
Level: 1

WAFFLES WITH CARAMEL BANANAS

Heat the butter in a medium frying pan over medium heat until melted. • Add the brown sugar and cream. • Cook, stirring constantly, until the sugar dissolves, about 3 minutes. • Simmer for 2 minutes. • Add the bananas. • Cook, turning them once, until slightly softened, about 3 minutes. • Toast the waffles until warm. • Top with the caramel bananas. • Serve at once.

$^1/_3$ cup (90 g) butter

$^1/_2$ cup (100 g) firmly packed dark brown sugar

$^1/_2$ cup (125 ml) light (single) cream

4 bananas, peeled and sliced diagonally

4 Belgian waffles

Preparation: 5 minutes

Cooking: 8 minutes

Serves: 4

Level: 1

CHOCOLATE FUDGE AND AMARETTI SUNDAES

Melt the butter in a medium frying pan over medium heat. • Add the brown sugar, cream, and cocoa powder. • Simmer until slightly reduced, about 5 minutes. • Let cool slightly. • Layer the amaretti cookies, peanuts, ice cream, and fudge sauce in individual sundae glasses. • Serve at once.

$1/3$ cup (90 g) butter

$1/2$ cup (100 g) firmly packed dark brown sugar

$1/2$ cup (125 ml) heavy (double) cream

2 tablespoons unsweetened cocoa powder

$3/4$ cup (90 g) amaretti cookies, crushed

$1/2$ cup (90 g) chocolate-coated peanuts, coarsely chopped

1 quart (1 liter) vanilla ice cream

Preparation: 15 minutes

Cooking: 5 minutes

Serves: 4
Level: 1

BAKED PEACHES WITH MERINGUE

Preheat the oven to 350°F (180°C/gas 4).
• Place the peaches, cut side up, in a
shallow baking dish. • Beat the egg
whites in a large bowl with an electric
mixer at high speed until soft peaks
form. • Gradually add the superfine
sugar, beating until stiff, glossy peaks
form. • Pipe the meringue on top
of the peaches. • Bake for about
10 minutes, until lightly browned.
• Dust with the confectioners' sugar
and serve hot.

8   canned peach
     halves, drained

2   large egg whites (at
     room temperature)

1/4 cup (50 g) superfine
     (caster) sugar

     Confectioners'
     (icing) sugar, to dust

 Preparation: 10 minutes

Cooking: 20 minutes

Serves: 4
Level: 1

RHUBARB AND CUSTARD PARFAIT

Mix the rhubarb, superfine sugar, and pear nectar in a large saucepan. • Cover and bring to a boil. • Decrease the heat to medium-low. • Simmer, stirring from time to time, until tender, 10–15 minutes. • Let cool slightly. • Layer the warm rhubarb and custard in individual serving glasses. • Drizzle with the honey. • Serve.

1   pound (500 g) rhubarb, trimmed and cut into small lengths

3/4   cup (150 g) superfine (caster) sugar

1/2   cup (125 ml) pear nectar or juice

2   cups (500 ml) vanilla pudding or thick custard

2   tablespoons honey

 Preparation: 10 minutes
Cooking: 10–15 minutes

Serves: 4
Level: 1

BRANDY SNAPS WITH MOCHA MASCARPONE

Beat the mascarpone and confectioners' sugar in a small bowl until smooth. • Mix the coffee granules, cocoa, and boiling water in a small bowl. • Use a large rubber spatula to stir the coffee mixture into the mascarpone mixture. • Place one cookie on each serving plate. Top with one-third of the mascarpone mixture. Repeat the layering twice, finishing with a cookie. • Dust with cocoa and serve at once.

1   cup (250 g) mascarpone cheese

3   tablespoons confectioners' (icing) sugar

1   tablespoon instant coffee granules

2   teaspoons unsweetened cocoa powder

1   tablespoon boiling water

16 brandy snap cookies

Cocoa powder, to dust

 Preparation: 10 minutes

Serves: 4
Level: 1

GRILLED DOUGHNUTS WITH COFFEE SYRUP

Mix the coffee, sugar, and vanilla in a saucepan over medium-high heat.
• Cook, stirring, until the sugar dissolves, about 3 minutes. • Simmer until reduced by half and syrupy, about 10 minutes.
• Stir in the coffee liqueur. • Meanwhile, place a grill pan over medium-high heat.
• Grill the doughnuts for about 2 minutes on each side, until warmed through.
• Place the doughnuts on individual serving plates. • Drizzle with the coffee syrup. • Serve warm with the ice cream.

1 cup (250 ml) strong black coffee, cooled

3/4 cup (150 g) superfine (caster) sugar

1 teaspoon vanilla extract (essence)

2 tablespoons coffee liqueur

6 cinnamon doughnuts, cut in half horizontally

Vanilla ice cream, to serve

Preparation: 10 minutes
Cooking: 17 minutes

Serves: 4
Level: 1

STRAWBERRY AND COCONUT DESSERT

Toast the coconut in a large frying pan until golden, about 5 minutes. • Mix the orange juice and passionfruit pulp in a small bowl. • Beat the cream in a large bowl with an electric mixer at high speed until soft peaks form. • Use a large rubber spatula to fold half the toasted coconut into the cream.

• Arrange half the cake in the bottom of a medium shallow dish. • Sprinkle with half the orange mixture and top with half the coconut cream. • Repeat the layering, finishing with the cream.

• Arrange the strawberries on top.

• Sprinkle with remaining coconut and serve at once.

3/4 **cup (90 g) shredded coconut**

Juice of 2 oranges

Pulp of 2 passionfruits

1$\frac{1}{2}$ **cups (375 ml) heavy (double) cream**

8 **$\frac{1}{2}$-inch (1-cm) thick slices pound cake or Madeira cake, crusts removed**

8 **oz (250 g) strawberries, hulled and thinly sliced**

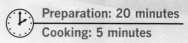

Preparation: 20 minutes

Cooking: 5 minutes

Serves: 4

Level: 1

CHOCOLATE TARTS

Preheat the oven to 400°F (200°C/ gas 6). • Combine the butter, chocolate, and superfine sugar in a medium saucepan over low heat. • Cook, stirring constantly, for 5 minutes. • Remove from the heat. Stir in the egg. • Lightly butter four individual tart pans. • Cut the pastry into four rounds to fit the tart pans. Line the pans with the pastry. • Spoon the chocolate mixture into each tart case. • Bake for 12–15 minutes, until set. • Dust with the confectioners' sugar and serve at once.

¼ cup (60 g) butter, cut up

4 ounces (125 g) dark chocolate, coarsely chopped

2 tablespoons superfine (caster) sugar

1 large egg, lightly beaten

1 sweet frozen puff pastry, thawed

Confectioners' (icing) sugar, to dust

Preparation: 10 minutes
Cooking: 17–20 minutes

Serves: 4
Level: 2

CARAMELIZED PEACHES WITH RUM SABAYON

To prepare the peaches, melt the butter and brown sugar in a large frying pan over medium heat. • Place the peach halves cut side down in the frying pan and simmer until caramel in color, about 5 minutes on each side. • Set aside and keep warm until you are ready to serve. To make the sabayon, whisk the eggs, egg yolks, rum, sugar, and lemon juice together in a medium heatproof bowl. • Place the bowl over a saucepan of simmering water and whisk continuously until the mixture has just thickened, about 5 minutes. Do not allow the sabayon to boil. • Remove the bowl from the heat and set aside. • Place two peach halves onto each serving plate or bowl and spoon the rum sabayon over the top.

Peaches

5   tablespoons butter

$1/3$ cup (70 g) firmly packed light brown sugar

4   peaches, halved and pitted (stoned)

Rum Sabayon

2   large eggs + 2 large egg yolks

$1/4$ cup (60 ml) dark rum

$1/2$ cup (100 g) sugar

2   tablespoons freshly squeezed lemon juice, strained

Preparation: 10 minutes
Cooking: 15 minutes

Serves: 4
Level: 1